HOW TO BE A GARDENER

Alan Titchmarsh

HOW TO BE A GARDENER
BOOK ONE

back to basics

Photographs by Jonathan Buckley

CONTENTS

Introduction

I've been entranced by gardening for as long as I can remember, but I know that for many people it's a baffling world out there. What makes plants grow? Is there such a thing as green fingers? Why do plants suddenly die for no apparent reason? Will I ever become a gardener when everything I touch seems to shrivel?

This book aims to answer all these questions. It will not only tell you *how* to garden, it will also tell you *why* certain techniques work better than others. Oh, you might not want to be bothered with the 'why', but if you can find the patience to stick with it, the background information can be fascinating and just as rewarding as the results of the craft itself.

Gardening is, in part, instinctive, but so many people have lost touch with that 'earthy' side of their nature in this technological age. They no longer rely on their instincts and intuitions – it's a great pity, as these are often the basic tools of the trade. *How to be a Gardener* will, I hope, put that right. I want you to get a *feel* for gardening as much as anything... to use all your senses – touch, taste, smell, sight and hearing – and, above all, to bring that common sense to bear that will make you a good gardener.

Traditionally, such skills have been handed down from generation to generation but, with so many wrinklies now into abseiling, surfing the tide and surfing the net, there's a real danger that such skills will be lost. How, then, do you acquire the necessary skills?

It's simple. Just getting to know your plants, your soil and your situation will make you a better gardener. It might also give you a different outlook on life and encourage you to do your bit for the environment, which, more than ever, depends on you for its very survival. A sound organic approach, backed up by a knowledge of science is, I reckon, the secret of success. We need gardens, and we need wise gardeners who can make sure that all forms of wildlife continue to thrive.

How to be a Gardener starts with the basics to help you understand what a plant is, how it grows, and what it needs to develop successfully. I have explained what gardening is and how the language works and, on a practical level, where and how to get started. Each chapter takes you through what you need to know to garden successfully, learning how to assess your site and soil, choose healthy plants, plan your borders and plant things properly. I want to show how the seasons affect what you do in the garden, and highlight routine gardening jobs – identifying what they are as well as how and why we do them. There's lots of useful information to help you identify, eliminate and prevent weeds and pests – always a big concern, I know! – and a whole chapter on your lawn.

There are practical, step-by-step instructions in my 'How to…' features and plenty of boxes and charts to highlight some of the more essential information or summarise things for you. I've also used 'Side stories' in the margins to include extra bits of interesting information that I thought you might find interesting and enjoy.

There's no great mystery to being a successful gardener – most of it is just plain common sense – but an appreciation of the natural world at work in our gardens helps. The first of two volumes, *How to be a Gardener Book One* aims to encourage this appreciation and help the first-time gardener get started, as well as enhance the understanding of the more experienced gardener. Later, *Book Two* will build on that knowledge and experience to explore planting and design further, and provide you with a complete reference manual for your garden. It's not all hard graft and earnest endeavour, I promise. There are sublime pleasures to be had from growing plants successfully and producing crops with a bumper harvest. As I hope this book will show you, it's not nearly as complicated or as difficult as you might think… whatever the weather!

1 GARDENING BASICS

What is gardening?

As a rule, I'm a fan of dictionaries, but the one thing they lack is any kind of passion. Look up gardening and you'll discover that it is 'the activity of tending and cultivating a garden as a pastime', which sounds to me just a bit casual. If you ask a gardener why he or she gardens you might just as well ask why they breathe – it's because they can't imagine life without it. Gardening is part art and part science, but more than anything else it's a craft that is fuelled by subterranean passion. It's all about nurturing and achieving, triumphing over nature and harmonizing with it. It panders to our primitive hunter-gatherer instincts. It can be incredibly satisfying and also very humbling; it can also be frustrating, annoying and, let's be honest, disappointing. But one thing I promise you is that once you get started and have the thrill of seeing your first seedlings flower, or your first new border bloom, you'll be hooked for life.

Formal gardens, like this one at Hatfield House in Hertfordshire, were especially popular in the 17th and 18th centuries and today they still appeal to lovers of straight lines and balanced proportions.

What are gardens for?

Today's garden, for the vast majority of us, is cultivated for pleasure and fun. More than ever before it's used like an outdoor living room – weather permitting – but it's also a place where you can pursue your own particular interest. If you are a keen plants-person, you can use it to collect and cultivate your favourite flowers; for creative souls, the garden makes a good outlet for design talents; families need somewhere for children and pets to play safely, while, for a lot of people, the garden is a place for relaxation – a place to sit, cook and eat in the open, or entertain friends.

But that isn't the way gardens have always been used. In the past, there was a huge distinction between the gardens of the rich and poor. The rich used their grand gardens and landscapes as status symbols – they were there to impress and were filled with expensive fittings like mazes, fountains and statues. Massive borders, shrubberies and lawns were maintained by a large staff. You can still see this type of garden when you visit stately homes – fascinating to look at, but not the sort of thing you can hope to recreate at home in a small space. (And anyway, good-quality staff are simply impossible to find!) The gardens of ordinary people were not only smaller, they were on-the-spot survival kits in the days when there wasn't a handy corner shop or supermarket down the road.

Self-sufficiency

Up until a century ago, the average garden was there for one thing only – to produce food. If you'd gardened then, you'd have kept animals and grown vegetables and herbs, not just for immediate use, but to store for the winter. You'd also have grown the ingredients of do-it-yourself medicines, cleaning products, fabric dyes and virtually anything else you wanted to use around the house. Even weeds were put to good use – horsetail (*Equisetum arvense*) makes a great panscrub. It's all a long way removed from how we live today, but the way our gardens look still reflects the way they are used.

The first 'real' gardens were probably enclosures, made by medieval peasants around their home-made hovels to stop livestock from wandering. As peasants became better off over the centuries, the enclosures developed into small holdings, which gradually became cottage gardens.

Traditionally, the working garden was at the back of the house, where there'd be the pigsty and poultry house, vegetable plot and fruit trees, and a well or pump providing the domestic water

The 'cottage garden' effect appeals to anyone with a nostalgic or sentimental streak.

However humble, a basket full of home-grown produce is always deeply satisfying.

supply. Round at the front was a pretty flower garden, where you kept hives of bees for honey that could be used for sweetening. Bee-attracting plants were a must!

Until as recently as the end of the last world war, cottage gardens still enabled their owners to be virtually self-sufficient; even today, country cottagers earn pin-money by selling honey, eggs and cut flowers at the garden gate, as they would have done in Victorian and Edwardian times.

Anyone who's ever sown a packet of seeds knows that one of the pleasures of gardening is the satisfaction of seeing the end result – serving up home-grown produce, cutting flowers for the house and raising plants for ourselves and friends, just as gardeners have done throughout history.

Decoration

The first garden flowers were useful plants, such as herbs, and what grew naturally – wildflowers – particularly the prettier variations with unusual colours or double flowers, which early cottagers dug up from hedgerow and field to plant in their gardens. Today, we're more conservation conscious and wild flowers are protected, which means that cultivated specimens must be bought in nurseries, or from seed merchants.

New plants brought from abroad by early traders, explorers or invaders meant that gardeners gradually had a greater variety to choose from. The biggest influxes of imported plants came in with the Romans, with knights returning from the Crusades, Elizabethan explorers and the Victorian plant hunters sent out by wealthy patrons. Such new plants always went to the owners of grand houses first, as they were the only ones who could afford them – ordinary people got the throw-outs via gardener's boys who lived in the village and passed them 'over the garden wall'. But plants also came back in Uncle Bill's kitbag when he returned from the Napoleonic wars, or other early campaigns.

By the 16th century, plants were being grown for their beauty alone, rather than simply for medicinal or culinary value. Naturally, it was the well-to-do who had the space, inclination and staff to grow such plants, but the idea rubbed off on the common herd who were, in spite of their lack of breeding, not insensitive to beauty!

In the 17th and 18th centuries, hobbyists bred and exhibited specially developed plants that became known as 'florists' flowers' – they included laced pinks and gold-laced polyanthus, some of which are still collected by enthusiasts today. Since then, the plant breeders have added an enormous range of flowers to our gardens that have never been seen in the wild and, today, they are available to anyone who will fork out a pound or two for a packet of seeds.

Entertainment

Now that we don't need a garden as a do-it-yourself supermarket, modern gardens can be all about having fun. For some people, it's the plants and design that matter most but, increasingly for others, the garden is used as an outdoor living room. The different ways we use gardens today is one reason why there are now so many styles of garden to choose from.

Gardens provide a creative outlet that is often lacking in modern life; you can practise arts and crafts, go organic, or experiment with interior decorating – outdoors. A garden is one of the few places in life where you can do what you like – a haven of peace where you can pull up the drawbridge after a hard day's work and indulge yourself.

Even a rooftop is today valued as an outdoor room for relaxation and for entertaining.

The garden environment

There's no getting away from it, a garden is a totally artificial environment. If you don't believe me, just leave a patch of ground alone for a year and see what comes up naturally – weeds, wild ivy, brambles and tree seedlings. The natural vegetation of Britain, historians tell us, was mostly giant beech or oak forests that were gradually cleared in medieval times to provide timber for housing, ship building, domestic enclosures and fires. Leave your garden to its own devices and, a century from now, it will be well on the way to becoming a wild wood. If we left our gardens alone now, in one hundred year's time, wild plants would have erupted from our gardens through our network of motorways and all but destroyed them. It's a thought I always find heartening.

A world of plants under one roof

The UK might not have a particularly big range of exciting native plants compared to places like the Amazon rainforest, but we have one huge advantage – our temperate climate. Without violent extremes of heat or cold, we can grow probably the widest range of plants from all over the world. Even quite a normal garden might hold rhododendrons from the Himalayas, eucalyptus from Australia, tulips from Iran, hardy cyclamen from Turkey and potatoes from South America.

How plants cope in a hostile environment

Wild plants have spent many thousands of years perfecting their survival techniques and some have adapted to living in pretty hostile conditions. In the garden, this means there are plants you can choose that will enjoy 'problem spots' where more ordinary, less suitable, plants often fail.

In dry regions, leaves may be very narrow, or have silver, grey or furry coverings to reduce water loss – plants such as artemisia, *Stachys byzantina* and pinks. Desert plants, such as cacti, have dispensed with their leaves altogether and just have fat, water-storing stems instead.

In tropical rainforests, where the humidity is high and plants are sheltered from drying winds by an overhead 'umbrella' of trees, they grow large, thin leaves that are the best sort for gathering low light. This is why they make good houseplants.

In boggy ground, plants don't have to worry about saving water, so they tend to have big leaves like giant solar panels. And in swamps, where the ground is short of nutrients, some plants, such as sundew and Venus fly trap, have turned carnivorous and obtain their nutrition by digesting insects.

Escapologists

Some imported plants have escaped from gardens to become naturalized nuisance 'weeds'. Japanese knotweed (above), *a foreign weed, was introduced by a Victorian botanist who thought it would make a good plant for his herbaceous border. It did – his and everybody else's.* Impatiens glandulifera *is a giant busy lizzie relative which invades river banks, spreading by seed flung from explosive capsules, and* Rhododendron ponticum *is so invasive that it has been banned from certain Hebridean islands.*

Climbers have 'learned' that they don't need to go to all the bother of growing rigid stems to get their leaves up to the light, because they can just scramble up somebody else's instead. They have developed all sorts of ways to hold on to other plants, from rose thorns that act like grappling hooks on twiggy stems, to the twining honeysuckle that corkscrews its way up anything upright.

Bulbous plants go into suspended animation when growing conditions get tough – a bulb is actually a complete plant in a time capsule. Some types, like tulips, go dormant in summer to survive a long, hot, dry spell, while summer-flowering dahlias have tubers that are dormant in winter when it's too cold to sustain growth.

Many plants that live where there's lots of competition have learned to spread fast and swamp their neighbours. That explains the success of weeds, such as greater bindweed and couch grass.

What this means for the gardener

Because most gardens contain a wide range of plants that don't grow there naturally, we have to match the varied needs of each plant to the actual growing conditions, which change slightly all around the garden. Because plants can't choose where they grow, we need to provide them with what they need – whether it's food and water, shelter, or something to climb up. We also have to make them behave, which might mean pruning, restricting their roots, or dead-heading to stop aggressive self-seeders taking over. It's all part of the taming of nature that we call gardening.

The tropics are all very well, but one of the greatest pleasures of gardening is to observe the effect of the changing seasons on the familiar patch of land around the house. Instead of everything staying the same all the time, you can see small changes taking place from one week to the next – new flowers coming out and new leaf tones developing. That's what makes walking around your own garden continually interesting, however well you know it.

Plants cope with their environments in various ways. The white furry covering on the leaves of *Stachys lanata* (*left*) helps to conserve moisture in the sun-baked environment where the plant originated. The lush leaves of the banana (*centre*) are large so as to absorb as much sunlight as possible in a tropical rainforest, and *Rodgersia* (*right*) grows in boggy ground and has access to plenty of water to support its large, fingered leaves.

Seasonal plants

Nothing ever stands still in the garden. Herbaceous plants (see page 28) die down for the winter and pop up again next spring; bulbs grow, flower and then die down again at different times of year – there are spring-, summer- and autumn-flowering bulbs, each with their own separate schedule.

Deciduous trees (see page 29) come into leaf in the spring and, during the summer, you'll gradually notice the leaf colour change from fresh lime-green to duller shades. Finally, the leaves fade or, in some cases, take on brilliant autumn tints before falling, to leave the bare shapes of trunks and stems visible in winter. Shrubs flower and some go on to produce colourful berries or fruits.

Some flowers bloom strongly all summer, while others stop early or go on to produce architectural seed heads that attract birds to feed. There are also short-lived seasonal flowers – annuals, or bedding plants – that are planted to provide a patch of colour for one particular season, in the garden or in containers, before being pulled out and replaced with something else for the next season.

Oh, I know that some gardeners can't keep up with this and feel that they can never get the garden 'sorted'. But once you stop thinking of the garden as ever being 'finished', you'll begin to enjoy the fact that it is always 'work in progress'.

Seasonal work

It's not just plants that are affected by the changing seasons. A lot of gardening activities are triggered at particular times of year and by the effects the seasonal weather has on plants.

Spring is the traditional start of the gardening season. It's the busiest time in the garden (see pages 124–26), when the warmer weather brings the spring flush of weeds, greenfly and other pests, and there's a lot of sowing and planting to be done. It's a good time for putting in perennials and, if you grow vegetables, there's a lot to do in the edible garden. You'll feel a bit like the circus performer who spins plates on tall sticks – sooner or later, some of them are bound to fall off. But don't worry – you can always pick them up again.

As the weather continues to improve, the big date in a gardener's calendar is that of the last frost. Once that has passed, it is safe to plant out frost-tender bedding plants, such as pelargoniums and fuchsias (see page 127) and that's when you start to see colourful summer displays in hanging baskets and tubs around front doors and on patios.

Summer is the most colourful season for flowers, when the roses, perennial plants (see pages 28 and 128) and bedding are at their best but, since most of the main jobs have been done, it's just a case of keeping on top of routine jobs, such as weeding, grass mowing and

British gardens, like this one at Glen Chantry in Essex, have one big advantage over their tropical counterparts – an ability to change the view through the seasons. Here, (*from the top, down*) silver birch trunks, red stems of *Cornus sanguinea* 'Midwinter fire' and drifts of snowdrops, *Galanthus* 'Atkinsii', provide interest in late winter and early spring. Daffodils, *Fritillaria meleagris* and spears of iris foliage arrive later. In summer, the lush foliage of blue hostas and green shuttlecock ferns, *Matteuccia struthiopteris*, as well as pink astrantias and feathery, pale green astilbe plumes give the border its full-blown glory. By autumn, the tints and contrasting shapes in the foliage still remaining from the herbaceous plants and the brown seedheads of astilbe, with the turning cornus leaves, are still providing colour and vibrancy in the garden.

Wait until the danger of late spring frosts has passed and then you can safely plant out summer bedding.

hedge clipping (see pages 127 and 129). For goodness sake, train yourself to relax at this time of year. Too many gardeners are incapable of sitting down. I know, I'm one of them – but I *am* in therapy!

Autumn is the end of the gardening season, when perennials, roses and bedding plants finish flowering and the garden is tidied ready for winter. It's a good time for planting fruit trees and bushes and ornamental trees and shrubs (see pages 130–34), as the wet weather means you won't have to do a lot of watering. The first frost of autumn means that cold-tender plants need bringing under cover if you want to keep them for next year. I like this time of year – I can move faster than the garden and once more get on top of things.

From November to February or March, gardeners try to do all their garden planning, soil preparation and construction jobs (see page 135), because the lack of routine chores means there's more time to spare. It's also the time when a lot of pruning is done – particularly clematis, grape vines and standard fruit trees – though other plants are pruned at various times during the growing season.

Looked at in this way, the garden seems a pretty demanding beast. But if you can learn to look at it in a more relaxed way, you'll appreciate it for what it is – a miracle of survival in an ever-more demanding world.

The growing season

Gardeners talk about 'the growing season' (see pages 114–21), by which they mean that part of the year when plants are growing actively – from spring to late autumn. The rest of the year, from late autumn to spring, is the dormant season, which is when deciduous trees and shrubs have lost their leaves and most plants are resting. The length of the growing season varies according to where you live. If you live in the far north of the country, or at high altitudes, the climate is colder and the growing season can be several weeks shorter than that close to the sea, or further south.

One thing you need to know when you start gardening, is the expected dates of the last spring frost and the first autumn frost in your area. This tells you when you can safely plant out frost-tender plants in early summer, and when you need to move them under cover in autumn. Because the climate varies so much around the country and the weather changes from year to year, it's impossible to give an exact date. Don't gamble – ask the locals – the hardened allotment gardeners and people at the gardening club. As a general rule, the last frost is usually around the middle of May in the southern half of the country and the first frost can be any time from mid-September onwards. In Cornwall, the last frost may be two weeks earlier and, in the north of Scotland, up to four weeks later.

What is a plant?

Plants are more like us than you might think. We have blood that flows through veins. They have veins through which flows a fluid called sap, which, like blood, also transports nutrients and other 'active ingredients'. Plants breathe and their lives are ruled by hormones and (admittedly basic) 'nervous systems'. They can reproduce themselves and even move. Sounds scary? Not really. I know a few people who are not such good company as a potted palm!

If you look back far enough into the past, it seems very likely that we once had a common ancestor. It may come as a surprise to you that we share half the same DNA as a banana and that our blood is almost identical to a plant's green pigment (chlorophyll) – except that blood contains a molecule of iron, whereas chlorophyll contains one of magnesium. OK, so it's stretching a point, but it makes you think.

Look at a traditional herbaceous border at the height of summer and you'll see plants at the peak of their performance.

Parts of a plant

To you and me, a chrysanthemum looks quite different to a pear tree, which in turn is nothing like a dandelion. But strip them down to their component parts and you find that all flowering plants have the same basic structure and work in exactly the same way.

Roots (1)

There are two sorts of roots. The big ones that you can see when you take a plant out of its pot, or dig it up, are there to anchor it in the ground. Most plants have branching roots that spread over a wide area, but some have tap roots that just go straight down. Seedlings grow tap roots first, to penetrate the ground, then they branch out later. Thick tap roots, such as carrots, are used for storing starches that the plant uses to fuel its flowering next year. None of these big roots take in water. That is done by the microscopic root hairs concentrated round the very tips of the main roots. Besides water, the root hairs take in dissolved nutrients – plants can't take in solid food, they suck up a mineral 'soup' that is drawn up through the plant by the 'pull' exerted by water evaporating from the leaves.

Stems (2)

Stems stiffen the plant so that it doesn't fall over and they hold leaves, flowers and fruit in the most advantageous positions for them to do their work. Some long-lived plants have thick stems in which part of the tissue turns to wood. This gives them an even stronger framework, which is vital in the case of trees that are big and have a lot of weight to carry.

Ringing in the years

Lignin (wood) in trees is laid down in distinct layers during each growing season, making the tree's characteristic rings. You can tell the age of a tree by counting the rings. The width of the rings shows which years were good or bad growing seasons, because, in a good year, a tree lays down more lignin, so creating wider rings.

Parts of a plant:
1 Roots absorb water from the soil, and tap roots, like this carrot, store food in the form of starch.
2 Stems are the 'pipes' that transport food and water to the parts of the plant where it is needed. The stem here has adapted and formed hairs to help prevent water loss in windy conditions.
3 Leaves and fronds – such as this tree fern – act like giant solar panels and factories, converting sunlight into food.

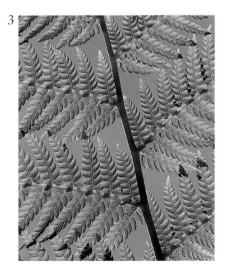

Stems also contain special tissue, 'xylem', that transports water and minerals all around the plant, and 'phloem' that takes starches and other things the plant has manufactured to wherever it's needed – usually to the roots where it can be stored.

Leaves (3)

Leaves are the powerhouse of the plant. Think of them as super-efficient solar panels with added technology. They absorb sunlight and, via the chemical wizardry of the green pigment, chlorophyll, use the sun's energy to transform carbon dioxide from the air and water from the soil into starches. Starches are ultimately used for building more plant parts, or for hoarding in underground stores, such as tap roots or tubers – think of carrots and potatoes. As a by-product of this process, known as photosynthesis, plants 'breathe out' oxygen – they are the lungs of the planet.

Flowers and seeds

Flowers are the way plants reproduce themselves. Male pollen from one flower is transferred to another of the same species, so that the female part of the flower is fertilized and can then produce a fruit or pod containing seeds, which eventually ripen and are shed to produce the next generation.

Each flower is made up of several parts. The petals act rather like an inn sign to attract pollinating insects. The stamens are the male part, made up of a stem (filament) with pollen-bearing anthers at the tip. The female part of the flower is the pistil, composed of a stigma (the sticky tip that traps the pollen), a tubular stem (the style), and an ovary deep in the flower, where the seeds form and which ultimately becomes a fruit or seed-pod.

Just like children, seeds need to leave home, otherwise the parent plant would be swamped with lively offspring competing for light, water and nutrients. For this reason, they have evolved all sorts of ingenious ways of travelling. Winged seeds, such as those of sycamore, literally fly away. Seeds inside hooked fruit, like burdock, latch on to passing animals for a free ride. Coconuts float on the sea for up to a year, travelling between islands without a thought of *mal-de-mer*. Seeds inside tasty fruits, such as blackberries, rely on animals or birds eating them and, later, depositing the seed elsewhere.

Most plants have flowers with both male and female parts, but some, such as birch and hazel, have separate male and female flowers on the same plant (monoecious plants). Others, like hollies, have male and female flowers on separate plants (dioecious plants). With these you need to grow a male and female plant close together to produce berries on the female. The sex life of plants makes our own look tediously straightforward in comparison.

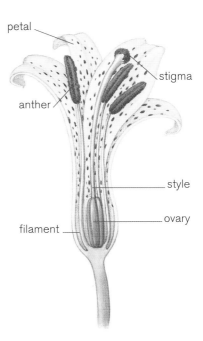

The stamen (male part) of the flower, is made up of the filament and anther. The pistil (female part) includes the stigma, style and ovary.

Doing the business

Some flowering plants are pollinated by insects and produce large, colourful, scented or nectar-rich flowers to attract bees and other pollinating insects. Others, like grasses and catkin-bearing trees, are wind pollinated and don't have colourful flowers because they don't need them. But some flowers are pollinated by creatures, such as bats, hummingbirds, flies or even, in the case of the aspidistra, by slugs. But then I've always thought the aspidistra a particularly desperate plant.

Different types of flower:
1 Daisy-like flower: rudbeckia.
2 Spike: lavender.
3 Raceme: verbascum.
4 Panicle: gypsophila.
5 Corymb: achillea.
6 Umbel: dill.

Types of flower

Flowers come in all shapes and sizes, as well as colours. There are 'proper names' for the various ways in which they are arranged on their stems and it helps to know them because that's the way they are often described on seed packets and in books. Knowing a bit of basic botany means you can picture the flower shape when there isn't a photo. There are several types apart from the solitary flower, like the tulip, which has a single flower at the end of each stem.

Daisy-like flower (1) The classic daisy flower is actually a mass of tiny 'disc' florets surrounded by 'ray' florets that make up a single 'flowerhead'.

Spike (2) A spike is a straight stem with lots of single, stalkless flowers evenly spaced out along it, as in lavender.

Raceme (3) Racemes are like spikes, except that each flower grows on a short stalk instead of straight from the main stem, as they do in verbascums. With me so far?

Panicle (4) Panicles are like racemes, except that each flower stalk is branched, so instead of one flower on the end of it, there is a whole bunch of them, as in gypsophila.

Corymb (5) A corymb is like a raceme, but the flower stalks are longer at the bottom than at the top of the stem, making a flat-topped flower, like those of achilleas.

Umbel (6) In an umbel, there are lots of florets on stalks radiating from the stem tip in a very geometrical pattern, like the spokes of an umbrella with flowers at the tips. Dill is a good example of this. And, if this seems a lot to remember, don't worry – you can look it up!

Plant names

There are a heck of a lot of plants out there. No-one knows for sure quite how many because, even today, new ones are being discovered in remote jungles but, at the last count, there were almost 300,000 different species. That isn't the total by any means – each species may include several wild varieties with different characteristics, such as flower colour. And it doesn't include the man-made forms (cultivars) that have been bred in cultivation.

What's in a name?
Even the most expert gardeners are familiar with only a fraction of the whole plant kingdom but, with so many to talk about, it's essential that we all use the same system of plant naming. The one used by botanists and gardeners the world over is based on that invented by the Swedish botanist, Carl von Linne (Linnaeus), in 1753. Once you get used to using the plants' Latin names, they are no more difficult to remember than your friends' forenames and surnames. And it still doesn't stop you calling them by their 'nicknames' or common names.

Plants have their 'surname' first, so all roses are called *Rosa*. The second name – equivalent to a forename – tells you which species it is, for example, *Rosa rugosa* (Latin names are always italicized). Wild forms of *Rosa rugosa* include several different colour forms, so you have a third name, such as *Rosa rugosa alba*, which tells you that it has white flowers – the lower case, italicized last name tells you that it occurs in the wild. Any variant of *Rosa rugosa* discovered or bred in captivity has the third name in Roman type and single quotes and always begin with a capital letter, thus *Rosa rugosa* 'Scabrosa'. Some plants are so interbred that nobody knows their precise parentage, so most modern roses are just known, for example, as *Rosa* 'Peace'. But you can still quite correctly call it a rose!

Infinite variety

The average garden centre probably stocks about 1000 different plants. Approximately 70,000 different varieties are currently on sale to gardeners in the UK. They are all listed, along with suppliers, in the RHS Plant Finder, an annual publication for plant enthusiasts, sold in bookshops and garden centres. If you want to know where you can buy any plant in cultivation, it will tell you.

Family trees

If you really go into plant names in detail, you can get a complete 'family tree' that shows you which plants are related to which others and share similar botanical characteristics, which means they are more likely to share similar needs in cultivation. This is what the family tree of two common roses looks like.

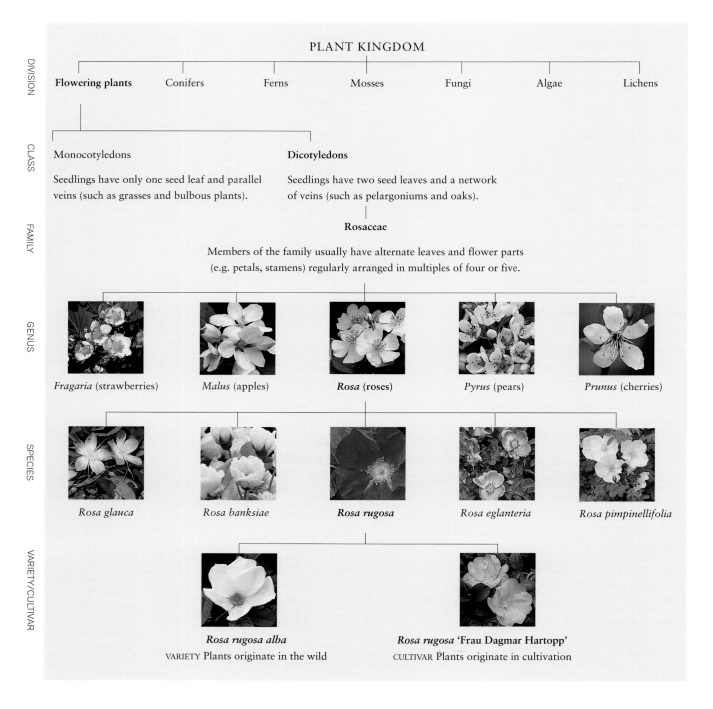

DIVISION

PLANT KINGDOM

Flowering plants   Conifers   Ferns   Mosses   Fungi   Algae   Lichens

CLASS

Monocotyledons

Seedlings have only one seed leaf and parallel veins (such as grasses and bulbous plants).

Dicotyledons

Seedlings have two seed leaves and a network of veins (such as pelargoniums and oaks).

FAMILY

Rosaceae

Members of the family usually have alternate leaves and flower parts (e.g. petals, stamens) regularly arranged in multiples of four or five.

GENUS

Fragaria (strawberries)   *Malus* (apples)   **Rosa** (roses)   *Pyrus* (pears)   *Prunus* (cherries)

SPECIES

Rosa glauca   *Rosa banksiae*   **Rosa rugosa**   *Rosa eglanteria*   *Rosa pimpinellifolia*

VARIETY/CULTIVAR

Rosa rugosa alba
VARIETY Plants originate in the wild

Rosa rugosa 'Frau Dagmar Hartopp'
CULTIVAR Plants originate in cultivation

Plant behaviour

Although plants don't 'behave' in the sense that animals do (but they can be just as tricky), they can do enough to take care of their own interests. In the wild, plants exist to reproduce themselves as quickly as possible and, if conditions are tough, they'll sacrifice leaves and other non-essentials in their effort to set (produce) seed. They'll stop flowering as soon as enough seed has been set, expending their energies on swelling and ripening the seed ready for distribution. Wild plants will also spread to colonize new areas for themselves and eliminate potential competition from other plants wherever possible.

In the garden, plants exist because the gardener wants them to be decorative; we want plants that keep flowering for as long as possible, with healthy attractive foliage. We are not usually bothered about collecting any seeds, but we do want plants to share the space happily with others. Gardening is all about making plants conform to what we want them to do, instead of letting them have their own way all the time.

Movement

Plants can't run around quite like animals, but some get quite close. To save water, the prayer plant (*Maranta*) folds its leaves up at night, when it's not using them to photosynthesize. *Mimosa pudica* has ferny leaves that collapse at a touch as a defence against predators.

Many plants show movement by opening and closing their petals in response to outside stimuli (though others keep their flowers open all the time once they start to bloom). Crocus flowers open when the air is warm enough, which makes sense, as early spring flowers stand a risk of being damaged by cold. Gazania and mesembryanthemum flowers only open when the sun is on them, and the evening primrose only opens at night – they are all responding to light intensity.

Family likenesses

You might be surprised to learn that plants as different as strawberries, roses and pears are related, but just take a close look at their flowers and you'll see that the similarity is evident (see page 24).

Plants move in different ways. An evening primrose flower (*left*) opens at the end of the day; a dandelion (*centre*) moves by dispersing its seeds; and a strawberry plant (*right*) sends out long stems, known as 'runners', on which grow small plants with roots to enable the parent plant to re-establish itself elsewhere.

Plants can move by sending out runners, like strawberry plants, or invasive roots, as with ground elder and nettles. But the way most plants move physically to a distant location is by shedding seed that is carried by the wind, or by animals, to a new site where the next generation can colonize. Think of dandelion 'clocks', which blow away as individual seeds on parachutes; sycamore seeds, which have built-in 'propellers'; explosive seeds like caper spurge, which are fired off a short distance, or blackberries, which are eaten by birds and then dropped with a built-in portion of nourishing manure, ready to grow into new brambles. Garden weeds are particularly good at doing this. But then that's why they've become weeds – wild plants growing where we don't want them.

Response to light

We all know about houseplants that lean over to face the light, which is why it's recommended that you give them a quarter turn every few days to keep them growing upright. But if you plant your clematis up a tree on the north side of the garden hoping their flowers will brighten up your view, you'll be disappointed because the plant will grow towards the light in the south and the flowers will turn to face it. The odds are that your next door neighbour will have a much better view of them than you do. This is regarded, in gardening parlance, as 'Sod's Law', but the plants are only following their basic instinct and responding to light. Roots do the reverse, growing away from the light to ensure that they grow down into the soil.

Response to gravity

Have you noticed how, if a potted plant falls over, the tip of the stem very soon bends upwards again? It's because it is responding to gravity – you can tell that it's gravity and not sunlight, because they'll even do it in the dark. Some plants don't have such a strong anti-gravity response, and these are the plants that naturally grow out along the ground, or trail down.

Response to daylength

Some plants (like chrysanthemums) are triggered to flower when the daylength shortens in autumn, while others flower in summer when the days are long. Commercial growers deliberately exploit this tendency in order to grow flower crops out-of-season, either by putting plants under artificial lights to lengthen the days, or by covering them with blackouts to give them shorter days. This is how growers get poinsettias to flower in time for Christmas – if left to their own devices, poinsettias would flower around Easter when the days and nights are roughly equal in length.

Learning the language

You don't need to learn a lot of gardening jargon to get growing, but the right word can say what might otherwise take a couple of sentences to explain. It's particularly handy to know the terms used on plant labels and in catalogues to categorize particular types of plants, as they tell you a lot of things you need to know at a glance.

Annuals

These are plants that last for one season only, that either die after flowering and setting seed, or, like bedding plants, are thrown away at the end of their first year. There are two sorts of annuals:

Hardy annuals stand the cold, so you can sow them outdoors in spring: March or April are the usual times. They'll germinate as soon as the soil is warm enough, and can flower several weeks earlier than half-hardy annuals. Examples are sweet peas (*Lathyrus odoratus*), sunflowers (*Helianthus annuus*) and nasturtiums (*Tropaeolum majus*).

Half-hardy annuals are killed by frost, but are also severely checked by cold. You can't plant them out until after the last frost, but then they keep growing till they are killed by the first frost of autumn. They include French marigolds (*Tagetes*), tobacco plants (*Nicotiana*) and petunias.

This really will be the scene 10 or 12 weeks after the seeds of hardy annual flowers are sown. Their life cycle is completed in a single growing season.

The native foxglove *(Digitalis purpurea)* is a biennial. Seeds sown in one year grow into plants that flower in the second year, after which the plant will die.

Biennials

Not so widely grown these days, biennials are plants that are sown one year and flower the next – such as wallflowers (*Erysimum cheiri*), sweet Williams (*Dianthus barbatus*), and foxgloves (*Digitalis purpurea*). Many are actually short-lived perennials – just to confuse matters – and may live for several years. But they are usually pulled out, after they have finished flowering the first time round, for tidiness or to make room for something else.

Perennials

Perennials are plants that die down to an overwintering rootstock each autumn and grow up again the following spring, like delphiniums and lupins. Years ago, we called them herbaceous plants and grew them in herbaceous borders. It's true that some perennials don't actually die down in winter – the evergreen kinds like hellebores, heuchera, bergenia and iris – but they are used in the same way in the garden and so they are conveniently lumped in the same category.

Hardy perennials are the ones you leave in the ground all year round, like hostas and delphiniums. In fact, you can usually leave them for three to five years before they need digging up and dividing (see pages 195–96).

Half-hardy perennials sound similar, but they differ in one major way. They include plants like pelargoniums and woody ones, such as fuchsias, that live for years but won't survive frost. These are plants that need to be kept under glass, or taken into a heated greenhouse, or indoors, for the winter. (Yes, I know some fuchsias are hardy, but many of the large-flowered kinds are not. Gardening has exceptions to every rule, mainly to prevent the likes of me from becoming too confident.)

Bedding plants

Bedding plants are any that are planted temporarily in beds, containers, or in odd gaps around the garden. These days, people usually mean half-hardy annuals or half-hardy perennials when they talk about bedding plants, but you can use bulbs and even shrubs as bedding plants if, for instance, you grow them for winter colour in the border, or in patio tubs.

Woody plants

This is a shorthand way of referring to plants that have a permanent structure of woody stems and branches above the ground, and they include trees, shrubs and climbers. A tree always has a trunk, even if it is only a short one with branches starting quite low down. A shrub has branches, but no trunk. Climbers and wall shrubs often cause a bit of confusion. Climbers have several stems where they leave the ground and scramble or climb naturally, but wall shrubs are normal free-standing shrubs that have been specially trained to grow flat against a wall, often because they are a tad too tender (fragile) to do well in the open, and they'll usually only have one stem where they leave the ground.

Deciduous and evergreen plants

Deciduous plants are those that lose their leaves every year in the autumn and replace them in spring, while evergreens keep theirs all year round – well, not quite. They do shed old leaves a few at a time throughout the year – often quite a lot of them in June, in the case of holly and evergreen oak (*Quercus ilex*) – but with most plants you'd hardly notice. Plants described as semi-evergreen, like *Cotoneaster horizontalis*, can't make up their minds. They'll keep their leaves in a mild winter, or a sheltered location, but shed them in cold winters or in exposed sites.

Most garden borders combine different types of planting, as found in this one:
1 Deciduous shrubs: *Physocarpus opulifolius* 'Diabolo' and
2 *Cornus alba* 'Elegantissima'.
3 Deciduous tree: *Gleditisia triacanthos* 'Sunburst'.
4 Grass: *Miscanthus sinensis* 'Zebrinus'.
5 Hardy perennial: hosta.

Bulbs

Lots of plants have storage organs, and there are several different kinds – true bulbs, corms, tubers and rhizomes – all with minor botanical differences that aren't of much practical interest to the gardener, so we usually lump them under the general term 'bulbs'.

A bulb (1) is a modified shoot; if you cut one in half vertically, you'll see it is made up of scale leaves (true leaves in embryonic form) and a 'bud' joined to a circular base plate, as in tulips and daffodils.

A corm (2) is an enlarged stem base, and is replaced every year by a new corm that grows from a bud on the original one. Crocus and gladiolus are examples of corms.

Tubers (3) are modified stems or roots, enlarged for storage. Examples are potato (stem tuber – the shoots or 'eyes' all over its surface are the give-away) and dahlia (root tuber – the shoots occur only at the top of the tuber).

Rhizomes (4) are creeping, horizontal, underground stems that produce roots. Examples are couch grass and bearded iris.

Types of bulb:
1 The daffodil is a true bulb.
2 The cyclamen is a corm.
3 The dahlia grows from a root tuber.
4 The German or bearded iris grows from a rhizome.

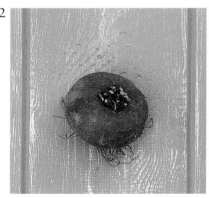

What plants need

Considering they can't get up and move around, plants are surprisingly sophisticated. They are like living factories; they manufacture some very complicated products – starches, fats and proteins, plus all their own colourings, hormones and enzymes – which is pretty good going when you think that they only have air, sunlight, water and soil to start with.

Every time you go around with the watering can, or a packet of fertilizer, you're helping to keep plants topped up with things they need, but how often do you really think about what you are doing? As in a real factory, plants need to be constantly supplied with all their various ingredients to work at peak efficiency; there's a very delicate interaction between ingredients. If one runs short, growth slows or stops until the shortage is made up. That's why commercial growers take such pains to manage the temperature, watering and feeding in their greenhouses so precisely – they may even add the carbon dioxide needed for photosynthesis to the air. Not at all surprising when you consider that it's their living.

At home we grow plants for fun, so it doesn't really matter if they don't work at peak potential all the time, though naturally we want them to grow well so that we have a garden that looks good. Even though we can't control the weather, keeping plants supplied with everything else they need is the secret of creating good growing conditions.

In the wild, plants grow in a natural situation that provides them with all they need – the rich woodland soil suits bluebells down to the ground.

Water

Plants are made up of over 80% water, but most of the water inside a plant isn't stored – it's in transit. Water is 'sucked' in through the root hairs (see page 20) and drawn up through the plant by the 'suction' created by evaporation through the leaves. A plant is just like a giant wick. On a hot summer's day, a big plant like a mature oak tree might lose up to 300 litres (66 gallons) of water through its 700,000 leaves, all of which has to come from the soil.

Water is the 'carrier' for all the things that move around inside a plant. Oxygen and carbon dioxide gases are dissolved in it; so are mineral nutrients taken in from the soil. As any gardener knows, the faster a plant grows, the more water it needs. That's because the hotter and drier the air is, the faster the plant loses water through the 'pores' (stomata) beneath its leaves. But there comes a point when the plant can't move enough water through itself to keep pace with demand, either because conditions are too hot or because there isn't enough water at the roots, so it craftily closes the whole system down by shutting its pores. This happens automatically when the water pressure drops inside special 'guard' cells round the stomata, which 'wilt' like deflating balloons, blocking the opening. Once the crisis is past and the temperature drops, or the plants are watered, the pressure returns to normal and the guard cells plump up again, which opens the pores.

Now, that might just sound like a bit of useless information, but it explains why a lot of pot plants run into problems on hot, sunny windowsills, or in a greenhouse in summer. Every time the soil in a pot dries out, or your greenhouse overheats in the sun, the plants stop growing until conditions return to normal. And if conditions just keep getting worse the plants lose more water and start to wilt. Wilting is what happens when all the cells – not just those round the pores – lose their water pressure. And if plants wilt badly enough or for long enough, even cooler temperatures and more water aren't enough to start the flow of water through the plant running again, and then there's nothing you can do to save it. Desiccation sets in and it dies. Crispy plants will not revive.

So if you didn't already know it, wilting plants need urgent attention, but it's much better to prevent them from wilting in the first place. That's why I'm always banging on about feeding and watering plants in containers, and ventilating your greenhouse or conservatory. Shading helps, too, in summer. The idea is to keep the temperature below 30°C (85°F), because that is the point at which virtually all plants stop growing temporarily until things get a bit cooler.

Water moves up through a plant and transpires through pores (stomata) on the undersides of the leaves. When its dry and hot, the plant cannot transport water fast enough, so its water pressure drops, closing the pores and the wilting process begins.

This water-loss business is also why newly planted bedding plants, vegetables and even woody plants, like trees, shrubs and climbers, need watering until they get established. Until new roots can grow out into the soil to find moisture, new plants can easily lose more water through their leaves than they take in through the roots. And in windy weather, they lose water even faster.

Nutrients

Plants might look pretty solid, but most of their bulk is made up of oxygen, carbon and hydrogen, obtained from air and water and transmuted into solid form during photosynthesis. The rest consists of around 30 chemical elements taken up from the soil, which are needed in different quantities and must be replaced regularly as they grow. Yes, I know all this is getting a bit scientific, but stick with me – it will all make sense in the end.

Domestic science

You can easily prove to yourself how much of a plant is water. Next time you cut a bunch of herbs to dry, weigh them as soon as you have cut them, then again after drying them in a warm oven until they are crisp. The difference is all water. Don't think of it as a scientific experiment – although it is – because you can still rub the leaves from the dry stems and store them in jars, ready to use.

Major nutrients	Deficiency symptoms	Natural sources
Nitrogen promotes leafy growth	Slow growth, upper leaves pale green and lower leaves yellow	Rain, nitrogen-fixing nodules on the roots of leguminous plants, like clover, peas and beans; garden compost and manure; nitrogen-fixing bacteria in soil containing plenty of organic matter
Phosphorus encourages root development	Stunted plants with very dark leaves with red or purple tinges; leaves tend to fall early	Some rocks and soils
Potassium promotes fruit and flower production	Tips and edges of older leaves near the base of the plant turn yellow and then die and turn brown	Some rocks and soils, especially clay soils, with sandy soil most likely to be deficient
Minor elements		
Magnesium		Dolomite limestone
Sulphur		Air pollution
Calcium		Limestone, eggshells, shellfish shells, hard tap water, bonemeal, calcified seaweed, superphosphate
Vital trace elements		
Iron, manganese, molybdenum, zinc, copper and **boron**		Bulky organic matter, seaweed products

Optional extras used by some plants: chlorine, sodium, cobalt, aluminium, bromine, iodine, vanadium and silicon

A tomato leaf (*left*) showing signs of magnesium deficiency, and a tomato plant (*right*) with healthy green leaves.

There are three main elements that are vital to plant growth – nitrogen (N), phosphorus (P) and potassium (K). Think of them as the proteins and carbohydrates of the plant's diet – the meat and two veg. Then there are several minor elements and 20 or so trace elements that are needed only in minute amounts. Think of these as the vitamins that plants need. They are all present in most garden soils, especially those that contain plenty of organic matter, but you can't keep taking material out of the garden – whether it is vegetables, cut flowers, lawn mowings, or fruit tree prunings – without putting something back (see pages 49–51).

Although you sometimes find plants suffering from a shortage of one particular mineral – tomatoes, for example, are very prone to magnesium deficiency – it is much more common to find them short of a whole range of nutrients because they are generally underfed. That is where fertilizers come in (see pages 52–53). But don't panic! If you improve the soil and use fertilizers properly, you'll rarely see deficiency symptoms.

Air

We take air very much for granted because it's all around us. Most gardeners think of air in terms of greenhouse ventilation. My old boss at the municipal nursery talked about 'putting on a crack of air' when he wanted the greenhouse vents opened only slightly. But there's much more to it than that.

Air provides plants with the oxygen and carbon that, with sunlight acting as the energy source and water providing hydrogen (it's H_2O, remember?), are the ingredients needed for photosynthesis, the process by which plants make sugars and starches (see pages 35–36). They don't stop there. Those sugars are converted into everything else plants need by more complicated chemical processes, using other elements taken up from the soil.

The air is also a source of nitrogen, one of the 'big three' plant nutrients, which gets into the soil in several cunning ways. Some of it is dissolved in the rainwater every time there is a thunderstorm. You can almost smell it. Nitrogen is also 'fixed' in the soil by bacteria in the nodules of the roots of leguminous plants, like clover, peas and beans, and by the soil bacteria that are found in healthy soils where there is lots of organic matter.

Light

Photosynthesis – the process that kick-starts a plant's entire internal factory – only happens in light, so it figures that if plants don't get enough of it, they can't work at full potential.

But some plants need more light than others. Some are adapted to work in low light – ferns, hostas, and the tropical plants we grow as houseplants that live naturally under tiers of trees. That's why they are so happy indoors. Living room conditions (apart from the central heating which can really dry out the air) are virtually identical in terms of shade and temperature to those of a tropical jungle – just think of that next time you plan an exotic holiday!

You can usually tell a plant that is used to shady conditions by its large, light-gathering leaves, which will be quite thin if it also likes moist soil or humid air. If you give shade lovers sunny conditions, some – such as hostas – will be all right provided they have enough moisture at the roots, so they don't dehydrate. But often, shade lovers, such as ferns, will 'scorch' in bright sunlight – the leaves just dry out and go brown, lacking the ability to absorb sufficient moisture to combat the drying effects of the sun – and then the plant dies.

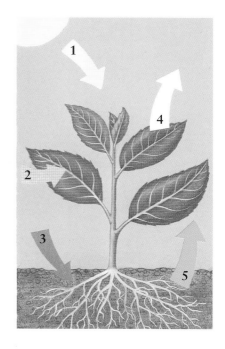

Photosynthesis enables plants to use sunlight (1), carbon dioxide (2) and water (3) to produce oxygen (4) and vital energy (5) with which to grow.

Plants, such as ferns, have adapted over millions of years to make use of the low light intensity in shady spots – so much so that in full sunlight their leaves can be scorched.

True sun lovers need a lot of direct sunlight on their leaves, otherwise they grow weak and spindly trying to reach the light. What's more, if they don't have enough light, they won't flower. Plants that are naturally adapted to life in really hot, bright sun have developed their own defences – their reflective silvery skins, furry or waxy surfaces are designed to protect them from overheating and prevent them losing too much water.

In the wild, plants can 'choose' where they grow. The parent scatters seeds, which will end up in all sorts of places, and it's only the ones that land in the right set of growing conditions that survive. In the garden, plants have to put up with where we put them, so that's why it pays to do a bit of homework and find out what conditions they need, so we can give them a place where they'll do well.

The plants growing in this gravel garden enjoy brilliant sunlight and good drainage at the roots – it mirrors their natural environment.

Warmth

Plants grow over virtually the whole surface of the planet Earth, including under the sea, and there are even a few that survive in deserts and areas of permafrost. But because the climates vary so much between the equator and the poles, the same plants don't grow everywhere – different plants have evolved to suit different temperature regimes.

The trouble is, we want to grow all of them – well, okay, a lot of them – in our gardens. Sometimes, we need the help of a greenhouse or conservatory to grow tender or exotic species, but, in many cases, we expect plants from all over the world to grow happily side-by-side in the garden. That's why it's useful to know what they are used to in the wild.

Plants that live in cold regions, or at very high altitudes, we usually refer to as alpines. They are adapted to life in harsh environments, with a short growing season between snow melt and snow fall and must get their growing, flowering and seed distribution over with quickly. Many have their own built-in, cellular 'anti-freeze' to keep them alive.

In hot areas, plants have to adapt to particular cycles of heat and cold, often with alternate wet and dry seasons that can be quite extreme. Tulips are a good example. They come from hot countries, such as Turkey and Iran, and grow in winter when the weather is mild and wet, flower in spring as the weather warms up, then duck underground to sit out the hot, dry summer as dormant bulbs safely insulated by a thick layer of soil.

Even in temperate zones you can experience different degrees of cold in winter and warmth in summer depending on latitude, and the plants that will grow happily in one place don't always survive in another. So it pays to know your own garden climate and how to pick the plants that will be happy in it (more later, on pages 115–21).

Soil

Soil has been created by nature from a strange mixture of ingredients. Most of it is rock that has taken millions of years to be turned into mineral dust. Sometimes this happened when glaciers picked up boulders and moved them slowly over bedrock, grinding up pebbles on the way. Chalk formed under water from the shells of trillions of tiny marine animals that lived and died millions of years ago. When the earth's crust buckled, it pushed the chalk up into cliffs – think of 'The White Cliffs of Dover' – and sun, wind and rain continually battered the outer layers of soft rock into dust. It's still going on now. The same kind of things happened to 'weather' other types of rock, from sandstone to granite, into soil, which is why soil types vary so much. They all depend on the kind of 'parent' rock.

The chemical elements found in soil also depend on the rocks it was made from – in Australia, soils are often very short of phosphorus because the parent rocks don't contain much. In some parts of the world, soil is composed largely of ash from volcanoes – it is rich in a huge range of plant nutrients and very fertile. The Indonesians never use fertilizer, yet produce enormous crops of rice and vegetables on their rich volcanic soil.

Soil also contains a proportion of organic matter, made from the natural decay of animal and plant matter, which is particularly high in woodland, where large numbers of fallen branches and leaves die and decay, enriching the soil. In the world's wetlands, there are areas of highly organic soil; in the fens and bogs, there are big peat

---

Not too hot, not too cold

As a good general rule, most plants that are hardy in temperate Britain grow actively between temperatures of 7–30°C (45–85°F). Below or above that range, photosynthesis ceases and the plants are just 'ticking over'.

Well-nourished soil produces well-nourished plants. Most of them will thrive in organically rich soil that is nevertheless well drained. You can almost see this lily-of-the-valley growing.

deposits that formed when prehistoric plants that died and were consumed by bogs could not decompose completely because of the high acidity and lack of oxygen.

But the soil you see on the surface of your garden is only the tip of the iceberg – if you dig down about a metre (3ft), you'll probably find things look quite different underneath (see pages 48 and 242–45). If you can stand the slave labour this is quite a good thing to do, because what's underneath may have a considerable bearing on common garden problems. You'll often find there's a layer of solid clay beneath a layer of good topsoil, which prevents plants rooting down deeply, or causes waterlogging in winter. Or you might find a band of sand or chalk that explains why plants dry out so badly in summer. Digging a hole, as well as doing a soil test to check the pH (the measure of acidity or alkalinity, see pages 90–94) is always a good first move when you take on a new garden.

From a plant's point of view, soil is the foundation of their home. It provides several things their roots need – nutrients, water and air, as well as a means of holding themselves upright.

Soil nutrients

Strange as it sounds, you *can* grow plants without soil. It's a technique called hydroponics, and commercial growers use it all the time for some types of crops – tomatoes and orchids are often grown in rockwool. At home people sometimes grow hyacinths in jars of water, or houseplants in containers filled with clay granules.

But if you grow plants without soil, you have to find other ways of providing them with the nutrients they'd normally get from it. Growing in soil is much easier, because plants take up what they want and leave what they don't want – the nutrient reserves in the soil act as a natural 'buffer' against hard times, and you don't get these in artificial growing media, or in peat-based growing mixes.

Soil, if it's healthy, actually generates a lot of its own plant food – naturally occurring micro-organisms all work away, making nutrients out of atmospheric nitrogen or organic matter and there are special fungi that cohabit with plant cells to help create a root-friendly feeding environment. Oh, soil might *look* brown and dreary but, as ever, you shouldn't be fooled by appearances.

Soil air

You never really think of roots needing air, but they do; they need oxygen to 'breathe' in order to function. They get it from tiny air spaces between soil particles. Soil is naturally porous, or should be.

Sandy soil is made up of large particles with correspondingly large air spaces in between them – that's why sandy soil dries out so quickly, because there's lots of room for water to run through it.

Clay and silty soils, on the other hand, are made up of very tiny particles with equally tiny air spaces in between, so water can't run through them easily. That's why clay soils tend to become waterlogged in persistent wet weather. Plants can literally die by drowning if the soil is waterlogged.

You can begin to see now why organic matter is so important. It is spongy, so it actually improves both types of soil. On sand, it helps bind the particles together to fill some of the gaps, and its spongy nature helps the soil to hold water. On clay, it binds tiny particles together to create bigger ones, which helps to form drainage channels. Organic matter also encourages earthworms, which improve the drainage by making tunnels. Adding gritty sand is even better for 'opening up' the texture of clay soil.

Soil anchorage

The thing that's easily overlooked about soil is the way it provides support and anchorage for roots. Roots grow out into the soil to keep the plant upright. It's easy to imagine big trees having roots like guy ropes to hold them upright, but that's not always so, as we saw when the Great Hurricane of 1987 blew so many big trees over in Britain. Looking at the trees that came down around my garden at Barleywood, I wondered how most of them had remained upright for so long. There was just a circle of roots fanning out round the bottom of the trunk, with nothing going down to any depth at all.

Since only the tiny roots at the very tip of the beefier ones actually take in water, this is pretty smart of trees. It means that all the water-absorbing roots are arranged round the drip-line – the circle of soil under the very edge of the canopy of branches where they'll find most of the water that runs off the foliage as if from a giant umbrella. But it also explains why if you have a huge tree in your garden nothing much grows underneath it – the soil is full of surface roots that take up all the available moisture and nutrients.

Look at a fallen tree and you'll see that most of its roots spread outwards from the trunk rather than going straight down. This is so that the fine feeding root tips reach the perimeter of the umbrella-like canopy where they can better absorb rainwater and nutrients.

What plants need	Why they need it
Water	To prevent stems wilting and leaves drying out
Nutrients	To prevent slowing or stunting of growth and unhealthy changes in leaf colour (fading, yellowing or purple tinging)
Air, light and warmth	To enable them to photosynthesize properly and convert energy to food in order to grow
Soil	As a source of nutrients, water and air, and as support and protection for the root system

What you need

My shed is groaning with gardening gear. I have special tools for everything from digging ditches to thinning grapes, but I never use them – they just decorate the walls. You could count the ones I use regularly on the fingers of two hands and you'd know straight away which ones they were because they are propped up just inside the door. They are usually dirty, either because I've just finished using them, or because I am just about to pick them up again, so they only get cleaned properly in winter.

Clean your tools occasionally (opposite) – it's really quite therapeutic – and sharpen them regularly.

The initial outlay

Considering that the spade I use belonged to my grandfather and was used by him on his Yorkshire allotment and by my dad (the plumber) for mixing concrete, it's actually doing very well in spite of the apparent mistreatment. But it just goes to show, if you've never done any gardening before, you don't actually need all that much to get started. Most people begin with a few old tools handed down from a parent or grandparent who has upgraded. Don't spurn these beauties. They'll be run in for you – with silk-smooth handles and well-honed blades. With luck! If you don't have a relative with an overflowing shed, then I'd suggest buying just the essentials from the economy ranges of any of the well-known garden tool manufacturers – you'll have no trouble finding them in most good garden centres. There's no need to spend a fortune. You can always add to your basic tool kit later, but for starters these are the things you'll really need.

The handles of spades and forks come in different styles – here a 'T' and a 'D' shape. Choose whichever you find most comfortable to use.

Spade and fork

These are the basic digging implements. A spade is better for digging sandy or loamy soil. Some people find a fork is best on clay soil, as it makes it easier to smash up the clods. A spade tends to get clogged if the ground is a bit stodgy, but a fork is definitely better on soil that contains stones as the prongs go between them, whereas a spade would just come to a grinding halt mid-stroke. A fork is also handy for moving manure or compost from a heap into a barrow and then spreading it around.

I reckon the fork is the most valuable implement in the garden. I even use it for final breaking down of soil on the vegetable plot. Hold it horizontally and bring it down at an angle on the soil, knocking the clods to shatter them. Using a rake to break soil down produces too fine a tilth that 'cakes' in a shower of rain. A rake is for final levelling – nothing else.

With spades and forks some people prefer a T-handle and others swear by a D-handle, so try out both before buying. Tempered steel blades are perfectly adequate. If you fancy stainless steel, be prepared to pay more, but beware of the cheaper models – they can be brittle and short-lived.

Tall people, or those with dodgy backs, might also find it worth trying the long-handled, American-style digging shovel, the sort you see gold miners using in old black-and-white films. They are said to be much less of a strain. Personally I'll stick to my grandad's old spade; it's like a family heirloom now.

Hoe

Garden tool catalogues are awash with fancy varieties of hoe, but they all do the same basic job: weeding. One is enough to start with, but hoes are something you tend to acquire as you find new models that you enjoy using just that little bit more. There are two basic types.

Draw hoes, or chop hoes, have the head at right angles to the handle; they are used with a chopping action and are best for hacking down big weeds, as you will need to do if you are clearing an overgrown vegetable plot. Short-handled versions with arched, 'swan' necks are known as onion hoes and they are brilliant for weeding between rows of any vegetables, on your hands and knees, where you need a bit more precision.

Push hoes, or Dutch hoes, are better for smaller weeds in borders, where the plants don't grow in rows. To use these, you just glide the blade forward through the soil. Some of the newer designs work on both the push and the pull strokes, so in theory you get double the work for your efforts. In practice, you can end up chopping off a lot of plants, too, if you aren't careful. Try several before buying, even if the other customers in the shop think you are a bit odd practising your hoe-swings out on the floor.

Remember, when using a hoe, skim it just below the surface of the soil so that weeds are cut off at their stocking tops – where the shoot meets the roots. Hoe too deeply and the weed will be dug up and can easily re-root after a shower of rain.

Hoes are most effective at controlling weed seedlings and annual weeds – things like groundsel, and chickweed (see page 141). They can weaken perennial weeds, such as ground elder (see page 146), and repeated hoeing can eventually wipe them out, but it takes a long time. Thick-rooted perennial weeds are always best forked or dug out of the soil completely.

Rake

The ordinary garden rake with short parallel teeth is meant for levelling soil, to make an even surface ready for sowing or planting. When used properly, the idea is to gather up large stones, bits of root and other rubbish behind it, which can be easily picked up and removed – you shouldn't end up with a great pile of soil as well. If you do, have another go. The idea is to redistribute the soil as you rake, and only gather up unwanted surface material. Don't over-rake, and don't remove too many stones. Plants' roots have no problem getting round them, and you'll only have to find a way to dispose of them.

The sort of rake with a wide fan of springy wire or rubber tines is meant for raking leaves off the lawn, or smoothing out footprints from gravel paths.

Trowel or hand fork

You need one or other of these for weeding, planting bedding plants and small perennials, and for fiddling about in pots on the patio. I like to use a hand fork for scuffling over the soil between plants to tidy up after planting a bed; it's just a habit, I suppose, but it does stop the soil from looking like a rugby pitch. But if you are going to have only one of these implements, choose a trowel – one that feels comfortable in your hand.

When you use it, don't hold it like a flour scoop. Position the handle so that the end of it sits right in the palm of your hand with the concave side of the blade facing you. A hole is excavated by pushing the trowel into the soil and pulling the earth towards you – rather like a primitive claw. Stainless steel trowels and hand forks are a good buy. They are relatively inexpensive, but last for years, unlike cheap hand tools which have a nasty habit of bending double or snapping off just when you've got used to them. I love old trowels which can often be bought for next to nothing and have blades that are razor sharp.

Various tools are needed for jobs around the garden. The push hoe (*left*), or Dutch hoe, is great for cutting off annual weeds, but keep it sharpened with a file so that it works efficiently. A stainless steel trowel (*centre*) is comfortable to use for planting, and very long lasting, and a rake (*right*) should be thought of as a levelling tool, not as a way of turning soil into dust.

Wheel barrow

Get a decent builder's barrow if you have some serious shifting to do. If you don't, then get a garden humper – a plastic tub with two handles – it's all you really need for carting weeds to the compost heap, or spreading soil improvers and mulches round the garden.

Watering can

A watering can is very handy for watering containers on the patio, and it's difficult to use liquid feeds without one. But if you want to use a watering can for liquid weedkillers, then I'd have a separate one clearly marked: WEEDKILLER. However well you rinse it out, there is always the risk that a trace will remain and that's often all it takes to kill susceptible plants. Tomatoes are notoriously sensitive to hormone weedkillers – even months after they were used in a can. Buy cans in two different colours, so there's no confusion.

If you have a big garden, or a lot of things to water, then it's worth getting a hosepipe, but then you really need to have an outdoor tap plumbed in – you'll soon get fed up feeding the end through the kitchen window. Liquid-feed dilutors, which make sure that the right strength of fertilizer is dispensed, can be bought to fit on to hosepipes.

Secateurs

Even in a brand-new, or labour-saving garden, you'll need to prune a rose or cut back an overgrown shrub sooner or later. There's no need to spend a fortune on 'professional quality' secateurs. An inexpensive pair will do very well to start with; then, when you graduate to a better pair later, you'll have an old pair to use for all the rough jobs.

Some people prefer the parrot-beak type of secateurs – the ones with two sharp blades that bypass each other like scissors – others plump for the anvil type – which have one sharp blade that cuts down onto a flattened base. It's entirely up to you – I'm a bypass man myself. A good pair, which may be guaranteed for life, can cost a reasonable sum, but it's money well spent. Choose secateurs with bright red handles, as they will then show up well when you put them down somewhere.

Normal, short-handled secateurs will cut through stems up to 15–20mm (½–¾in) thick. For thicker stems, a pair of long-handled loppers is handy – they have wider jaws and longer handles that give you more leverage. If you need to cut back climbers or tall trees, you can get long-reach pruners, which are like secateurs on a pole, with a trigger handle at your end.

Secateurs are a vital pruning tool, so keep them well oiled and rub the blades with emery paper to remove any dried sap which can make them stick.

Where to start

Before you can start any serious garden-making, the ground nearly always needs clearing. You might have inherited a jungle of weeds and overgrown shrubs from a previous owner that needs clearing completely, or you might just want to turn a patch of grass into beds and borders. Even if you start with what looks like a virgin site on a new housing estate, you might find the ground has been badly churned up by heavy machinery and needs a bit of sorting out before you can grow things in it.

I know it's very tempting to get some plants in straight away and worry about the weeds or the dreadful soil later. Everyone does it at some time, because they are so keen to start seeing some flowers. But if you don't tackle the serious problems first, you'll be struggling with bindweed, or wondering why nothing wants to grow for years – and it can cost a fortune in failed plants. Soil improvement is vital too, so, at the risk of sounding like a kill-joy, do the groundwork first. It won't take long if you pull your finger out.

Second-hand gardens

When you inherit someone else's old garden, you never know what you are going to find. There might be some real treasures, or whole borders that are basically okay apart from being a bit overgrown with weeds. On the other hand, you might be faced with an overgrown tangle that you just want to clear away so that you can start again from scratch. If there are only a few plants worth saving, it's probably easier to dig them out and put them in pots to keep them safe while you tackle the undergrowth.

Digging weeds out by hand is the safest way to clear them when they are growing close to plants that you want to keep. If you are razing whole beds to the ground, it is much quicker to burn them off with a flame gun, though that won't kill perennial roots and you'll probably need to do it several times to kill the regrowth if the ground is very weedy.

If you don't mind using chemicals, then weedkiller is often the easy answer if the 'jungle' contains a lot of hard-to-get-rid-of perennial weeds, such as bindweed and ground elder (see pages 145 and 146). Even though I don't usually use chemicals, this is one situation in which I'd seriously suggest using a glyphosate-based product to eradicate them, because it kills them roots and all. The residue of glyphosate is non-persistent and safe to pets and wildlife, once dry. One or two doses, about six weeks apart, applied at any

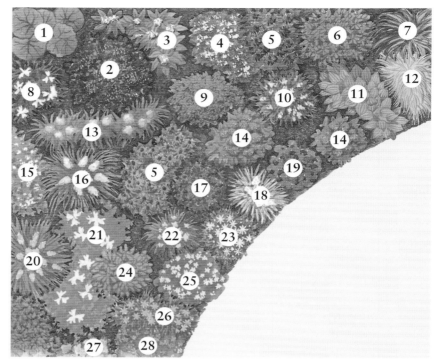

Revive an old bed (*above*) by keeping some established plants to provide structure, and adding new plants around them. A simple, or detailed, planting plan (*right*) can help you envisage the finished border (*below*). The plan shows plants at their peak and not all of them can be seen here.

time the weeds are growing strongly, is usually all it takes to do the job, unless there is a very serious infestation (see pages 153–54). You can garden without chemicals from then on.

Real organic fans will sometimes opt for the old carpet method, which involves smothering weeds out under a complete layer of old carpet, or black polythene. This starves the weeds by depriving them of light, but it takes about two years to work (see pages 155–56).

Whatever you do, don't just plough the lot in with a rotavator. If there are perennial weed roots, all you'll do is chop them up and propagate them. Each piece turns into a root cutting that grows into a new plant.

If you need to get rid of whole trees or tree stumps, hire a qualified person who knows what they are doing. A tree surgeon will cut the branches off a big tree and then reduce the trunk in stages, which is much safer than chopping it down in one go, especially if it's close to buildings. Tree stumps can sometimes be winched out if there is room for the equipment, otherwise get in a contractor with a stump grinder. It looks like a rotavator and chews the stump to sawdust; then you shovel out the remains. If you refill the hole with topsoil, you can plant something else later the same day.

Lawn conversions

Maybe you have an existing garden and fancy digging up a patch of the lawn to make a new bed. If so, don't just rotavate or dig it in, or you'll have grass growing up as weeds in your new bed for ever more. Either kill off the grass with glyphosate and dig it in after four to six weeks, or strip the turf right off to leave bare soil. You can skim off the turf to about 2.5cm (1in) deep with the back of a spade – unless you feel like hiring a mechanical turf stripper. Use the turf to re-turf a new piece of ground, or stack it up in a heap somewhere out of the way, grass side down, for a year. By then it will have decomposed and turned into good topsoil that is handy for topping up a bed.

Ground that has been under grass for several years usually has a very good structure. The old roots provide fibre and the worms will have worked through it. But on the downside, it'll have a high population of soil pests just waiting to nibble off the roots of any plants you put in. Turf and grassland are the preferred habitats of such root-eating pests as leatherjackets (daddy-long-legs larvae), wireworms (click beetle larvae) and chafer grubs. If you don't want to use a soil pesticide, then it's best to turn the soil over several times in winter. This exposes the soil-dwelling beasts to hungry birds, who'll be happy to deal with them for you.

Key to the plants chosen for the border (*left*):

1 *Darmera peltata.*
2 *Cotinus* 'Grace'.
3 *Verbascum* 'Raspberry Ripple'.
4 *Cimicifuga simplex* var. *simplex* Atropurpurea group.
5 *Echinacea purpurea.*
6 *Skimmia fortuneii.*
7 *Phormium* 'Maori Queen'.
8 *Lilium regale.*
9 *Weigela florida* 'Foliis Purpureis'.
10 *Penstemon* cultivar (white).
11 *Hosta* 'Halcyon'.
12 *Hakonechloa macra* 'Aureola'.
13 *Eremurus* hybrids (mixed).
14 *Sedum spectabile* 'Indian Chief'.
15 *Cimicifuga simplex.*
16 *Cortaderia selloana* 'Sunningdale Silver'.
17 *Rosa* 'Indigo'.
18 *Sisyrinchium striatum* 'Aunt May'.
19 *Geranium sanguineum.*
20 *Kniphofia* 'Yellow Cheer'.
21 *Melianthus major.*
22 *Sisyrinchium striatum.*
23 *Osteospermum* 'Buttermilk'.
24 *Rhododendron yakushimanum.*
25 *Geranium sanuineum* 'Album'.
26 *Gazania* cultivar (yellow).
27 *Trollius x cultorum* 'Lemon Queen'.
28 *Geranium* 'Johnson's Blue'.

First-time gardens

If you've just moved into a brand-new house, don't assume you'll have good soil all ready to garden on. You might be lucky... but take a good look around. New houses often have piles of builders' rubble left around outside, or ground that has had the life squashed out of it by heavy vehicles. Sometimes there are oil spillages or, most frequently, infertile subsoil has just been dumped and spread out, so the ground needs quite a bit of work to get it back in good shape before anything much will grow. It's a soul-destroying process, but later on you'll be glad you sorted things out at the beginning.

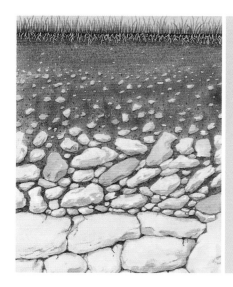

A worm's-eye view

The cross section of any soil is known as a soil profile – a sort of worm's-eye view of the different layers within the ground. On the surface, just below any living vegetation, will be a layer of rotting and rotted organic matter. This is known as humus, and is a vital source of soil improvement when dragged under the surface by worms. It enriches the topmost layer of earth known, not surprisingly, as topsoil. This is where most plant roots grow. Beneath it is subsoil – it may be clay or gravel or sand. It is usually lacking in nutrients and not nearly so hospitable to root growth as the richer topsoil. Below the subsoil will be a layer of fragmented rock and, eventually, a layer of bedrock. The depth at which these layers occur varies from garden to garden, but the deeper the layer of topsoil the better the conditions for plant growth.

The first thing to do is hire a skip and get rid of all the old breeze blocks and bricks (well, okay, save a few if you think you'll need them – they're often handy for odd jobs) and any baddies, such as lumps of concrete, or piles of building sand. Bright yellow builders' sand is no good for the garden – it's very fine and contains a lot of lime, unlike horticultural sand which is grittier and lime-free.

If the soil has set in big, hard lumps, is yellow or blue in colour, or forms a glutinous mess in wet weather, then take a spade and dig down to see if there's something better underneath. The odds are that you've had a heap of subsoil dumped on your patch and the original topsoil may be several inches down. You can improve subsoil, but it takes years of work. Frankly, you are much better ditching it, loosening the ground underneath with a fork to repair the compaction, and buying some decent topsoil to spread on top. Builders! Don't ya just love 'em?

Soil improvement

Unless you are lucky and have naturally good ground, it'll need improving. The time to do this is when you are first making a new bed or border because that's usually the only time the ground is completely clear and at its most 'get-at-able'. There are two ways of improving the soil – one is by digging in bulky organic matter, such as manure or garden compost, and the other is by adding fertilizers. People often confuse the two substances, or they imagine you can use one *or* the other, but don't need both. Actually, you *do* need both because they each have a different job to do. The task of digging them in also helps to improve the soil.

At Barleywood, where I reckon to be about 95 per cent organic, my standard soil improvement technique consists of digging in lots of organic matter (on newly cultivated soil), or mulching the surface of the soil (on established beds) in winter. I use masses of well-rotted stable manure and home-made garden compost. I fork in a good sprinkling of a general organic fertilizer just before sowing or planting, and established borders get the same treatment in early spring. Keen vegetable growers often add seaweed meal to their vegetable plots in the belief that the extra trace elements make everything taste better.

At Barleywood, I use manure and garden compost as a surface mulch on established beds and borders – it keeps down weeds and helps retain soil moisture, while the worms slowly drag the mulch material beneath the surface, enriching the soil.

Organic matter

Bulky organic matter is 'roughage' – it improves the structure of the soil and, as it breaks down, releases small amounts of nutrients when worked over by soil bacteria. That's what organic gardeners are on about when they say 'feed the soil, not the plant'. But though organic matter is a good source of trace elements, the quantities of major nutrients released in this way aren't enough for serious gardening, so, along with organic matter, you need to use fertilizer as well (see pages 52–53).

For most people, the cheapest and most convenient form of bulky organic matter is garden compost (see page 51). You can make it yourself and it costs you nothing. In country districts, manure is often available cheaply through small ads in the local paper – some horse owners give it away free at their yards just to get rid of it.

There are also various soil improvers that you can buy in bags at the garden centre, and mushroom compost or spent hops are sometimes available locally. They all have their pros and cons (see pages 51–53). When in doubt, go for whatever you can get most of at the price you can afford. But don't miss out on your own free soil improver – make a compost heap, if you don't have one already.

Manure (1) varies in quality according to the type of animals and farming system used. Manure from racehorse stables, for instance, tends to be much better quality than that from intensive cattle farms where little bedding is used. Keen organic gardeners prefer to use manure from non-intensive systems on the grounds of animal welfare.

Fresh manure of any kind needs stacking for six months so that it rots down before use – if it is used fresh, it releases a lot of ammonia that can scorch or even kill plants. But manure needs to be bought with care. If it has been stacked in a weed-infested corner of a field, it is often full of weed seeds or roots and it's easy to find you have imported something nasty, such as bindweed, to your garden, along with a load of muck. If manure has been stacked for too long, then most of the nutrients will have been washed out by the rain and run away into the soil beneath the heap, so, though you benefit from the roughage, you miss out on the trace elements that your garden should benefit from.

Leaf mould (2) is something you'll only get if you have a patch of woodland in your own garden, or if you can collect a lot of dead leaves to rot down and make your own. Don't, whatever you do, go digging leaf mould out of forestry land or woods – it's illegal and you're likely to get arrested! It's really too precious to use for general soil improvement but, if you are making a shady bed for choice woodland plants, then it's the best thing to use.

Mushroom compost (3), these days, is usually based on peat rather than rotted manure, as it once was, and tends to be alkaline due to the chalk used in the casing material. But if you live in a mushroom-growing area, then it's a useful source of organic matter.

Chipped bark (4) is good for mulching, but composted bark is the next best thing to leaf mould and most garden centres sell it. It holds moisture, but doesn't go boggy in very wet conditions, as peat does.

Garden compost (5) is potentially a much richer source of nutrients than other forms of bulky organic matter, especially if you use a good mixture of ingredients to make it. Use kitchen waste, such as tea leaves, orange peel, potato peelings, crushed eggshells and vegetable waste, as well as lawn mowings and weeds. It's really worthwhile to build a bin and re-cycle all this waste that would otherwise just be thrown away (see pages 204–7).

Peat (6) used to be the gardener's first choice for improving the soil but, now that we realize how damaging peat-extraction is to wetland habitats, it's best avoided. Peat doesn't contain any nutrients, so other forms of organic matter are a much better bet.

Types of organic matter:
1 Stable manure needs to be stacked for six months before being used on the garden.
2 Leaf mould needs at least a year to rot down to a brown and crumbly texture.
3 Mushroom compost, which contains bits of chalk, is especially useful on acid soils (see page 93).
4 Chipped bark is a good mulch, but composted bark is more useful for soil enrichment.
5 Garden compost is one of the best soil conditioners of all...
6 ... and peat the most overrated – to be avoided for conservation reasons, also.

Recycled materials are increasingly being investigated since peat has been off the soil-improvement shopping list. Manufacturers have experimented with all sorts of alternatives, based on everything from municipal waste to composted bank notes – no, there's no chance of finding the odd, half-digested fiver, they've all been carefully shredded first. Ask your local authority for details of their own recycling schemes and keep an eye on what's on offer in garden centres.

Fertilizers

Fertilizers are concentrated plant foods. They come in two types, organic and the other sort – inorganic. In gardening terms, 'organic' means those that come from natural sources like plants, animals or naturally occurring rock (see pages 53 and 164–66), instead of manufactured 'chemical' feeds, but plants can't tell the difference. So long as they get what they need in a way they can use it, they really don't mind. Organic fertilizers have the advantage in that they keep soil bacteria busy breaking them down into an absorbable form and busy bacteria are happy bacteria.

The thing you need to do is look at the label to see what you are getting. Fertilizer packets have, by law, to be printed with a declaration that lets you know the amount of each of the three main elements, N:P:K.

N (nitrogen) is good for promoting leafy growth, P (phosphorus alias phosphate) helps the roots, and K (kalium, the ancient name for potassium or potash) is vital for producing flowers and fruit. If the declaration on the packet is 6:4:4, it means that in every 100 grams of the fertilizer you get 6 grams of nitrogen and 4 grams each of phosphate and potash (the rest is bulking agent). This tells you straight away which applications the product is best for – a product high in N but low in P and K is a high-nitrogen feed for encouraging leafy growth – the sort of thing you'd put on the lawn in spring. Nowadays, you don't really need to bother working it out for yourself as it tells you on the label what it's for – when in doubt, read the small print. But there are various types of fertilizers for use in different situations.

Granular or powdered fertilizers are the kind to use on the open garden, when you are first preparing the soil ready for planting. You can also use them to 'top up' the nutrients in spring, at the start of each new growing season. With heavy-cropping plants, such as sweet peas, roses and vegetables, it's a good idea to sprinkle some more fertilizer around the plants during the summer and water it in, or use it to pep up the ground on the vegetable plot between crops.

Fertilizers are an essential supplement to bulky manures, and much easier to apply.

General purpose fertilizer, such as Growmore (inorganic), or blood, fish and bone (organic), is good for preparing soil before planting or sowing, and it's also good for feeding all around the garden. If you only want to buy one kind of fertilizer, this is it. The three main nutrients are present in equal quantities, making this a 'balanced' fertilizer – the plants' answer to a good square meal.

Rose fertilizer contains more potash and magnesium than a general purpose feed and, though not essential, it's good to have if you grow a lot of roses. Fork rose food into the ground before planting, sprinkle it all around the plants and fork it in in spring, then again in summer, just after the first flush of flowers. The fact that plants can't read means that you can also use rose food on other flowering shrubs and perennials, as they'll all enjoy the same blend of nutrients and it saves you using two different products.

Straight fertilizers contain just one of the main nutrients; sulphate of ammonia supplies nitrogen; sulphate of potash supplies potassium and superphosphate supplies phosphate. Use them if you know what you are doing. An onion grower, for instance, would use super-phosphate for preparing the bed for his prize-winning exhibits. But for most gardeners – me included – compound fertilizers that contain a balance of all the main nutrients are best for most 'everyday' uses, as they contain a bit of everything plants need.

Organic feeds, such as dried blood, bonemeal or hoof and horn provide an unbalanced mix of nutrients – dried blood is a fast-acting nitrogen feed, and hoof and horn is a slow-acting nitrogen feed. Bonemeal is a very slow-acting high phosphate fertilizer that is trad-itionally used when planting trees or shrubs, especially in autumn and winter. In reality, most of the phosphates are 'locked up' by the soil, which is why I have stopped using bonemeal and prefer to use bulky manure at planting time instead – the improvement of soil structure is, I reckon, more conducive to root establishment than the addition of fertilizers. It's rather like giving an invalid chicken soup instead of fillet steak.

Blood, fish and bone is the organic equivalent of Growmore, but since the potash in it comes from sulphate of potash, organic purists prefer to buy special truly organic general fertilizer from specialist organic suppliers.

Seaweed meal is a particularly good source of trace elements, though it doesn't provide the main nutrients in worthwhile quantities. Think of it always as a supplement that helps provide a balanced diet.

Most plants need fertilizer if they are to grow to their full potential – vegetables are especially greedy due to their rapid growth rate.

Digging

'Why bother?' is the reaction you hear from a lot of new gardeners to this most traditional of gardening jobs. There are several good reasons for digging and, even with no-dig techniques, you still need to prepare the ground by digging it in the first place – it's just that from then on you don't need to dig it again.

Digging controls weeds by burying them. By turning them in on the spot, instead of composting them first, you cut out an extra job. This only works if you are turning in annual weeds before they form or 'set' seed. If you bury ripe seed heads, the seeds will grow. And if you dig in roots of perennial weeds, you are simply spreading them, too. Even with annual weeds, if you let them grow big, there is too much leafy growth to bury properly.

Digging fluffs up the soil, aerating ground that has been squashed down (compacted) by being walked on, or by heavy rainfall. Loose soil has bigger spaces between the soil particles for air to move through and for surplus water to run away. It also makes it easier for roots to penetrate, so plants grow better and, because the soil is soft, it makes sowing and planting much easier.

But the main reason gardeners dig is to incorporate organic matter, which improves the soil structure and adds nutrients before planting. Years ago you were always told to double-dig the ground to make a new bed. Frankly, that's incredibly hard work and you just don't need to do it, unless you want to grow award-winning parsnips or giant dahlias. And if your garden has a thin layer of decent topsoil over chalk, stones, or a layer of nasty yellow or blue clay subsoil, then the last thing you want to do is bring that lot up to the surface. No, for most people single digging is quite enough.

The no-dig technique

With the no-dig technique, as used on the deep beds that are very popular with organic vegetable gardeners, you do have to dig – deeply – when you prepare the beds in the first place. But from then on, you add new organic matter by mulching thickly on the surface (see pages 154–55) with well-rotted manure or compost whenever the soil is vacant between crops. You then simply wait for the worms to pull the mulch down into the soil and do the digging for you.

You can achieve the same result without digging by making a raised bed. Use low walls of planks to outline the bed and fill it with well-rotted compost laid on top of the existing soil.

Bear in mind that the no-dig technique only works if you avoid walking on the soil, otherwise it becomes too compacted.

How to... **single dig**

If you want to get the ground ready to plant trees, shrubs, or perennials with well-established roots, this is all you need to do. If you want to sow seeds, or grow small plants, such as annuals or vegetable seedlings, then you need to dig it over, then rake the ground lightly to reduce the surface layer to what gardeners call a 'fine tilth' – a fine-textured surface that looks more like cake-crumbs.

Don't overdo the digging – if you aren't used to it, it can be hard work. Divide the area into several bits and do it in easy stages. If you are working in autumn or winter, you can leave the ground rough dug for the weather to work on. Birds will ferret out a lot of soil pests for you. If you are only adding a thin layer of organic matter to previously worked beds, it's easiest just to spread it over the ground and turn it in as you dig, instead of actually burying it in the trench.

What you need
• *digging fork*
• *sharp spade*
• *organic matter*
• *wheelbarrow*

1 Before you begin to single dig to prepare the ground in your patch, bed or border for planting, fork out perennial weeds and clear any rubbish. Start at the top of the patch and, using the spade, dig a trench in a straight line along the shortest edge. Put the soil you've dug out in a heap close to the far end of the plot.

2 Spread organic matter along the bottom of the trench with a spade or fork. If you are making a new bed on previously untouched ground, add a 7–10-cm (3–4-in) layer of organic matter to give it a really good start. On ground that has been dug over before, a thinner layer of organic matter is okay.

3 Dig a second trench alongside the original one, flicking over each spadeful of soil, so it lands upside down in the first trench. That'll bury any small annual weeds and cover the organic matter. Remove any perennial weed roots as you work and bash down any large earth clods with the fork into walnut-sized lumps. When you get to the end of the row, the first trench will be full and you'll have created a second one about 23cm (9in) further down the plot. Keep doing this until you've dug the whole area, and use the original soil pile to fill in the final trench.

2 GROWING AND PLANTING

How plants grow

Producing seeds is the ultimate goal of most plants, and seed heads, such as the round heads of *Echinops*, the bluish *Perovskia* and the golden *Stipa gigantea* in the background, can be a valuable addition to the autumn garden.

Just like us, plants pass through several distinct phases of life. In their natural state, they begin as seeds that germinate and become seedlings. They pass through a non-flowering, juvenile phase before reaching the mature, adult stage, when they flower and produce seed to complete the cycle. They'll sometimes have a short senile phase, when they don't bear much fruit, as in the case of old apple trees, for instance, but with a lot of plants, such as annuals, producing the next generation leaves them exhausted. I have two daughters. I know how they feel.

Seeds

When you think about it, seeds are pretty amazing things. The tiny acorn in the palm of your hand might not look like an embryo oak tree, but that's exactly what it is. Like a bird's egg, it contains everything the new life inside it needs to get growing. It just needs something to trigger it into 'hatching'. But, unlike birds' eggs, which are very fragile and need intensive care, seeds are very rugged and are designed by nature to withstand adverse conditions. They'll lie dormant until conditions are right for them to spring into life.

What seeds need is air, a suitable temperature and moisture. They don't even need nutrients to germinate, as they have their own supply stored in the seed leaves (cotyledons) packed inside them, which is enough to last until they have formed roots. The bigger the seed, the more food reserves it contains. In the wild, seeds have to take their chance. Lots of them never germinate at all because they land in unsuitable places. A fair percentage will be eaten by animals, and there's a high mortality rate among the seedlings that do make it. Life is tough from the outset, and that's why most plants shed huge quantities of seed to allow for natural wastage.

But in the garden at home, when you are paying for seeds by the packet, you want as many to reach maturity as possible, which is why the germinating seeds and small seedlings are normally treated very carefully. If you've never tried growing plants from seed, give it a go. It's about the most rewarding gardening activity of all.

Seed packets

Virtually every kind of seed has its own ideal set of conditions for germination, and the closer you match them the better your results. Don't just guess. Seeds are expensive and there are a limited number in the packet, so do your homework – read the instructions!

Lots of useful information gets thrown away along with the seed packet, so write a plant's name on a plant label to stick into the pot or at the end of the row when you sow. Copy out useful details such as height, what type of plant it is (hardy annual, half-hardy etc), sowing date and so on, on to the back of the label to act as a reminder. A seed packet stabbed on to a stick rots or blows away.

The small print

Name: you might be given the full botanical name or just the variety name, depending on the supplier; with vegetable seeds, you'll usually be given the type of vegetable and variety name only.

Description: designed to whet your appetite. Allow seed merchants a bit of leeway... they're not quite estate agents, but they can sometimes get a bit over-enthusiastic.

Height: lots of popular old varieties, such as flowering tobacco plants, are being bred in ultra-compact versions nowadays, so make sure you're buying what you need for the place you have in mind.

Sowing information: gives times and places for sowing indoors and/or outdoors, and a required temperature range for fast, even germination.

Spacing: the distance apart to thin out seedlings or plant out young plants, allowing them to grow to full size without competition from neighbours.

When you buy seeds from a garden centre, the packet has a picture on the front and instructions on the back. If you buy direct from the seed companies' catalogues, you'll have a bigger choice of varieties, but the seeds are often sent out in plain white packets with no instructions – just the name. You can look up the description or photo in the catalogue, but there's usually little growing information. Some firms supply a booklet with detailed germination requirements for different types of seed, otherwise you'll need to look up advice in a good plant dictionary or encyclopedia.

Seed diversity

Seeds range in size, from coconuts to specks of dust, and, in shape, from long, thin quills, as in French marigolds, to winged maple seeds. The reasons for their odd shapes and sizes are mainly to do with the way the seed is dispersed naturally: on the wind, by hitching a lift with animals or birds, by firing from an explosive capsule, or by being shaken from pepper-pot-style pods. Seeds also have some elaborate survival tricks up their pods. Think what would happen if seeds all grew as soon as they were shed. You'd have some coming up just as winter was around the corner, when seedlings would stand no chance of survival. The seed's internal chemistry makes sure it remains dormant until there's the right combination of warmth, light and moisture, but some won't grow until they've experienced a particular set of conditions.

Eucalyptus seeds, for instance, only germinate after a bush fire, so to help them germinate you need to simulate one. Australian growers buy smoke pellets to imitate the chemicals released by burning wood; at home you'll get eucalyptus seeds to germinate quicker by pouring a splash of boiling water over the compost in which they've been sown.

Unless you know about such 'special requests' in advance, seed raising with certain plants can be a bit slow. But even a 'normal' seed needs special care as it's coming up. The critical time in any germinating seed's life is the 12 to 24 hours during which the seed coat cracks open and the first tiny shoot starts to emerge. If it dries out, becomes chilled or waterlogged, then the seed will just die and you don't get a second chance.

Golden rules for good germination

Germination is a seed's first stage of growth, when the first root and shoot emerge. Different types of seeds need to be sown in different ways to ensure they germinate properly. (See pages 64-67 for step-by-step instructions on sowing seeds and pricking them out.)

Storing seeds

Ideally, don't! It's much better to buy what seed you need and use it the same year. The percentage of seeds that will germinate drops for every year they are stored, even in good conditions. Don't leave packets of seed lying around in the greenhouse – keep them at a low, steady temperature somewhere out of the sun. If you really want to store part-used packets for future years, tape them shut and put them in a screw-top jar in the salad compartment of the fridge. They'll become a delightful source of family disputes.

1

2

3

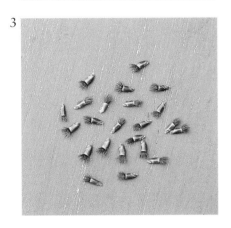

Seeds come in all shapes and sizes and
produce plants of different habits:
1 These sweet pea seeds will
    produce clambering plants with
    lots of delicate flowers.
2 The sunflower seeds give tall stems
    with big, bold, yellow flowers.
3 And the cornflower seeds
    produce shorter plants with small
    flowers in mixed colours.

Big seeds (e.g. runner bean)

To start the germination process, seeds must first soak up moisture. The bigger the seed, the more moisture it needs, which is why it's worth soaking pea and bean seeds for 12 hours before you sow them. Don't soak them for longer though, as that's as long as seeds can go without air; after that they'll literally drown. As a rule of thumb, when sowing large seeds, cover them with their own depth of compost. Large seeds are so easy to handle that you can space them out in the seed tray, or sow them in individual pots, which saves pricking out seedlings later.

Medium-sized seeds (e.g. French marigold)

These are seeds from apple-pip size down to mustard-and-cress size. They are usually sown by scattering them thinly over the surface of the compost in a seed tray or pot, so that they rest about 5mm (¼in) apart. They are then covered with more compost until they *just* disappear from view. To get a really fine, even layer of compost, shake it through a sieve. Never bury seeds too deeply – they are not moles.

Very small seeds (e.g. begonia, busy lizzie)

Very small to dust-like seeds won't germinate if they are covered with compost. Scatter them on to the gently firmed, level surface of compost in a pot or tray. To moisten, stand the pot in a few centimetres of water for about 10 minutes until you can just see moisture glistening on the compost surface. Watering with a can just washes the seeds to one end of the tray. Then cover the top of the pot with plastic film, or slip it into a loosely tied plastic bag, to keep the humidity high and prevent the seeds from drying out.

Hard seeds (e.g. canna, strelitzia, sweet peas)

Built like ball-bearings, these seeds won't germinate until the outer casing has decomposed enough to let water in to start the germination process. To speed things up, you can 'chip' a hole in the seed coat. Use a sharp knife to carefully pare away a sliver of the seed coat, so you can *just* see the greenish or white layer of live seed inside.

Chipping seed is a pretty risky business, but you can play it safe and just rub one side of the seed with fine emery paper instead. Don't do the whole seed – you only need to do a tiny patch, and just enough to get a glimpse of the live seed inside.

Seeds needing cold treatment

Some trees, shrubs and many alpines won't germinate until they have experienced one or more periods of very cold weather. Sow

Sweet peas germinate faster if their tough seed coats are chipped with a sharp knife – watch your fingers!

them in pots or trays in the autumn, as for ordinary seeds, and cover the tops with fine-mesh wire netting to protect them from birds, mice and squirrels. Stand them out in an open cold frame, or in a safe place in the garden, for the winter. If they don't come up next spring, keep them watered all summer and leave them out again next winter. Be patient – some kinds can take three years to come up.

Alternatively, you can give slow-germinating seeds an artificial winter in the fridge. Sow in pots and water them in as usual, then place them in the salad drawer of the fridge for six weeks. Bring them out into a temperature of 15–21°C (60–70°F). If they don't come up within 12 weeks, put them back in the fridge for another six weeks – some will actually germinate there. Seedlings raised by the 'fridge method' are often not as robust as outdoor-grown seedlings, so it's best to prick them out and grow them on under glass until they are well established.

Moisture-loving plant seeds (e.g. candelabra primulas)
Sow these seeds thinly on the surface of compost in pots and, to keep them moist, stand the pots in a dish or tray containing 2.5cm (1in) of water. Keep it regularly topped up until the seedlings are pricked out. Don't try this trick with anything except real moisture-lovers – other types of seed won't appreciate standing in water.

Seeds with wings or tails (e.g. clematis, sycamore)
Sow very thinly, so the wings or tails don't overlap with their neighbours, then cover them with a thin layer of fine grit, which weighs them down so they can't blow away. Or break off the tails and wings and just sow the seeds as usual – but that's a pretty fiddly job.

Primula seeds need light to germinate, and moisture-loving candelabra primulas need very damp compost, too.

How to... **sow seed indoors**

What you need

- *clean pots or half-sized seed trays (one for each variety to be sown)*
- *fresh seed compost or multi-purpose compost*
- *plant labels and a soft pencil*
- *seeds*
- *kitchen or garden sieve*
- *clingfilm*
- *plastic bag or heated propagator*
- *clean seed tray*
- *a dibber, or use the pointed end of a pencil*
- *watering can with a fine rose*

The most reliable way to sow seeds is under cover, where you can control the conditions. Keen seed raisers use a cold frame or greenhouse, ideally with a heated propagator. If you don't have special facilities, then small numbers of seedlings can be raised on a bright windowsill indoors, as long as it is out of direct sunlight. Check the temperature needed for germination and sow all the seeds that need the same temperature at the same time, especially if they are sharing a heated propagator. It sounds obvious, I know, but you'd be surprised how often people don't bother with heating a propagator and it makes all the difference to your success rate.

You won't often need to use a whole packet of seed, but sow in a tray if you do need lots of plants. Sowing too thickly will encourage fatal fungal infection. Check your 'nursery' daily. If the compost starts to dry out, water again by the dunking method (see step 3). When the first seedlings germinate, remove the plastic cover, or open the vent in the propagator lid, to give them fresh air. If any seedlings keel over, or grow fluffy grey mould, remove them with tweezers to avoid contaminating healthy seedlings.

1 Loosely fill a pot or tray with seed compost. Spread it evenly and use the base of another clean pot/tray to firm the compost down gently – don't steamroll it. Write the plant name and sowing date on to the label so that it can be pushed into the pot after sowing.

2 Tip the seeds on to the palm of one hand. Hold it 10cm (4in) above the compost, and tap it with the other hand, so the seeds are dislodged onto the compost. Move your hand from side to side to get a thin, even distribution over the surface.

3 Cover the seed thinly with sieved compost. If it's very fine seed, leave it uncovered and stretch clingfilm over the top of the pot. Stand the pots in tepid water until moisture has soaked up to the surface of the compost. Let all excess water drain away, then place the pots inside a large, loose plastic bag, or in a heated propagator. A germination temperature of 18–21°C (65–70°F) suits most seeds.

Pricking out

Once most of the seedlings have opened out the first true leaf (and before they become tall and spindly), they are ready for spacing out – or 'pricking out' as gardeners call it. True leaves look like miniature versions of adult ones, as opposed to the small, rounded 'seed leaves' that are the first to emerge on germination (see pages 59 and 60–63). To avoid passing on fungal infections, never re-use compost from the original pot of seedlings – put it on the garden and use fresh seed compost here. Pricking out is easiest if the compost is slightly on the dry side; don't water the seedlings just beforehand.

Keep seedlings carefully watered while they are growing into young plants, but don't overdo it. They need to be evenly moist, not waterlogged. From now on, the seedlings will need bright light; only shade from hot, direct sun, which would otherwise scorch or shrivel the leaves. The seed compost contains all the food they need for the first six weeks but, after that, begin feeding them once a week with general-purpose liquid fertilizer, diluted to the correct strength. By the time the pots or trays are full of roots, the young plants will be ready for planting out, or potting up into larger pots.

4 Fill a clean seed tray with fresh seed compost and bang the tray gently on the work surface to level it off. Firm it gently. Use a dibber to gently loosen clumps of seedlings and separate their roots from excess compost. Don't handle seedlings by their stems or true leaves; the slightest bruise can become infected by grey mould, which usually proves fatal.

5 Lift each seedling by a seed leaf and lower it into a finger-sized hole in the new compost. If necessary, coil the roots round the bottom of the hole, so that the seed leaves rest just above the surface of the compost. Don't leave long stems sticking out, or you'll end up with weak, leggy seedlings. Nudge compost round the seedling to fill the hole and cover the roots.

6 Space the seedlings about 3.5cm (1½in) apart. You will get between 28 (seven rows of four) and 48 (eight rows of six) seedlings in a standard-sized seed tray. Water them in, either by standing the tray in water, or by using a fine rose on a watering can. If you only want a few plants, you can either use a half-sized seed tray (a half-tray), or individual 9-cm (3½-in) pots.

How to... **sow seed outdoors**

What you need

- *digging fork*
- *general fertilizer, such as blood fish and bone*
- *rake*
- *soft sand*
- *garden line or a length of bamboo cane*
- *packets of seed*
- *plant labels and soft pencil*
- *twiggy pea-sticks*
- *watering can with a fine rose*
- *hand trowel or fork*

This is the best method to use for hardy annuals and vegetables. You can also use it for seeds of perennial and biennial flowers in early summer. Don't bother trying this method with half-hardy plants, as you can't sow them outside until after the frost and so there won't be any flowers until late summer, when the season is nearly over.

You don't need any special equipment but, because you can't control the growing conditions, it's essential to pick your moment. Even hardy annuals won't germinate if conditions are very cold in spring and, if the soil is also too wet, many seeds, such as peas and beans, will rot before they have chance to germinate. It is always best to wait until the weather improves. If you are impatient, place a row of cloches (mini-greenhouses) or plastic sheeting over the soil for a couple of weeks to dry and warm it slightly first.

The other big thing to watch out for is weeds. If your ground is full of weed seeds, sow seeds in rows: yes, even annual flowers. It makes weeding much easier, because you can see clearly which are weed seedlings and which are sown ones. If necessary, you can always move them to their flowering positions later.

1 To produce a colourful border like the one shown on page 67, you first need to make a fine seedbed by forking over the soil to loosen it. Remove any weeds, then sprinkle general fertilizer evenly over the surface and rake it lightly in, leaving a fine, cake-crumb-like tilth. Hardy annuals are usually sown in 'drifts' – mark these out with a trickle of sand – a different variety is then sown in each area.

2 When sowing in drifts, a garden cane can be pressed into the soil at 7.5–10-cm (3–4-in) intervals to make shallow furrows or drills. On the vegetable plot, mark out a row with garden line and make a furrow with the corner of a rake, about 1cm (½in) deep, alongside it. Scatter small seeds thinly along the row, or 'space sow' larger seeds, setting them out individually a few centimetres apart.

3 Cover to roughly their own depth. Remove the garden line, if sowing vegetables, and push a plant label in at the end of the row or drift, marked with the plant name and sowing date. Cover with twiggy pea-sticks to protect from digging cats. Water well with a can fitted with a fine rose, or sprinkler bar. If no rain is forthcoming, water again before the soil dries out.

4 Start thinning out the seedlings as soon as they are large enough to handle. It's a good idea to do this in several stages as the seedlings get bigger.

5 Aim to leave the strongest ones growing about 2.5–5cm (1–2in) apart. Thin again as the plants grow larger, so that the remainder are about 7–10cm (3–4in) apart. If the plants are to be left in the same row they were sown in throughout their lives, they'll need a further thinning to leave them at their final spacing.

6 To transplant plants to a different position, prepare their new bed beforehand by forking over the soil and removing all weeds. Dig up each plant carefully with a good ball of roots and soil. Set them out at the correct distance apart and dig a planting hole for each. Pop them in at the same depth at which they were originally growing. Firm gently and water thoroughly.

A sight that most of us remember from school, when we would germinate bean seeds inside a jar against a sheet of damp blotting paper. The root pushes down first and then the shoot emerges into the light.

The developing plant

It's not often you get the chance to watch a seed germinating, but think back to the 'bean in a jar' experiment at school. Remember the seeds sandwiched between damp blotting paper and the side of the glass jar? You could almost see the seed growing daily. The seed would swell, then the first root (the radicle) would push downwards. The first shoot (plumule) would uncurl from between the fat seed leaves (cotyledons) and push up to the light, while the fine root hairs started reaching out in all directions, exploring for moisture and food.

When a seed germinates, the resulting young plant is very basic with just one or two leaves and a short stalk. Monocotyledons (plants with one seed leaf, such as palms and grasses) live up to their name. They produce one spear-like seed leaf, followed closely by further leaves, one at a time, which look very similar to the original seed leaf. Dicotyledons have a pair of seed leaves. As the two seed leaves open out at the tip of the emerging stem, one on each side, you can often recognize them as being the two halves of the seed that has burst out of its surrounding coat. They look nothing like the plant's true leaves, which appear later from between the seed leaves. When seedlings have one or two true leaves, that's the best time to prick them out, as they are just about big enough to handle at this stage, but the root system is small enough to move without damage. The nutrients from the seed leaves are absorbed as the seedling develops and these eventually dry out and drop off – which is why you use them as 'handles' when picking up seedlings (instead of the more vulnerable stems). It won't matter if you bruise a seed leaf slightly as it's dispensable, but a damaged stem is unlikely to recover.

Once they have been given more room, seedlings really put on a growth spurt and quickly turn into young plants. By the time they have been potted up, or planted out in the garden, they are really in top gear and have begun to develop mature characteristics – a bit like us giving up rented flats and clubbing after a while, in favour of settling into paying the mortgage and putting down some more permanent roots. Some plants go on to produce entirely different leaves at maturity, for example, many eucalyptus have sickle-shaped adult leaves, while the juvenile ones are disc-shaped.

While they are settling into grown-up life, it's important for maturing plants to gather as many resources as possible – water, food, light and space – ready to produce a family. Although most plants are content to jostle for space in a border, there is one type of plant that always seems to want more than its fair share, and that's the climber.

Clingers and climbers

Climbing plants produce fast-growing stems fitted with all sorts of nifty devices for getting a leg-up on whatever comes to hand – other plants, fences or trellis – and some can even attach themselves to the sheer face of a wall. Their aim is to leap-frog over the heads of competitors and hog the light, and some of them aren't worried about the trouble they cause on the way. If you are planting climbers, it's as well to know their little ways and it helps to understand the climbing techniques that they use to further their own ends.

Thorns on plants, such as climbing roses, are curved backwards like hooked claws. As stems grow longer, thorns act like grappling irons, grabbing hold of branches to help the rose scramble over other plants. The more strongly curved the thorns, the harder it is to pull the stems down because you are pulling in the opposite direction to hundreds of hooks. If you want to pull out a stem you've just cut off a climbing rose, do so from the tip and it'll slide out quite easily. But unless you grow them through a tree, you need to treat climbing roses like wall shrubs and tie their main stems in to some form of support to keep them in place. Thorns are hopeless at clinging to flat surfaces like walls.

Tendrils are stems or leaves that have been modified for climbing. Plants like sweet peas and grape vines use tendrils for 'strap-hanging' from branches, netting, twiggy pea-sticks or trellis. Clematis don't have tendrils, but the leaf stalks twine round branches or trellis in much the same way, so they, too, hold on without harming anything. Tendril plants are among the most docile climbers for garden use but, though you need to give them something to climb up, there's no need to tie them in once they get going.

 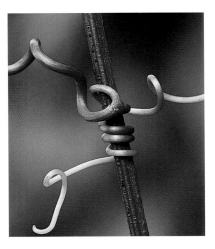

Roses (*left*) climb and scramble through other plants using their thorns as grappling hooks, while plants like this vine (*right*), use tendrils to clamber upwards.

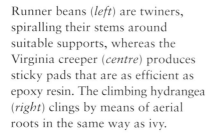

Runner beans (*left*) are twiners, spiralling their stems around suitable supports, whereas the Virginia creeper (*centre*) produces sticky pads that are as efficient as epoxy resin. The climbing hydrangea (*right*) clings by means of aerial roots in the same way as ivy.

Twining stems are used by a lot of plants, including honeysuckle, wisteria and runner beans, which climb by sending their stems out in a spiral motion. Instead of growing straight, they wind themselves around anything they touch, which might be another plant, a cane, twiggy stems or trellis. Some twiners follow the direction of the sun and twine clockwise, while others do the opposite. If you are winding bean plants around canes to help them get started, observe which way they want to go, because if you try to go against their natural inclinations they'll just unwind themselves and flop on the ground. Big twiners, such as wisteria, need watching. Don't let them wrap themselves around guttering or down-pipes, because the thin shoots fatten with age and will eventually wrench the pipework off the wall.

Sticky pads on Virginia creeper (*Parthenocissus quinquefolia*), and its cousins, enable them to hang on to bare walls. The sticky pads are rather like the rubber suckers on the tips of toy arrows, but they hold on tighter and for longer, so they can damage less-than-perfect masonry. They are fine for a sound surface, such as a concrete block wall, or if you want to cover a hideous old outbuilding in a hurry, and they are magnificent let loose over a pergola, a steep bank, or up a big tree.

Aerial roots are used by ivies and climbing hydrangea to cling to bare walls or tree trunks. First, short, bristly roots grow out from the stems when they touch something solid; then aerial roots reach out to penetrate cracks, thickening out to wedge themselves into place. If the surface is an old brick wall, they can enlarge cracks and make the surface crumble. Again, sound surfaces, or structures that don't matter, are the best places for this type of climber.

Flowers and pollination

It's only when plants reach maturity that they will flower, which explains why it sometimes takes plants such as passionflower several years to bloom if you grow them from seed. From the plant's point of view, flowers aren't just there for decoration, they are a vital step towards their final goal – producing seed to ensure the species' survival.

Pollination is how plants reproduce, transferring pollen from the male anther on to the female stigma (see diagram page 21) in order to produce seeds. Not all plants bother with fancy flowers. Grasses, bamboos and some trees, such as willows (*Salix*), just have greenish tufts or catkins – a sure sign of a plant whose flowers are pollinated by the wind. Plants that use the wind to pollinate usually give out vast clouds of pollen to make sure there's a sporting chance of at least some of it reaching a mate. It's a numbers game.

Plants that have elaborate and colourful flowers do so in order to attract the right sort of creature to pollinate them. This means that the flowers don't need to produce so much pollen, but they'll often have scent to attract helpers, with a supply of nectar as a reward. Most flowers are pollinated by insects, such as bees or hoverflies. Those that open only at dusk may be pollinated by night-flying moths. At home, if you want your melon plant to produce melons (known as 'setting' in the trade), and there are not many bees about, you simply cheat and take a small artist's paintbrush to do the job by hand – dusting the pollen from male anther to female stigma.

Bright flowers are produced for a reason – to attract pollinating insects. This leads to seed production and ensures the plant's survival for another generation.

In some parts of the world, flowers may be pollinated by bats or humming birds, and some have evolved into special shapes so that they can only be pollinated by one particular species. Flowers that are pollinated by humming birds, for instance, have elongated throats the same length as the bird's beak. As the bird drinks the nectar, pollen sticks to the top of its head and is transferred to the next flower it visits. A neat trick for effecting pollination.

In the interests of beautiful gardens, we've done plenty of cheating on nature. In the wild state, most plants have single flowers, which come complete with a full set of sexual organs. By selecting accidental mutations or freaks, or by deliberate plant breeding, we've managed to increase the number of petals for our own enjoyment. But, in most cases, it is the reproductive parts of the flower that have been 'converted' into extra petals, so double flowers rarely produce any seed. The extra petals can take the place of scent-producing organs, which is why some sumptuously double flowers are lacking in fragrance. And, since they don't yield seed, you have to divide them (see pages 195–96) or take cuttings, to get more plants from such 'sterile' varieties. Crude genetic engineering has been going on for centuries but, in such instances as these, the 'engineering' is allowed by nature.

Why cross-pollinate?

Unlike cuttings, which are 'clones' with exactly the same genetic make-up as their one parent, seed-raised plants have two parents, each contributing half their genes. All of the offspring have a slightly different genetic mix. Although still recognizably the same type of plant as the parents, they have tiny differences – maybe bigger leaves, different-coloured flowers, or more drought resistance – which may give them the edge in the survival game.

In the wild, cross-pollination gives a species the 'bounce' to adapt to changing conditions. It's such a good, long-term survival strategy that some plants have built-in mechanisms to prevent self-pollination. Most hollies have male and female flowers on separate trees, so are almost invariably pollinated by another individual. Slipper orchids (*Cypripedium*) have a complex one-way system for bees to negotiate through, which ensures that their own flower's pollen never reaches their own female parts.

In cultivation, plant breeders make use of cross-pollination to produce desirable new varieties, known as hybrids, like this *Rosa* 'Graham Thomas'. By crossing two parent plants with the required characteristics, they can create a super-strain with bigger leaves, more flowers, or tastier tomatoes. And all with no artificial 'genetic engineering', which involves introducing genes from unrelated plants, or even things like jellyfish, that could never have got it together naturally.

For this apple tree, the reproductive cycle and natural progression of plant growth, in a single season, is:

1 The bursting of shoots.
2 The production of flowers, which will be pollinated.
3 Developing fruitlets, which turn into...
4 ... the full-sized fruit, bearing seeds inside.

Fruit and seed

Once pollination – the transference of pollen from the male anther to the female stigma – has resulted in the flower being fertilized, the petals drop and the ovary at the base of the flower begins to swell and turn into a pod, berry, or fruit full of seeds. At this stage, a short-lived plant, feeling its job is nearly over, starts to shut up shop. The first thing it does is stop producing any more flowers, concentrating its energies instead on swelling and ripening the seeds.

Unfortunately, that doesn't always suit us, since we don't want our border plants to give up after the first flush of flower and produce a load of tatty old seed heads. So we deadhead them, picking off the dying flowers. The plant's immmediate response is to form some new flower buds in its effort to set seed. The same thing happens with peppers – pick them green and the plant promptly grows some more. But if you leave them to ripen and turn red, the plant thinks it has done its job and stops producing new flowers, so you don't get such a big crop. It's the same story with sweet peas and courgettes. These also need harvesting regularly to prevent them from feeling their work is finished.

Choosing and planting

Some plants are just not practical to raise yourself. Maybe they need nursery facilities, complicated production techniques, or take a long time to reach planting size, so there's a lot to be said for buying ready-grown plants. Visiting nurseries or garden centres also introduces you to new plants you might not meet otherwise, and it's the obvious answer if you want instant results.

When and where to buy

Years ago, you could only buy trees and shrubs that had been dug up from a nursery field in winter, once they had lost their leaves. You ordered them during summer, they were delivered any time between leaf fall in autumn and bud-burst in spring, and you planted them straight away, if only temporarily (known as 'heeling them in').

Garden centres changed all that by selling their plants in pots. Because there's less root disturbance, you can plant them at any time of year, even when in full flower – provided that the soil is in reasonable condition, and that you plant them properly and keep them watered until established. Opening up all the year round for plant sales paved the way for garden centres to grow into one-stop garden shops. Now, as well as providing essential garden tools and products, they also sell anything you can think of for the garden – and much else besides.

Nowadays, nurseries tend to specialize in particular types of plants – perhaps unusual shrubs, old-fashioned cottage-garden plants, trendy perennials, cacti or conservatory climbers – especially the less common ones that you won't find so readily in garden centres. Because such nurseries are often out in the sticks, you may have to be prepared to travel some distance, but the best place to find them and their plants is at flower shows and plant fairs.

Busy people increasingly buy plants by mail order, or from Internet gardening sites, but here, it pays to know your supplier because you can't see what you are getting until it arrives. You are relying on somebody else to pick out good plants, pack them carefully and see that they are sent out by a speedy delivery system. If a specialist nursery runs a mail-order business, you can usually be sure that the plants will be healthy and carefully packed. Such businesses are, by their very nature, run by enthusiasts and can usually be relied on when it comes to quality of plant and speed of despatch. Mail order is an especially popular way of buying young plants and 'plugs', which being small, are easy to pack and cheap to post.

Check plants over carefully before adding them to your trolley.

Choosing healthy plants

You can usually tell a good nursery or garden centre because it's busy. If the plants were of poor quality, people wouldn't keep going back. One of the reasons plants tend to be good at busy outlets is precisely because the turnover of stock is rapid, which allows you to buy plants in nursery-fresh condition. Few garden centres grow their own stock these days, but many nurseries do and are always worth patronizing. Word of mouth is the best recommendation for nurseries that are a bit off the beaten track. They are worth the travelling because many supply a specialist range of plants that are unobtainable elsewhere. But wherever you shop for plants, get into the habit of checking them over before adding them to your trolley, to make sure you are buying the best.

What to look for when buying plants

Flowers	Leaves	Stems and branches	Compost	Roots
Should match the picture or description on the label.	Should be healthy, unblemished and free of signs of pests or diseases.	Should be sturdy and evenly spread around a central stem.	Should have a soil surface free of moss and liverworts – signs of over-watering and nutrient shortage.	Should be plentiful. By the time they are offered for sale, most plants have filled their pots with roots.
If not, the plant may be wrongly labelled – it happens in even the best-run nurseries (often because customers stuff labels back into the wrong pots!).	Leaves (unless they are meant to be golden or variegated) should be a rich shade of green, not pale and pasty. Why trouble yourself with extra feeding and pest control when you can choose a perfect specimen?	Standard plants and trees should have strong, straight stems, with well-branched heads at the top. Avoid lopsided or broken plants, and trees whose leader (main central shoot) is missing or broken.	Hairy bitter cress spreads, so weed it out, but don't reject an otherwise healthy plant just because of a few weeds. Avoid plants where compost has shrunk from the pot sides due to drying out.	Roots through the pot's bottom are not a problem; standing pots on a damp sand bed for a long time, encourages the roots to wander. If the plant is healthy, buy it and cut the pot off carefully.

How to... **plant**

There's an old gardening saying that goes 'spend as much on the hole as the plant'. Some people will happily spend a small fortune on a tree, and just dig a hole and shove it in without any preparation at all – and very indignant they are too when it dies. A barrowload of organic matter (garden compost), from a couple of handfuls for a small plant to about two bucketfuls for a large tree, and sufficient water would have made all the difference.

The same basic planting technique works for almost anything, from a semi-mature tree to a tiny alpine, though there are a few small variations on the theme that are worth knowing for particular plants (see pages 77–79). And, after planting, keep new plants well watered if the weather is dry, so that the roots are encouraged to grow out into the surrounding soil.

1 If the plant's compost is bone dry, stand the pot in a bucket of water until it's thoroughly moist. On well-prepared soil, dig a hole twice the diameter of the pot, and fork a bucketful of organic matter into the bottom of the hole. If planting in spring, when you want to encourage growth, fork in a sprinkling of general fertilizer, too. If you are planting a tree in grass, or on ground that hasn't been cultivated for a long time, make the hole about four or five times the diameter of the pot and add correspondingly more organic matter.

2 Remove the plant from its pot. If it is pot-bound, tease a few of the biggest roots out from the bottom and sides of the rootball. Some gardeners bash the rootball to break up the cylindrical shape. This is advisable with conifers and other tough-rooted trees and shrubs that are excessively pot-bound, but with fleshy-rooted plants, such as magnolias, it can set them back years. In this case, leave well alone. Stand the rootball in place in the hole. If the plant has a best side, make sure it faces the direction from which you'll normally view it.

3 Check that the top of the rootball is level with the surrounding soil, and that the plant is standing upright. Mix more organic matter with the excavated soil and shovel the mixture back around the rootball, firming it gently with your foot. When you have filled the hole, tidy up and level the area, then water thoroughly. Spread an 8-cm (3-in) layer of mulching material, such as manure or bark chippings, over the cultivated area, and that's it – job done.

Variations on the planting theme

While most plants respond well to the basic planting technique (see page 76), there are a few variations on the theme that are used to guarantee success with more specialist plant groups.

Alpines

Most rock plants need very good drainage and rosette-formers, such as houseleeks (*Sempervivum*), need especially good drainage round their 'necks' (where the stem meets the roots), otherwise they rot off at soil level. When planting alpines, set the top of the rootball 1cm (½in) proud of the soil and then spread a layer of gravel, granite chippings, or slivers of slate around the plant neck and all over the soil surface as a top dressing. Besides setting the plants off well, it prevents mud splash, improves surface drainage and lets air circulate beneath the rosettes.

Bulbs

Bulbs generally need planting a lot deeper than you'd think. The rule of thumb is three times their own depth, so for a daffodil bulb that is, say, 6cm (2½in) long from top to toe, you'd be looking at making a hole 18cm (7in) deep. Yes, really. Deep planting places bulbs safely below cultivation depth, so you won't accidentally chop them up with a hoe, or spear them with a fork when you're weeding. It also ensures they have good supplies of moisture. It's not disastrous if you get the depth wrong because most bulbs can winch themselves down into the ground using special, contractile roots – it takes time, but they get there eventually. If you're planting bulbs on rather heavy soil, put a shovelful of grit in the bottom of the hole first, to ensure good drainage.

Alpines adore good drainage, which is why they grow well in shallow sinks – with the plug left out!

Plant narcissi and snowdrops (*below left*) deeper than you might think. When planting spring-flowering bulbs, your rule of thumb is to plant them at three times the depth of the bulb (*below*).
1 crocus.
2 snowdrop.
3 tulip species.
4 Dutch iris.
5 tulip.
6 hyacinth.
7 narcissus.

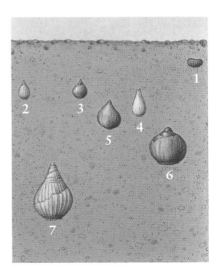

A few bulbs prefer shallow planting, so put Madonna lilies (*Lilium candidum*) in with their 'noses' (the tip of the bulb) just showing above ground. In the case of crown imperials (*Fritillaria imperialis*), which have hollow-centred bulbs, lay them on their sides so that water can't collect in the hollow and make them rot.

If mice or squirrels are in the habit of stealing your bulbs, plant them with a layer of small-mesh wire netting or lots of holly leaves over the top to put them off.

Plant clematis deeper than normal to ensure recovery after an attack by clematis wilt and to keep the roots cool.

Clematis

Clematis are the major exception to the normal rule about planting depth; they need deep planting. The top of the rootball should be buried 10–15cm (4–6in) below the surface of the soil. The usual reason given for deep planting is so that clematis can recover if they are attacked by clematis wilt. This disease affects new plants in particular, first making the plant droop as if it were short of water before it dies down to ground level. Deep planting means there is sufficient stem from which new growth buds can develop, so you don't lose the plant and it's not long before new shoots appear. Deep planting also helps to keep clematis roots cool and moist (they love this), and if you do happen to go a bit wild with the hoe, or nylon-line trimmer, a butchered plant can still re-grow.

Evergreens

Planting evergreens is pretty standard (see page 76); it's the after-care that you might need to vary a bit. Evergreens are very keen on turning brown if they dry out after planting, so it's especially important to keep the soil moist. Severe 'scorching' can kill a young plant completely, and conifers may end up with permanently brown patches, since the browned-off bits never re-grow.

It's not only dry soil at the roots that causes scorching – strong winds and hot sun can do it too. Scorching happens when the leaves lose water faster than the roots can take it up and, on new plants, the full complement of roots has not yet developed. If you live in an exposed area, protect newly planted evergreens and conifers by hammering in a circle of poles and tacking windbreak fabric around them. It's not an object of great beauty, it's true, but it'll only be for a few months. Oh, and wandering neighbourhood dogs cocking their legs can have a similar effect.

Grafted plants

Quite a few garden plants – such as fruit trees, some ornamental trees, roses, and the more expensive shrubs, such as Japanese maples – are grafted or joined together. Grafting is done because it's the most convenient way to raise named varieties that can't be grown from seed, or that are very slow or difficult to root from cuttings. What you are buying is actually two plants in one: the roots of a reliable 'good do-er' (the rootstock) and the named variety on top, which is known as the scion. The point where the two have been joined by grafting is called the graft union. It can usually be identified by a pronounced bulge in the stem.

With ornamental trees and fruit trees, where the eventual size of the tree is controlled by the vigour of the rootstock, you don't want the scion to take root, so it's essential to plant with the graft union about 10cm (4in) above ground. When you buy grafted shrubs growing in pots, they will already be planted at the right depth, so just plant with the top of the rootball flush with the ground. The same is obviously true with a few trees, such as some weeping, ornamental cherries, that are 'top-grafted' at the head of a long, straight stem.

Roses are different. They are generally budded on to rootstocks for reasons of cheapness and efficiency of production; several buds of one variety are used to make each bush and the vigour of the rootstock is not the main reason for grafting. With roses, you might as well encourage the scion to root for additional stability, so plant bushes with the union about 2.5cm (1in) under ground, even if they were riding higher in their pots.

When planting most grafted plants, make sure the graft union is kept clear of the soil.

Trees

It's a good idea to stake any new tree in excess of 2m (6ft) tall, through its early life, while it's getting properly rooted in. The tree experts have changed their views lately about a lot of things we once regarded as holy writ. Now there's no need to use tall stakes and tie the trunk in two places, unless you are planting a variety with a notoriously feeble root system, or a very well-developed crown. All you need is a 100–120-cm (3–4-ft) stake that is hammered in at an angle of 45 degrees, a short distance from the rootball. The top end of the stake should point in the direction of the prevailing wind. Use a proper tree tie to fix the trunk to the stake about 30cm (12in) from the ground – the buckle of the tie should rest against the stake, not the tree.

By holding the base of the tree firmly in this way, the roots can't rock loose in the wind, while the top is free to sway. This movement encourages the trunk to strengthen so that when you remove the stake, the tree can stand up on it's own. You can usually take the stake out after two years. In the 'bad old days', it was quite common to find that apparently established trees fell over the minute their 'crutch' rotted.

In a garden afflicted with rabbits, slip a spiral tree guard round the trunk after planting to stop the bark from being chewed off. It's normally in winter, when food is short, that this happens but, if the bark is ringed right round, the tree will die.

Tall trees need staking. To do this, use a single short stake at an angle of 45 degrees, and fasten the trunk to the stake with a proprietary tie.

Moving house

If you are thinking of moving plants with you to a new garden, think again because, unless you have formally agreed with the new owners exactly what you are taking, you can land yourself in legal hot water. Garden plants are considered part of the fixtures and fittings, just like the bath and kitchen units. Although you can take plants growing in patio pots and tubs, don't roll up the lawn, or walk off with the newly planted hedge. If you know you are going to be moving, collect seeds and take cuttings well beforehand – or else just regard the new garden as a blank canvas where you can start again with a completely new collection of plants.

Moving existing plants

Sometimes it's necessary to move established plants – maybe because you've re-designed part of the garden, or something has outgrown it's space, or you just think it will look better elsewhere.

Moving perennials

Border perennials present no problem, since they are regularly dug up and divided anyway. Spring is the best time for dividing or moving most perennials, but there are a few exceptions: bearded irises should be split and shifted about six weeks after flowering; move primroses and polyanthus immediately after flowering. Autumn suits tougher plants, like Michaelmas daisies (*Aster novi-belgii*) and, on light soils, many robust perennials are happily moved at this time.

A few perennials, such as hellebores, never really move well. Look out for self-sown seedlings around the original and transplant them in spring. Peonies move perfectly well, if you do the job in spring, contrary to popular belief. The secret is to dig up a good rootball and not to bury it too deeply – the tuberous roots should rest just beneath the surface of the soil.

You can move spring bulbs at any time during summer, when they are dormant. You can also dig them up as soon as they finish flowering and move them 'in-the-green'. This is certainly the best time to move snowdrops and winter aconites (*Eranthis hyemalis*) which don't transplant at all well if the bulbs are allowed to dry out.

Moving existing shrubs

Most shrubs will move with no trouble at all, provided that they have not been growing for more than a few years. Shallow-rooted kinds, like rhododendrons, which form tight, fibrous rootballs, move very easily. Evergreens move best in early autumn or early spring. (Christmas tree spray is an effective anti-transpirant, so use it to spray evergreens just before moving them, and again two weeks later, to reduce water loss.) Move deciduous shrubs when they are not in leaf, which means any time between autumn and early spring.

Whatever the shrub you are transplanting, take it up with as large a ball of roots as possible. Shift it straight to a new, well-prepared planting hole, with lots of organic matter forked into the bottom, and get the roots tucked in quickly. Make sure that the shrub is replanted at the same depth as it was growing before, and ensure that a big plant faces the same direction as previously. Water it in well, and keep it watered during dry spells.

Before moving a large plant, plan ahead. It's advisable to dig right around it, during the spring before you want to move it. By doing this you'll sever some of the big thick roots, and this encourages the plant to make lots of new fibrous roots, which form a dense rootball that transplants better. By the time you move it, six months or a year later, the plant will have girded its loins for the disturbance.

It just isn't worth the risk of moving some shrubs, unless you absolutely have to, as they rarely recover – magnolias, for instance. And frankly, it's not worth moving established roses. Damaging their roots usually means they produce a forest of suckers from the rootstock, and damaged roots are often more susceptible to soil-borne diseases. Roses are usually past their best after 10 years anyway, so it's better to buy new plants.

Moving existing trees

Trees will move happily if they have only been planted for a year or two, provided that they are shifted in the dormant season. Otherwise, they'll have developed a deep tap root system that simply doesn't transplant well. The only exception is if you are buying semi-mature trees from a nursery. Such big trees will have undergone a special process of preparation before they are offered for sale. They are grown in what I can only describe as underground cages – giant mesh containers filled with good, fertile soil. The root system is regularly undercut as they grow, so they never get the chance to develop tap roots and the container becomes filled with fibrous roots that transplant perfectly.

They are harder to establish than a younger, smaller tree and, as they are expensive, you'll need to look after them well. Have the planting hole ready with lots of organic matter worked in, so the tree can be swung straight into it from the crane. To make sure that the tree establishes well, keep it very well watered in dry spells for the first two years. Guy ropes, or short, stout staking, will be necessary for stability. Expensive I know, but at least you can have a tree in your garden instantly that looks as if it's been there for years.

Planting time

You can plant container-grown trees and shrubs at any time of year except when the ground is really difficult to cultivate (i.e. if it's waterlogged, frozen solid, or set really hard), but the best time is at the beginning or end of the growing season.

Autumn is the best planting season if you garden on lightish soil, as the soil stays warm, and winter rains help new roots to get established without you having to do any watering. Spring is better if you garden on cold, wet clay soil, as plants still have time to get going before the weather turns hot and dry, and there's no risk of new roots rotting because of poor conditions over the winter.

Summer is fine, too, but if the weather's dry, you will need to keep the new plants watered through the dry weather – all season, if necessary.

Foolproof planting checklist

Location	Preparation and planting	Aftercare
Check soil type (see pages 90–91)	Dig soil and improve it (see pages 49–55)	Water
Check site: is it sunny, shady, boggy, dry, etc?(see pages 86–88)	Water plant while in pot	Stake if necessary (see page 79)
Check situation: is it affected by geographical location and aspect? (see page 89)	Prepare hole (see pages 76–79)	Mulch
	Plant and water in	Check for signs of wilt, disease, etc (see pages 32–33 and 221)

3 PLANNING AND MAKING BORDERS

Making a start

The golden rules with gardening are, first, don't take on too much at once, and second, never expect your garden to be completed. A garden evolves – it doesn't stand still and it's always changing. You're not going to rush into the house one day and say 'That's it Mildred, it's finished'.

I still haven't 'finished' my garden at Barleywood, and I've been here 20 years. But planning and planting up an individual bed or border is a different matter entirely. If it's properly sorted out in advance, you can usually reckon to complete a new border, or make-over an old one, in a single weekend, instead of the job trailing on for weeks, with you feeling that you're getting nowhere fast.

The list of preparatory tasks seems daunting – far more than a weekend's work. But work out the basics first, and enjoy doing so, and the job itself will be more straightforward.

You'll be surprised at what you can achieve in a short time if you get your act together. This hardy annual border, planned (*right*) and sown in spring (*above*), is in full bloom by mid-summer (*opposite*).

1 *Agrostemma githago* 'Milas'.
2 *Amaranthus caudatus*.
3 *Nigella damascena* 'Miss Jekyll'.
4 *Nicotiana* (white).
5 *Tropaeolum majus* 'Alaska Mixed'.
6 *Convolvulus tricolor* 'Blue Ensign'.
7 *Cosmos* 'Seashells Mixed'.
8 *Calendula officinalis* 'Pacific Apricot'.
9 *Limnanthus douglasii*.

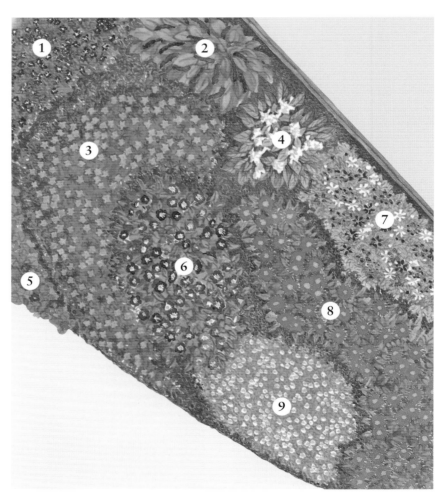

Order of working

We are about to deal with all this in detail but, in a nutshell, when you start to work in the garden there is a basic order of working through the jobs that need doing. Assessing your site to check your soil type and the site location in terms of which way it faces and how it is affected by sun and shade is vital as this information helps you plan your design on paper. (Bear in mind colour, height and spread of plants suitable to your site.) Marking out the border shape on the ground is important to ensure it's where you want it, and weed and rubbish clearance, as well as soil preparation and improvement, must be done before you plant. Place your plants in position and judge the overall effect, before planting the major trees and/or shrubs and evergreens to create a framework. You can then add your perennials and fill the gaps with annuals while you wait for the shrubs to grow and fill in the space. You'll then need to fork the soil over lightly and mulch it well to give your plants a really good start.

Assessing the site

Step into David Attenborough's shoes for a moment and look at your garden as a series of mini-habitats. Each area provides different growing conditions that make one place more suitable than another for particular plants.

Before planting anything, check out the amount of light, shelter and soil type so that you know the facilities that are on offer in the spot where you want to make your bed. Once you know what cards you are holding, it's a heck of a lot easier to start dealing with plants. If you've set your heart on growing shade lovers in a hot, sunny garden, or drought lovers on wet clay soil, there's a certain amount you can do to make the growing conditions more suitable. These are things to tackle before you start planting but, to avoid future disappointment, it's important to accept that there is a limit.

Light

Lie in a hammock on a sunny summer's day, and watch what happens as the shadows move around the garden. Resist rude remarks from the family. They may suggest you are just lazing around, when you are actually engaged in valuable research. What

From early morning to late evening, the sun moves across the garden (*below*). Take time to sit in your garden on a sunny day and see just which areas get the most sunlight, and which stay in the shade.

you are looking for are areas that are in shade all the time, those that are shaded for about half the day, and those that remain in full sun throughout the day. Are the shady areas in deep shade – can you see to read a book easily? If not, then it's too dark to grow even shade-loving plants, unless you do something to improve matters.

Light shade beneath a canopy of trees produces an attractive dappled effect, where it is very pleasant to sit and enjoy a cold drink. Both shade-loving plants and choice woodland species will enjoy it too, as long as there is some shelter from cold or strong winds. Once you know your garden well, taking account of light and dark corners becomes second nature, but, in a new garden, mark them on a sketch plan of the garden, to help you work out what to plant where.

While you're enjoying the sun, don't forget that, in winter, the picture will have changed quite a bit. Deciduous trees will have shed their leaves, so some areas will be a lot brighter. The winter sun is lower in the sky and shadows are longer, so some previously sunny places may now be in shade for some of the time. You probably won't want to wait and see through the whole gardening year before going ahead with your plans, but at least be aware of the way the light levels change as the year rolls around. But what if your light levels don't tally with what you want to grow?

Creating shade

It's very easy to introduce shade into a sunny garden. You can plant trees with a light canopy: birches (*Betula*) and crab apples (*Malus*) cast enough shade to cool things down without blotting out the sun entirely. For additional summer shade, you can plant a screen of tall grasses, such as *Miscanthus*, which you could then cut down in winter, when they turn brown, to let in more light. And arches, pillars and pergolas will introduce a nice spot of dappling.

Let there be light!

If the garden is too shady, you can often increase the amount of light it receives. Every little helps! So, prune overgrown shrubs and remove trees and shrubs that don't contribute much to the garden. Ask a tree surgeon to thin out the over-dense canopies of big trees, or remove the bottom branches to 'lift' the crowns. You can also paint walls in pale, pastel colours, or use mirrors or water to reflect all available light and add some sparkle to shady areas.

Shade lovers will enjoy areas beneath shade-casting shrubs, while sun lovers will prefer full light at some distance from the shrub's canopy.

Aspect

The direction a garden faces has the most significant bearing on the amount of light it receives. It figures that a garden with a south-facing aspect is going to be sunny, while one that faces north gets little, if any, direct sun – although it won't necessarily be gloomy. As long as it has a wide-open horizon around it, a north-facing garden may enjoy quite reasonable light levels and the lack of direct sun can make it ideal for delicate plants that are easily scorched.

A garden's aspect can lead to problems that are not easily foreseen. For example, it's not a good idea to plant early-flowering plants in an east-facing garden, because the petals can 'scorch' if early morning sun hits them while they are still frozen by the previous night's frost. It's bad enough having all your camellias ruined, but if you grow fruit trees in an east-facing garden, this is probably why you don't get very good crops. If late frost coincides with flowering time, it 'burns' the petals and scorches the pollen-bearing anthers, so it's curtains for that year's crop of fruit.

On the other hand, a west-facing garden receives late afternoon and evening sun, so as well as being safe for early spring flowers, it's a fine place for sitting after work. A west-facing niche is a really good site for your favourite, fragrant plants and you can enjoy them in warmth and comfort.

Locality

Gardening conditions are also affected by geographical location. A high altitude garden, or one surrounded by wide-open countryside, is likely to be very windy. If it's on a cliff top, or close to the sea, the odds are that the garden will also be exposed to the abrasive action of blown sand, or the burning action of salt spray. In these situations, you have to decide whether you want a conventional garden, in which case you'll need to put lots of shelter around it first, or whether you'd prefer to keep the wonderful views and settle for a more natural effect, using plants that can rough it a bit.

If your garden is next to a busy road, you can expect to have dust blown over it on a regular basis, so you might want to settle for a scheme that includes lots of glossy-leaved evergreens that are easier to keep clean. You might also need to consider taking a few basic security precautions: avoid putting containers or garden ornaments where they can be seen or easily whipped away. And make the most of plants that are naturally prickly, to make screens or hedges round a garden that needs protection from intruders, vandals or animals.

In a seaside garden, use plants that are resistant to wind and salt spray.

Assessing your soil type

To most people soil is just dirt, but, to a plant, it's life or death. It's not hard to identify your soil type, given a bit of basic detective work. Whether you garden on clay, sand, chalk, or on the perfect loam soil, it affects what will grow well. Loam is generally regarded as the best garden soil and traditional soil improvement is designed to turn whatever soil you inherit into something as much like loam as possible. You don't have to take that route – if the soil is particularly extreme, it can often be easier to design a garden that uses plants that are naturally at home in such conditions. But first, you need to assess what you have before you can make the best of it.

Simple soil analysis
You can discover a lot about your soil just by looking at the garden shortly after it's rained, and by rubbing a handful of soil between your fingers.

Sandy or gravelly soil (1) feels gritty when rubbed between the fingers and won't hold together if you try to form it into a ball. After rain, surface puddles drain away in next to no time.

Different types of soil:
1 Sandy soil is free-draining but often lacking in nutrients.
2 Clay soil is fiendishly difficult to work and slow to drain.
3 Chalky soil will not suit acid lovers such as rhododendrons.
4 Loamy soil is everybody's dream.
5 Peaty soil is rich in organic matter.

Clay soil (2) feels smooth and takes a surface polish when rubbed between the fingers. If you roll a ball of clay into a sausage shape, it will hold together without crumbling and allow you to shape it into a ring without breaking. Clay soils turn rapidly into sticky mud after rain, and long-lasting, surface puddles form easily. But when clay soil is dry, it sets like concrete and may crack.

Chalky soil (3) is usually pale in colour, and white chunks of chalk are often visible, especially if the chalk rock is close to the surface – chalk hills or outcrops nearby usually give the game away. Chalk soils drain very freely, so puddles don't last long after rain.

Loamy soil (4) is dark brown in colour and holds moisture quite well, but excess water drains away after heavy rain, so puddles don't last more than a few hours. If you roll it into a sausage, it will hold its shape, but it will break when you bend it into a ring.

Peaty soil (5) is almost black when moist, being composed almost entirely of partially decomposed organic matter, such as moss or sedge from bogs or fens. It crumbles if rubbed between the fingers and, after rain, glistens with moisture. It absorbs water like a sponge, so surface water only forms puddles if the soil is totally saturated.

Elementary chemistry
There's also a very simple test you can do. Take half a handful of soil and stir it into a large jam-jar full of water. Leave the mess to settle, then take a look after a couple of hours.

Sandy or gravelly soil will have sunk to the bottom, forming a distinctly gritty layer with slightly dirty water above it.

Clay soil is full of very fine particles that don't settle out quickly, so the solution will still look very cloudy with only a thin layer of fine muddy material sitting on the bottom of the jar.

Chalky soil makes the water turn a pale greyish colour and there will be a layer of gritty white fragments at the bottom of the jar.

A good loam settles slowly into fairly even layers, with the biggest particles at the bottom and smaller particles on top. This is as it should be, because a good loam contains some clay, some sandy particles and plenty of organic matter.

Naturally peaty soil contains a large amount of floating material suspended in dirty water.

Improving the soil

Well-rotted organic matter is the closest you will get to a universal panacea in soil improvement terms, and it comes in many forms (see pages 50–51). If you have sandy, chalky or gravelly soil, you can improve it by digging in organic matter in spring and autumn, mulching heavily where you can't dig. But this type of ground is very fast-draining and 'hungry', absorbing organic matter fast, so you'll have to add organic matter on a regular basis – as part of your annual garden routine. If your patch is also hot and sunny, I'd recommend you make a Mediterranean or seaside-style garden and save yourself the hard labour.

Clay soil turns into good, fertile earth if you add plenty of organic matter and dig in enough grit to open it up. Use horticultural grit, coarse, sharp sand, or fine, river-washed gravel. Don't use builder's sand, which contains too much lime, or gravel dredged up from under the sea, as it is too salty for plants. Dig in at least a bucketful of grit per square metre/yard, or sprinkle it on as a mulch along with some well-rotted organic matter. Then let the worms do the work.

Good loamy soil needs occasional helpings of organic matter to keep it in good condition, especially if you crop it heavily, but it takes a heck of a lot of the hard work out of gardening if the soil is on your side to start with.

Peaty soils, though moisture-retentive and free-draining, are very short of nutrients and very acidic. Organic matter provides a range of essential trace elements and adds 'body' to a thin, peaty soil. Excessive acidity can be countered by applying lime (see page 95) and you will also need to use a general-purpose fertilizer regularly, especially for vegetable crops (see pages 52–53). But many gardeners positively yearn for soils like this – it's perfect for a huge range of choice, lime-hating plants, such as rhododendrons and azaleas.

A Mediterranean-style garden is a good choice on hot, sunny sites, particularly if your soil is very free-draining.

Acidity and alkalinity

If you have chalky soil, it's almost certainly going to be alkaline, and you can usually guess you have acid soil if your neighbours can grow wonderful rhododendrons. But the safest way to tell for sure is to do a pH test – the accurate measure of acidity and alkalinity. You can buy a soil-testing kit from any good garden centre.

Doing a soil test

First take your soil sample. It's no good just grabbing the first handful of soil you find and expecting it to tell you about the soil all over the garden. You need to test a sample that is typical of the whole area, avoiding those places where you have had bonfires, or mixed cement, which might affect the result.

Use a trowel to dig several 'cores' of soil from different areas around the garden. Carefully remove the top 2.5cm (1in) of soil from the core, so that you are testing soil from just below the surface. Mix the samples together well and use a small portion to do the test.

If your garden clearly has several different types of soil within it, then do a separate test for each area, again mixing several soil samples from within each area to ensure truly representative results.

Spread the sample out on a clean glass dish to dry, then follow the instructions in the soil-test kit. The box contains almost everything you need: a test tube, pH indicator fluid and a colour chart. You will also need some distilled water (from a car accessory shop or pharmacist).

After mixing the soil sample, put some in the test tube, adding the chemical and the distilled water, shake it up well and leave it to stand. When the soil has settled at the bottom of the test tube, it leaves a layer of coloured liquid above it. Compare the colour of the liquid with the colours on the chart and read off the pH value (see below).

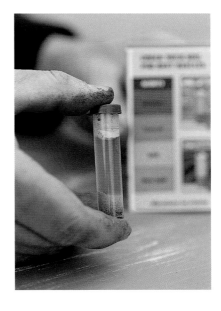

Simple soil-test kits tell you in a matter of minutes whether your soil is acid or alkaline – something that affects the types of plant you can grow in it.

Soil acidity and alkalinity

The result of the test tells you the pH of your soil, which shows how acid or alkaline it is. If the pH is 7.0, you have neutral soil, which means most plants will grow happily and you can safely skip reading the next bit altogether because you don't need to do anything about your pH.

Most garden soils are in the pH range 6–8, that is, slightly acid to slightly alkaline. Most plants grow in such soils without problems, except for real acid lovers, such as rhododendrons and most heathers. To all intents and purposes, the soil pH is controlled by its calcium content. If the pH reading is 7.5 or more, then the soil is alkaline. The higher the number, the more alkaline it is and the more calcium it contains – mostly in the form of lime (calcium carbonate). At pH9 or more, the soil would be seriously limy.

Stone fruits like plums and cherries do well on alkaline soils, as they need calcium to make their stones. Encrusted saxifrages will get all the calcium they need to make the silvery, limescale encrustations that are such a feature of their leaves. Plants such as clematis, pinks (*Dianthus*) and scabious will be very happy, although they also grow in less alkaline soils. They are natives of chalk soils (chalk being a form of calcium carbonate).

A pH reading below 7 means your soil is acid; the lower the number the more acid it is and the less lime it contains. Soils of pH3 are so acid, you'd only find them on boggy moorland, where a limited range of very specialized plants grow, such as cotton grass (*Eriophorum*) and cranberries (*Vaccinium*). In a slightly acid soil, you can grow plants like camellias, rhododendrons and heathers, and also more choice lime haters, such as *Crinodendron* and *Berberidopsis*. The terms 'lime haters' and 'acid lovers', by the way, mean exactly the same thing.

In alkaline (chalky) soil, encrusted saxifrages can happily produce the white powdery deposit on their leaf rosettes.

Why is soil pH important?

The big problem with soils that are very acid or very alkaline is that certain nutrients are chemically 'locked up' and so are unavailable to plants – that's when you may see deficiency symptoms.

On alkaline soil, iron and some trace elements are locked up. That's why, if you try to grow rhododendrons on limy soil, their leaves turn yellow – it's a symptom of iron deficiency. On the plus side, earthworms, nitrogen-fixing bacteria and the soil bacteria that break down organic matter are more active in alkaline soils, which is good news for organic gardeners. Vegetables, especially the cabbage family, are usually happier on slightly alkaline soils, as the nutrients they need are more available in those conditions. Club root disease is less of a problem – it was once a tradition to lime allotments to prevent its occurrence. Potatoes, however, are more likely to be affected by scab on limy soil, so the potato patch was always left unlimed.

On acid soil, phosphates are locked up and some trace elements, such as aluminium, are unlocked and are toxic to plants in large quantities. Some plants, particularly ericaceous, or acid-loving types, like rhododendrons, camellias and most heathers, only grow happily on acid soil. Most conifers and a few other plants prefer it, though they'll also grow in neutral or slightly alkaline soil.

Altering the pH

If you have extremely acid or alkaline soil, it's expensive and difficult to make drastic changes to the pH, and 'cures' are rarely permanent. You might make a special effort to alter a small patch, perhaps, but for a whole garden... forget it. Although it's relatively easy to raise the pH by adding lime, it's important not to overdo it or you'll just scorch the plants. Don't try to make a big change in the pH all at once; it's safer to use enough lime each autumn to alter the pH one point at a time. Test again a year later and then add more if necessary.

The amount of lime you need to add depends on your soil type – clay soil needs more than sandy soil. As a rough guide, it takes about 500g of lime per 1sq.m (1lb per sq.yd) of soil to raise the pH by one point. You'd need half that amount on sandy soil but half as much again on clay. Never use lime at the same time as organic matter or fertilizers, as they react with each other and spoil the effect. The usual system is to put lime on in the autumn, dig organic matter in during the winter, then put the fertilizer on in the spring when you are ready to plant.

If you have chalky soil and you want to make it acid enough to grow lime haters, you'll have a difficult job on your hands. You can dig in acidic forms of organic matter, such as well-rotted pine needles or leaf mould, but it will make only a tiny difference. Once upon a time, moss peat would have been used to make an acidic peat bed, but this is rightly frowned on these days due to the need to conserve our fast-disappearing peat bogs. One alternative is to dig in sulphur chips and feed lime-hating plants in spring with chelated iron (sold as sequestered iron), but you need to apply both regularly and they are too expensive to use in anything but a small area.

So, if you pine to grow rhododendrons or other lime-hating plants when you are saddled with chalky soil, the best way is to grow them in containers, using a lime-free (ericaceous) potting compost. There are several peat-free brands available.

Liming

Years ago vegetable growers used to lime their allotments the way they took baths, whether they needed to or not, in order to avoid diseases like club root. It's far better to be a bit scientific about it and do a soil pH test, then apply lime if the results indicate that it is needed. The sort of lime to use on the garden is sold as garden lime or hydrated lime. Lime doesn't last in the soil for very long, so undertake a soil test every year and re-apply (or not) depending on what the test tells you. Although it supplies calcium, lime isn't really a fertilizer but, by reducing the acidity of the soil, it releases nutrients that have been chemically locked up, so, in a way, it acts like one.

If your soil is badly drained, make a bog garden – go along with nature rather than fighting her.

Moisture levels

Some gardens are naturally wet and some are very dry for most of the year due to a combination of site and soil type, but you can have problem 'pockets' within an otherwise fairly normal garden, so it's worth taking a look round.

Gardens on heavy clay tend to be boggy in winter and during prolonged rain. Elsewhere, wet soil can be caused by natural springs, or a high water table. The water table is the level below which the ground is saturated with water. You can easily check the height of the water table in your own garden just by digging a hole. Make it about 60cm (2ft) deep and watch it over a couple of days. In winter, in low-lying areas, the water table can be very close to the surface, which is no good at all for the roots of those plants – such as many Mediterranean natives – that must have well-drained conditions.

Wet soil can be drained, but it means burying porous pipes to take the water away. This can be a very costly undertaking and, in any case, only works if you have somewhere for the water to run to, so it's no good for flat sites. Under such circumstances, it's much better to turn the conditions to your advantage by making a bog garden. Where there's a high water table, it's usually only high in winter, so grow tough plants that won't mind wet winters and drier summers. Springs can be turned into a natural water feature, perhaps surrounded by outcrops of rock, or they can be piped away underground (at more expense). Make raised beds for treasured rock plants, herbs and Mediterranean plants that hate having wet feet.

It's usually chalky, sandy or gravelly soils that are prone to drought. This type of very light, fast-draining soil can be improved by adding organic matter, but it decomposes so quickly in these conditions that you need to apply it twice a year, in spring and autumn. I'd rather make the most of the superb drainage by making a gravel garden and planting it with drought-lovers. If you want to make the odd 'conventional' flower bed, dig in plenty of coarse or incompletely rotted organic matter and work in some of the water-retaining gel crystals sold for hanging baskets. Do the same where you want to grow vegetables, which are also a problem to grow if they keep drying out.

As a general rule, whenever you are faced with 'problem' places, my advice is, don't try to fight the conditions, but make the most of plants that like to grow naturally in the given circumstances. It's cheaper and much less labour-intensive, and you'll enjoy your garden much more if you don't turn it into a battle ground, fighting your soil all the time.

Designing a bed

I'm not going to tell you about designing a complete garden here. Instead I'll concentrate on individual beds and borders. There are several different planting styles and types of border, and the ones you choose help to create your garden's character.

Planting styles

The style of planting you choose makes a big difference to the 'feel' of your garden. Style is largely a matter of taste and personal preference, but each of the different planting styles has its own advantages.

Traditional herbaceous borders are the sort you see in the grounds of stately homes, ablaze with mid-summer flowers, such as delphiniums and lupins, often set against a yew or a beech hedge. Such borders can be a lot of work, as the hedge may harbour weeds and pests, and the tall plants that form the back row often need staking. And once the summer display is over, there is nothing much to see.

The traditional herbaceous border offers wonderful form and colour and is at its best in high summer. Choose plants like:
1 *Alchemilla mollis*.
2 delphiniums.
3 achillea.
4 nepeta.

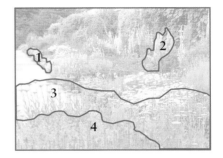

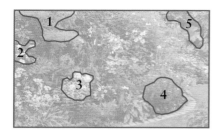

In a huge garden, that doesn't matter much, as other seasonal hotspots can become the centre of attention. In a small garden, it isn't so clever, and you'll probably be better off planting a mixed border, perhaps in an island bed (see page 101) so that perennials are shown off by a backbone of winter-flowering shrubs and bulbs. There's less work involved in this kind of planting scheme and everything is within easy reach.

Mixed borders are the best choice for most gardens. For example, this border has:
1 *Gleditsia triacanthos* 'Sunburst' (tree).
2 *Gladiolus callianthus* 'Murieliae' (bulb).
3 *Phlox paniculata* 'Norah Leigh' (perennial).
4 anthemis (perennial).
5 *Gunnera manicata* (perennial).

Mixed borders include a bit of everything. The great advantage of a mixed border is that there is something to see during most of the year. These areas of your garden are the original pick 'n' mix selection and you can choose your own blend of 'ingredients' to fill a mixed border.

You can include trees and shrubs to give the border height and bulk, and to give it some interest during the winter. Bulbs will provide a spring show to brighten up the bed and perennials will add the summer colour. Bedding plants can then fill any seasonal gaps you find you have.

Contemporary areas (1) are easy to care for; they include plenty of open space, interesting surfaces, such as pebbles, cobbles or decking, and dramatic clumps of 'architectural' plants, like phormiums and bamboos, grouped together to make eye-catching features. Quite unlike a traditional bed, the effect is more like living architecture.

The cottage garden (2) style is an easy-going one, created by planting beds of self-seeding annuals and perennials that will spread without needing regular digging up and dividing. But modern cottage gardeners are often plant addicts, who use this style as an excuse to house their ever-expanding collections. In this case, it's a good idea to keep invasive plants in beds of their own, so that they can't smother slower-growing treasures.

Prairie planting (3) is a stylish and fashionable form of perennial planting. Here, you can forget about lawns and beds and, instead, have a solid carpet of low-maintenance perennials and ornamental grasses that you walk between on winding, bark or gravel paths. It's quite easy to look after, as long as you don't have masses of perennial weeds in your soil.

Various planting styles:
1 Gardeners who like a minimalist approach will position carefully chosen plants alongside pebbles, cobbles, timber and ornaments.
2 Traditionalists will probably prefer the cottage garden approach with its show of old-fashioned flowers.
3 The prairie garden uses a mixture of grasses and wild-looking plants for a more natural 'untamed' effect.

Border types

Traditionally, a border is the type of wide bed that runs round the edge of the garden, though you might have a narrow one that runs along the edge of a path or patio. Borders often have straight edges, which gives them a formal style. For softer, more informal effects, create borders with generously curving edges. But beware! Make your curves broad and sweeping – lots of tight bends tend to make a garden look fussy and are a real pain when it comes to mowing. And make your borders as wide as you can so that you have room to plant with lots of interesting variation in height without cramping the individual plant's style.

There are several variations on the theme that you can use to get away from the 'ribbon-development' effect – if that's what you want:

The wider the border, the more dramatic the effect and the more room plants will have to grow. Straight-sided borders have a clean, formal feel.

Island beds are the sort that are sited within the garden, to form planted 'islands' surrounded by lawn, gravel or paving. They usually have informal, curving outlines and may be, for example, teardrop- or kidney-shaped. Island beds look particularly good when landscaped to fit into existing hollows, perhaps in a sloping lawn, to give them a natural appearance. Again, tight curves and sharp angles are best avoided.

Raised beds are much more artificial creations. They are made with brick, timber or dry-stone walls and filled with soil. Raised beds might be specially built to bring the garden up to easy working level – ideal for gardeners who are becoming a bit creaky in the back! In this case, it's a good idea to build a wide top edge that doubles as a seat.

They are often built to create better drainage for plants that hate wet feet – Mediterranean plants and most alpines, for example. If so, you'll need to put lots of drainage material at the bottom (it's a good place to get rid of all your old half-bricks) and fill the beds with a mixture of soil and horticultural grit. One of their other big advantages is that your favourite plants are brought much closer to eye (and nose) level.

Borders sculpted in sweeping curves have a more natural, relaxed look.

Where plants need really good drainage (or when you reach that time of life when bending becomes more difficult!), raised beds are a good idea.

Creating planting plans

The plan becomes reality – the mapped out 'winter interest' border (*below*), will also look great in summer (*right*).

1 *Corylus avellana* 'Contorta'.
2 *Carex fraseri* 'Frosted Curls'.
3 *Cornus sanguinea* 'Midwinter Fire'.
4 *Erica x darleyensis* 'Silberschmelze'.
5 *Mahonia aquifolium* 'Smaragd'.
6 *Erica x darleyensis* 'Kramer's Rote'.
7 *Bergenia* 'Sunningdale'.
8 *Eleagnus x ebbingei* 'Limelight'.
9 *Pennisetum alopecuroides* 'Hameln'.
10 *Hamamelis x intermedia* 'Westerstede'.
11 *Mahonia japonica* 'Hivernant'.

Once you've worked out a shape and decided on a style for your bed, make a planting plan that shows you which plants to put where. Why not just go to the garden centre and buy whatever takes your fancy? Well, the trouble is, impulse buying is fun at the time, but you'll probably pick plants that look great on the day. When they've finished flowering, it may be ages before they 'peak' again. It's impossible to resist the most eye-catching plants, but they don't always make good neighbours – they may not even enjoy the same growing conditions. No, we need to be a bit methodical – sorry!

Do your research

One of the best ways to plan your bed or border is to take a sheet of paper and write at the top the theme of your bed – say a mixed border, prairie bed, exotic island bed, or whatever. Make a note of the soil type, site and aspect – hot, sunny and sandy, or cool, wet and shady maybe – and start jotting down the names of plants

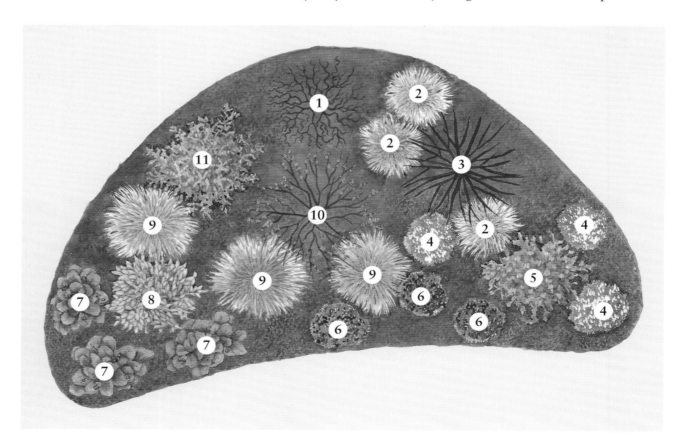

that will grow well in such circumstances. Where to look? Plant reference books contain useful lists of plants for particular situations and, if they have illustrations, so much the better. It may be worth buying a book that covers gardening on clay or chalky soil, if that's your particular situation, as it will contain far greater detail about plants that grow best there. If you belong to a gardening club, other members often have pertinent advice to offer.

Try spending a fact-finding morning in a garden centre. Some centres group plants for particular situations together, or make special display gardens. Even if the plants are arranged in alphabetical order, you'll still find vital information on the labels attached to individual plants.

But the most enjoyable way of undertaking research is to visit other gardens looking for inspiration. If you live in a problem area, maybe near the sea, then visit gardens close to home with similar conditions. Look out for open gardens with features you admire, such as bog or gravel gardens, or particular planting styles. Take a notebook and camera and, when you see a planting scheme you like, take notes, or take a picture of the plants to act as a reminder later.

Labels in the garden

If you don't like to see your plant labels, save them and file them in an old shoe box. If you think you won't remember what's where, draw a map and mark the positions and names of your plants on it.

If you like to keep your plants labelled, I'd still remove the plastic pictorial tags as they quickly fade, get buried, or break off and blow away. Copy vital information, such as name and pruning instructions, on to a metal label to push down into the soil by a clump of plants or bulbs, or tie it discreetly to an inner branch of a tree or shrub, where you can still find it.

Read the plant label

This is the type of basic information you should find on the back of a plant label in a garden centre.

Name: Latin and common names.

Height and spread: average size after five years. Don't expect plants to follow this to the letter; actual size varies according to growing conditions.

Flowering time: often represented by a number that corresponds to the month (or months).

Hieroglyphics: symbols representing sun, partial shade, shade etc.

Special instructions: pruning instructions, or other critical information.

Arranging shapes

Choosing plants that enjoy the growing conditions in your garden is only half the battle. It's the way you put them together that really gives your planting scheme star quality. When you analyse what makes a border successful, you'll see that there are several basic plant shapes: tall and upright, low and spreading, spiky, domed, rounded and foamy 'filler'. Forget about plant names for now; the best way to start designing is just by arranging the shapes on paper.

It's a good idea to cut out different-sized triangles of paper, sketch in rough plant shapes – spiky, weeping, upright, domed and so on – and put them together to get an idea of the finished effect. Then arrange them on your plan. By working in black and white, you can see instantly which contrasting shapes have dramatic effects when positioned beside each other.

Don't try to tackle a whole bed at once. Start with small units and then put them together. The units that work best for me are triangles or pyramids. A typical triangle might contain an upright tree, a rounded shrub and a low, spreading plant. These will work well together if you just want a free-standing trio of plants to form a small contemporary feature, surrounded by a carpet of gravel, perhaps with a single large cobble for dramatic focus.

A traditional, plant-filled border works in exactly the same way – there's just a lot more of it. Go about it in the same way, and keep putting triangles together until you've filled the whole area. Use different-sized triangles: large ones for upright tree-shapes, rounded shrubs, and low, spreading perennials; smaller triangles for evergreen herbs, perennials and bulbs.

You can use triangles to fill any shape, from a long, narrow border with the tallest plants along the back row, to an irregular island bed in which the tallest plants are grouped along the 'backbone' so that you can see everything as you walk round the margins. Above all, try to avoid making your planting scheme look like a plate of buns.

Think in triangles and your beds and borders will end up having an interesting and flowing shape.

Adding colour

This is the point where I feel a quick watercolour coming on, but you don't need to be at all artistic to have a go for yourself. Start filling in the triangles using splodges of colour. The effect will be more Picasso after a wild night out than Gainsborough doing a detailed landscape. There's no need to be realistic in terms of shape or detail, because what you want is just an impression of which colour goes where, and how they go together.

If you're making a traditional border, you'll probably want to include a lot of different colours. To stop them all clashing, and looking artlessly garish, it makes sense to have a preponderance of green – provided by evergreens and foliage plants – with blobs of colour sprinkled throughout. Avoid placing colours that shriek right next to each other. You could be very co-ordinated and stick to shades of purple, mauve and pink, or blues, pinks and whites; or go for hot and trendy using red, yellow and orange. A word of advice though, don't mix these two colour ranges, or the result will be like an explosion in a paint shop. Oh, and don't worry that you still haven't put any plant names in, or thought about how to keep colour in the border throughout the seasons, because that comes later (see pages 122–34 and 197–99).

The colour wheel

Artists have some of the most brilliantly colour co-ordinated gardens, even if they don't know all that much about plants. They instinctively apply the same 'colour theory' for putting plants together as they do when they are painting.

An artist's colour wheel shows immediately the relationships colours have to each other. Imagine a rainbow bent round into a complete circle. Red – orange – yellow – green – blue – indigo – violet. That's a colour wheel. Any time you are planning a colour scheme, you can use it to see at a glance which colours 'go' together well.

They say opposites attract, and that's certainly true with colours. Some of the most striking combinations are the contrasting colours that lie immediately opposite each other on the colour wheel, such as red and green, purple and yellow, orange and blue. Three-way combinations make slightly more subtle contrasts. The most successful are based on three colours that are spaced at equal distances around the colour wheel – red, blue and pale yellow, or purple, green and orange-yellow.

Instead of choosing contrasting colours, you can make harmonious effects by using three colours that lie next to each other in the colour wheel. You might choose yellow, orange and

Different colour combinations:
1 The contrasting green *Paris polyphylla* and red *Lobelia* 'Fan Scharlach'.
2 Purple *Verbena bonariensis* and yellow *Patrinia scabiosifolia*.
3 Blue agapanthus against a background of orange crocosmia.
4 A multicoloured confection of electric blue *Eryngium x oliveranum*, scarlet *Crocosmia* 'Lucifer', yellow *Coreopsis verticillata* and magenta *Lychnis coronaria*. Stunning!

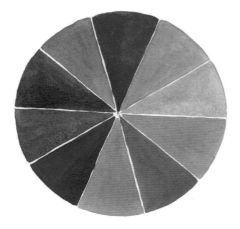

Use this colour wheel to work out the colour scheme of your planting. Adjacent colours harmonize; those opposite one another on the wheel, such as red and green, will make dramatic contrasts.

1

2

3

4

red, or mauve, purple and violet; it's exactly this technique that works so well at Sissinghurst Castle, in Kent.

I find it really helps me to paint my plan for a garden or border to assess how the colours will come together. Remember, there are more than just pure colours that you can put together; colours come in all sorts of variations and flowers come in all sorts of tints and tones. Their foliage, also, has an almost infinite number of variations in colour – yellowy greens, bluish-greens and soft greys, right through to deep bottle green, burnt copper and almost black.

Crimson *Astrantia* 'Hadspen Blood' (foreground), the ruddy pokers of *Sanguisorba menziesii*, and the rose 'Dusky Maiden' combine to make a hot, monochromatic scheme.

Monochrome schemes

If you want a monochromatic colour scheme, you can go about it by putting together the colours from one segment of the colour wheel only but, for that to work in a garden, you must also think laterally. Vita Sackville-West's famous white garden at Sissinghurst Castle actually contains lots of grey, silver and glaucous-blue foliage, plenty of gold- and silver-variegated leaves and a few lilac flowers. The variety gives it depth and brings it to life. White gardens planted with white flowers alone would look flat and dull.

The only colours that don't appear on the colour wheel are black and white. White is 'off the scale' at one end, as there is no colour at all. Black would be a single spot in the centre of the wheel, because black is what you get when all the colours are present. To the gardener, black and white are 'neutral' and go with everything, though they are not colours to use in large quantities. Remember, above all else, that green is the most important colour of all because it complements all the others and acts as a buffer between flowers of different shades. What's more, leaves are interesting for a greater part of the year than flowers.

Putting it all together

Once you have designed the shape and size of the bed, worked out what shaped plants and what colours to put where, it's simply a matter of putting plant names to the specifications and making sure that they'll all be right for your soil and situation.

Plants-people with a bit of past experience in putting plants together often cut out the formal planning process and do the job 'by eye' in the garden centre. They pick out several groups of plants with contrasting shapes that look good together, and experiment by arranging the groups in various combinations to see how they might work best as a team.

Large plants, like trees, shrubs and evergreens, are relatively easy to position, but smaller plants, such as alpines and perennial flowers, are not always so simple to sort out. The secret is to go for trios of contrasting shapes that have something in common – maybe colour – then put the various trios together until they fill the area.

Timing

Remember that however carefully you plan your scheme, it is going to change with the seasons and as it matures over the years. Start by planning for the main summer effect, and then try to stretch the season of interest by adding evergreens and spring bulbs, etc. I never said it was going to be easy. Just easier!

Professional planting

If you still don't feel very confident about putting groups of plants together, try organizing them with a common theme running through the area. This is a valuable concept garden designers call 'unity'. In the case of a rock garden, for example, you might use a mulch of stone chippings to tie the design together. In a border, you could repeat groups of one particular 'filler' flower throughout, or use skeins of silver foliage running through a whole flower border to 'pull' trios of more individually striking flowers together and stop them from clashing.

The do's and don'ts of planting schemes

Do...	Don't...
Choose plants that suit your soil aspect and situation	Go for plants with widely varying growth rates or the strong ones will smother their weak neighbours
Place plants in threes so that they create 'triangles' and form a clump	Choose plants with identical shapes or you'll end up with a very tedious effect – lots of variety is needed
Think about colours that will go together well or contrast well	
Have a theme of some sort running through a bed, whether it's a colour scheme, a regularly repeated flower, or rustic accessories	Make beds with lots of sharp bends and acute angles, as they are a pain to mow around

A basic framework of shrubs and perennials can be thinned out in an established garden, and new plants added to refresh the scheme.

Renovating or restoring an old bed

It's all very well planning a completely new bed from scratch but, if you want to make-over an existing bed, you'll need a slightly different approach since you aren't starting with a clean slate.

First, you need to work out what's already there. Make a plan of the border with the plants marked in, then decide what you think you'd be better off without. Maybe the bed has been there a long time and is a bit overgrown, or you might have been inspired by something you've seen on TV and feel like giving an old border a new look. It's a great opportunity to weed out some of the old plants you've lost interest in, and to replace them with something more exciting. And, while you're at it, take the opportunity to replenish the soil now there are gaps in the border. After digging out the unwanted plants, work some well-rotted compost and a dressing of general fertilizer into the ground.

When deciding what else to plant, if you draw a plan, it's quite easy to get an impression of the effect when the surplus ingredients have been erased. You can then sketch in new plants that will look good against the existing background, in just the same way as if you were planning a completely new border from scratch.

Unplanned arrivals

Very often, what happens is that you've had a very good day out at a show or a nursery, gone mad with the credit card, and come back with the car full of new plants. We've all done it and, frankly, it's part of the fun, but the trouble with buying on impulse is that you usually have no idea where you are going to plant your new 'finds'.

A lot of people try to accommodate their new plants by making new beds, or enlarging existing beds and borders. This is fine if you happen to have a rambling, informal cottage garden, or a natural, prairie-style one. But in a formal or a contemporary garden, you can find you've lost the whole thrust of your design if you clutter the clean lines with extraneous matter that wasn't part of the original plan.

I find that the best way of working new plants into an established scheme is to leave them in their pots and just stand them in gaps all round the garden. That way, you can move them around until you find the best combination of plants and gaps before finally deciding where to plant them.

But don't go worrying about it too much, the great thing about plants is that, if you decide you don't really like the result later, you can always dig them up and move them again – it's a lot easier than moving house.

How to... **remove unwanted old shrubs**

When you are renovating an old border, you need to remove the items you don't want, or that are diseased, without disturbing or damaging the plants that you have chosen to keep. There is a simple way to do this, but it's hard labour, so take care of your back when you're doing it. Some of the more 'macho' gardeners prefer to work bare-handed, but I'd advise wearing a pair of stout gloves to protect your hands and help you keep a good grip.

Old tree stumps can be quite a feature in the wilder type of garden and, if you have to have a tree taken down, it's often a good idea to leave a fairly tall stump and train climbers over it. The best way to remove an unwanted stump is to have it winched out, provided that there's room to get the equipment into the garden. Otherwise, hire in a stump-chipping service. The stump chipper is a machine that looks rather like a rotavator; it chews up the stump, roots and all, to sawdust. Just shovel out the sawdust and refill the hole with new topsoil. You can replant once the ground has settled.

What you need

- *secateurs or loppers*
- *spade*
- *flat-bladed pick (mattock)*

1 Cut the stems back to about 60cm (2ft) above ground level with secateurs or loppers. These stems can be used as a lever when you dig out the roots, making the plant less unwieldy, so reducing the risk of damage to nearby plants and yourself. Beware of the cut ends – it's very easy to give yourself a nasty poke in the eye as you bend over the butchered shrub.

2 Dig around the stump with a spade to reveal the roots, and chop through them bit by bit with the spade or one of those flat-bladed picks that we call a 'beck' in my part of Hampshire. In other areas, it is known as a mattock. The secret is to tackle the main roots individually.

3 Use the remaining stems to lever the rootball back-and-forth. This will reveal any remaining roots. Continue chopping through them and, eventually, you will be able to remove the whole thing. Fill the hole with fresh soil and, after a bit of a lie-down, you're ready to re-plant.

4 FROM SEASON TO SEASON

The growing season

One phrase that crops up all the time in gardening parlance is 'the growing season' – that time between spring and autumn when plants are actively growing. For the rest of the time – the winter – most outdoor plants are dormant and barely ticking over, a bit like hibernating animals.

For us, the start and finish of the growing season are the signals that trigger the changing routines of the gardening year. There are particular jobs that need to be done either when plants are just starting to grow – such as seed sowing and re-potting – or when they are safely dormant – such as moving deciduous shrubs, or pruning grape vines. Life would be so easy if you could just look at the calendar and say, 'Right, March 15th, prune the roses' and know you should do the same thing on the same day each year.

At the height of the growing season plants produce lots of lush growth. Some grow so fast you notice the difference daily.

Unfortunately, it doesn't work out quite like that. The climate varies all around the country, and the weather means that each year's growing season is different. You need to know your local climate and observe natural signs that show when plants are starting or stopping for the year.

Deciduous plants are the big give-away. They detect subtle changes of light and temperature, which start the sap flowing and hormone levels surging. When their growth buds start swelling and bursting open, that's the start of the growing season and, when they lose their leaves in the autumn, that's the end of it… regardless of the precise date on the calendar.

Climate

It's easy to confuse climate and weather. It's probably a tad un-scientific, but the way I think of it is that climate is created by major geographic features that affect local conditions on a permanent basis, and weather is the stuff that changes from day to day.

If your garden is close to the sea, or at high altitude, or in the far north or south of the country, or in the middle of a large city, you're probably well aware that you have a rather different climate from the standard conditions of middle England, which is the one place targeted by anyone giving gardening advice in books and magazines. That's why you'll need to adjust any dates you are given accordingly.

If you've ever driven north to south through the country in spring, you'll have noticed how the daffodils seem to come out during your journey. That's due to the effect the changing climate has on the growing season. In the far north of Scotland, the growing season often starts three to four weeks later than in middle England. The Scottish daffs will hardly be showing through the ground, while at the far tip of Cornwall, where the season may be up to two to four weeks earlier, the daffs will be in full bloom. Since the growing season also ends correspondingly later in Cornwall than in Scotland, it follows that garden plants have a lot longer to complete the season's growth at Land's End than at John O'Groats. That's why your chances of harvesting a good crop of sweetcorn is much better in a southern garden; the shorter, northern growing season may not permit the crop to grow and ripen before the frost. A short growing season also condenses your summer bedding displays and limits your chances of a good show of late-flowering perennials. It's not fair, I know, but it's a fact of life.

It's not just when travelling from north to south that you notice the difference in climate. For every additional 300m (1000ft) above sea level, you can knock roughly two weeks off the growing season

Even when the growing season has come to an end, it doesn't mean the garden has to be dreary – frost can actually brighten a view.

because the higher you are, the colder it gets; even those few degrees can make all the difference. Close to large bodies of water, like the sea, or a huge inland lake, the water acts like a giant, night-storage heater. In these areas the temperature is less likely to fall as low in winter, or rise as high in summer, as it does even a few miles inland, where the night-storage-heater effect peters out.

In the middle of the city, the climate is different again, because the heat leaking out of buildings warms the air to create an unusually mild micro-climate. This is why you'll often see the tougher indoor plants, such as cyclamen and azaleas, flourishing outdoors in window boxes, even in the middle of winter. City dwellers can also grow tender plants outdoors that you'd otherwise only be able to leave out all year round if you lived at the tip of Cornwall. If this irritates you, tell yourself that you wouldn't want to live in the city – whatever the compensations!

Frost pockets

People in mild, southern gardens might think they've got off lightly when it comes to the climate, but don't bank on it. Frost pockets can occur anywhere. When frost covers a garden at night, the cold air sinks to the lowest point. If your garden is in a dip, or at the foot of a slope with high walls at the bottom, the cold air can't sink any further and collects there, creating a frost pocket. It might only be a small part of the garden, but plants in that area will be later starting into growth, tender-ish plants will be more prone to frost damage, and half-hardy bedding will need planting slightly later than the rest of the garden. It pays to know.

On a cold, sunny morning, you can spot frost pockets immediately because you can see the frost lingering there when the rest of the garden has thawed. If you are half-way down a slope, you can often get rid of frost pockets by removing obstructions, such as fences or hedges, or by making gaps in them, so that the cold air can drain away down the slope.

Hardiness zones

The islands that make up the UK form a chain of fairly small land masses warmed by the temperature-modifying effects of the sea, so, although the climate varies from end to end, this variation is not massive when you compare it with continental land masses like the USA. If you think there's a lot of difference between the plants that will grow at the tip of Scotland and on the toe of Cornwall, just think of the problems faced by gardeners in the USA, working out what will grow where. Their climates range from perma-frost in Alaska to baking deserts in Nevada, from vast areas of featureless prairie to great lakes and huge mountain ranges and even the odd bit of temperate rainforest.

The way the Americans get around it is by dividing the country up into a series of 11 climate zones, as defined by the US Department of Agriculture. They act rather like council tax bands, except that they tell you how cold it gets in winter. Once you know which zone you live in, you can match that to the hardiness rating given for each plant, which is part of the standard cultural information given in gardening books in the USA.

Summer and winter

Hardiness zones tell you the lowest winter drop to expect, but they don't tell you how long it will last. The official definition of winter is when the temperature falls below 6°C (43°F).

In those parts of Scotland and northern England that are far from the coast, winter lasts for over a third of the year, while in central England, it lasts for around three and a half months. In the West Country and along the south coast, it's about two and a half months long, and at the tip of Cornwall, it is just one month long.

It's summer when the temperature rises above 18°C (64°F). Gardeners in the Home Counties experience the longest summers, which last for almost a third of the year. Summer may be only half that long in Scotland and much of northern England.

Now that so many books are sold in English-speaking countries all around the world, we are becoming aware of hardiness zones here, too. Many of the big plant encyclopedias in this country will now include the words 'hardy to zone 8', or give a zone number in a box marked 'hardiness'.

Most of the UK falls into three hardiness zones: 7, 8 and 9. The way it works is that if a plant is hardy to zone 7, then it'll also grow perfectly safely in zones 8 and 9, which are warmer. But if you want to grow a plant that's hardy to zone 8 in zone 7, you'll stand a good chance of losing it unless you bring it in for the winter.

But it's not just the UK and the USA that use hardiness zones – they cover most of the world, and it's quite entertaining to see which other places have the same climate as you do. But don't get carried away: remember that hardiness zones only relate to *average* minimum winter temperatures. The weather can still vary enormously between one zone and another.

The weather

You've only to listen to any group of gardeners talking for a few minutes before they get around to the weather, but it's not just because they want to know if the lawn will be dry enough to cut this weekend. The weather doesn't only affect the gardener's plans, it affects the plants in the garden, too. Nasty outbreak of tomato blight? Blame it on the weather. Mildew on the roses, courgettes rotted off, plagues of toadstools in the lawn, hanging baskets fried to a crisp? Yes, the weather is often at the root of the matter. Each season is different, and thank goodness. How boring gardening would be if each year was the same as the last. Where would the challenge be?

Bad weather

In winter, many plants become dormant to avoid wind, rain and cold. There's a lot you can do to protect plants from bad weather at each end of the growing season – by providing shelter for newly planted evergreens when it's windy, or by covering late or early vegetables with cloches. But when bad weather strikes in summer, it can have a very serious effect on plants. A cold summer means that bedding plants in containers and hanging baskets will be slow to start growing and won't peak until towards the end of summer; vegetables and salads will take longer to mature and fleshy fruits, such as courgettes and strawberries, will be more likely to rot, especially if they touch the soil. If a cold, wet spell coincides with the start of the rose season, many blooms might go mouldy before they have the chance to open fully (a condition called balling that often affects some of the old-fashioned varieties).

Hardiness zones in the UK:

Zone 7 is the coldest and, if you live in central Scotland, you'll know what it feels like. In winter, the average temperature can go down to between −12.3°C and −17.7°C (10 and 0°F), which is… cold!

Zone 8 covers most of England (apart from a small blob over the East Midlands and a strip all around the coast), and all of Scotland (except the bit in zone 7). Here the winter temperature can drop to anything between −6.7°C and −12.2°C (20 and 10°F).

Zone 9 includes a strip all round the west, south and east coasts and the East Midlands. If you live here, you'll experience average winter temperatures between −1.2°C and −6.6°C (30 and 20°F).

Zone 10 has winter lows between +4.4°C and −1.1°C (40 and 30°F), and just kisses the toe of Cornwall, so here and the Scilly Islands can just about expect to stay free of frost in all but the worst winters. That's the same as southern Florida, but they do have better weather over there!

Sudden spells of hot dry weather can put plants under stress and, with roses, that often leads to an outbreak of powdery mildew.

Small transparent plastic tunnels, or 'cloches', are handy for protecting early vegetables from severe weather conditions.

There are some combinations of bad weather that are predictors of outbreaks of plant disease. Cool, damp weather with dull days provides ideal conditions for fungal diseases, so you can expect blackspot on the roses and grey mould in the greenhouse. Mid-summer rains almost guarantee an outbreak of potato blight, which also affects outdoor tomatoes (the two plants are closely related). Take precautions as soon as you realize the risk.

Although hot, dry weather is generally considered to be good weather by gardeners, that's not always how plants see it. It's bad for most plants if they become too dry, or if the temperature in the greenhouse rises so high that plants scorch in the burning sun. Plants need protection from high temperatures by shading and ventilating greenhouses, and by the vigilant watering of those plants that are susceptible to drying out (see pages 32 and 169–72). The most 'at-risk' are plants in containers, shallow-rooted annuals and any recently planted youngsters that haven't yet established a far-ranging root system.

Dry, late-summer weather may prevent spring-flowering plants forming flower buds, which is why you should water rhododendrons in August if the soil is dry. And a prolonged dry spell at any time in summer creates conditions that encourage powdery mildew to develop on roses, honeysuckle, Michaelmas daisies, or other susceptible plants.

Because the weather can vary so much from year to year, it's easy to be caught out. In recent years, five hot, dry summers with hosepipe bans, and light winter rainfall in between, convinced some people in Britain to plant drought-resistant gardens – just in time to be battered by the worst floods since 1947! But then, as H.E. Bates said, 'Gardening, like love, is a funny thing, and doesn't always yield to analysis.'

Frost

The dates of the first and last frost of the season are turning points in the gardening year. The last frost of spring signals the start of the bedding-plant season, as that's when you can start planting half-hardy annuals outdoors. The first frost of autumn finishes them off, so then you pull them out and put in your wallflowers, making sure all your tender plants have been carefully stowed in a heated greenhouse or brought indoors.

Frosty weather is fine when it happens on schedule. Cool autumn temperatures that slowly sink to a cold snap in mid-winter lead plants into a proper dormancy, and kill off all sorts of bugs, snails and slugs. That's what used to happen when we had old-fashioned winters with a white Christmas and tobogganing in January. The problems occur when the cold snap comes late, after a long, mild autumn, which is what happened in the late 1990s. Mild weather ran right into what should be winter and, by early spring, a few sunny days triggered plants out of a sort of shallow sleep, just in time for tender buds and newly opened young leaves to be clobbered by frost. Weeks later, when the real spring arrived, all sorts of odd symptoms appeared; many new leaves had brown edges or peculiar wrinkling. The tight buds had been 'nipped' by frost, which killed part of the leaves so that they distorted as they unfolded. In severe cases, a late frost can kill all the buds on a plant and it may look dead for weeks until it manages to produce a new crop of buds. Don't be in a hurry to dig out 'dead' plants after a late frost. They may be resting and recuperating. Give them until early summer and, if there's no sign of life by then, you're probably right to ditch them.

The odd late frost can occur anywhere, once in a while, and it's just bad luck, but if you garden in a frost pocket, or have an east-facing site, avoid growing early-flowering plants, like camellias, and choose late-flowering fruit varieties. Frosted early flowers are killed if the frozen tissues defrost too quickly, and that's what happens if they are hit by early morning sun. At best, you've lost a season's flowers and, at worst, you've lost a whole crop of fruit. But grow shrubs and trees that flower from early summer onwards in that situation and you won't have a problem.

Frost damage on this gunnera has produced typical 'scorching' symptoms.

First and last frosts

In 'middle England' you can usually anticipate the last frost of the season happening sometime around mid- to late May, and the first frost of autumn can come from mid-September onwards, though in the last few years it's been more like early November. But remember to adjust the dates based on whereabouts in the country you live, and take into account the weather, which can advance or delay frost dates from two to six weeks in any one year.

The year-round garden

Proof (*opposite*) that there can be colour and interest in the garden at any time of year:

1 Tulips are spring bloomers.
2 Vines colour up well before their leaves fall in autumn.
3 Evergreens like this euphorbia look good when rimed with winter frost.
4 In summer, the whole garden seems to erupt into flower.

There's no mysterious secret to creating a stylish, good-looking garden with all-year-round appeal. It just takes a bit of planning to ensure there's a constant stream of plants reaching their peak at different times of year. To make sure it's always interesting, your garden should contain some plants from each of the key seasonal groups (see also pages 16 and 27–29).

Gardening work-planners help to plan the year, but they aren't meant to be followed slavishly. You can't take it for granted that the ground will be in a fit state for seed sowing in March, just because that's what it says on the packet, so read the signs and adjust the dates to suit local conditions and the vagaries of the weather.

The key jobs I've given here for each season are by no means a comprehensive list, but I've included them to make the connection between the things that gardeners need to do and the seasons. Experienced gardeners feel this connection instinctively but for first-timers, often living or working in urban environments and being somewhat removed from the seasonal changes, the association is not so obvious. There are many more jobs than I've listed, but at least these will give you a clue as to what areas of maintenance need thinking about at what time of the year.

Overview of the gardening year

Season	Plants at their best	Main seasonal jobs
Spring	spring bulbs fruit tree blossom	cleaning planting and sowing weeding and mulching rose pruning
Summer	roses herbaceous perennials bedding plants	mowing hedge clipping hoeing vegetables feeding and watering
Autumn	autumn leaves fruit berries	bulb planting planting trees and shrubs cutting down and tidying up lawn maintenance
Winter	coloured shrub stems tree bark evergreens	digging and preparing soil planning and designing construction general maintenance and repairs

Spring

Spring bulbs, tree blossom and flowering shrubs are the highlights of spring, and most people are so relieved to see a bit of colour after a long, dull winter that they aren't too worried about creating tasteful colour combinations. They want whatever there's most of, and I'm inclined to agree with them.

Bulbs

The great thing about most spring-flowering bulbs is that you can grow them beneath trees knowing that they'll put on a darn good show when you need it. You don't have to worry about the deep shade that envelops them when the trees come into leaf, as that's when they die down anyway. In borders, this useful habit means that you can grow summer-flowering perennials in practically the same spot as your bulbs. Snowdrops and winter aconites are especially worthwhile for a first carpet of colour, and they like being naturalized – planted and then just left alone to spread. Once they are in, they don't make any more work.

Daffodils and crocuses are fine for naturalizing in a lawn, as long as you plant in drifts, but if you want a wildflower meadow, then go for species daffs, such as *Narcissus poeticus,* or the spectacular *Fritillaria meleagris* (snakeshead fritillary) with nodding, chequer-patterned, mauve or white bell-flowers. The starry blue squills (*Scilla*) and chionodoxas are also good for naturalizing in a wild-style garden.

In borders, carpets of dwarf daffs are much more practical than the gigantic 'picking' daffs, as they don't leave tall, untidy foliage littering your flower beds when they are over. 'Jetfire' is one I'd recommend – neat plants, masses of flower, and it clumps up well too.

As soon as buds start to break in spring, and these shuttlecock ferns (*Matteuccia struthiopteris*) push up their bright green shuttlecocks in ground that will soon be shaded, there is a great feeling of renewal in the garden. Savour every moment!

For containers, the earliest dwarf daffs like 'February Gold' are good, but it's bulbs like tulips and hyacinths that are going to make a real splash when spring arrives in earnest.

Trees

Mid- to late spring is blossom time and you'll be spoiled for choice. If you have a small garden – especially if it's not very sheltered – don't be seduced by trees such as lilacs and flowering cherries, whose flowers don't last long before turning brown and blowing away at the first puff of wind. They leave you with nothing very interesting to look at for the rest of the year. In a larger, more sheltered garden, yes, grow them if you love them. Just make sure they have plenty of company to keep the garden colourful when their weeks of glory are over.

For my money, some of the best blossom trees for a smaller garden are those that give you a second spectacle later in the season – they make better use of the space. *Amelanchier* (snowy mespilus), for example, has white flowers that open at the same time as the bronzed young leaves in spring, followed later by wonderful autumn colour. Similarly, crab apples are first wreathed in spring blossom before bearing a generous crop of bright autumn fruits. Where there's more room, the edible quince (*Cydonia oblonga*), is a superb tree with large, pale pink blossom in spring and golden pear-shaped fruits to follow.

Spring-flowering evergreens have a good chance of looking handsome all year round, if you choose those with attractive foliage and a strong shape. In mild sites, you might choose unusual early-flowering trees, such as *Azara microphylla*, with fluffy, yellow, vanilla-scented flowers in late winter and early spring. *Ceanothus arboreus* 'Trewithen Blue', which flowers for weeks on end in late spring, also has an interesting shape and dark, glossy, evergreen foliage the rest of the time.

Shrubs

The bulk of the best-known shrubs flower in spring. This is when you can enjoy camellias, rhododendrons, berberis, forsythias, mahonias, many viburnums, the flowering currants (*Ribes*) and ornamental quince (*Chaenomeles*). But it's always good to include a real star like *Magnolia stellata* – that's the shrubby one that doesn't mind a bit of chalk in the soil. It makes a good 'specimen' if you don't have room to grow it in a mixed bed. Perhaps plant a few of the less common spring shrubs that you don't see everywhere, especially if you want to make a small garden special. Mezereon (*Daphne mezereum*) doesn't suit everyone's soil, but the scented, pink-purple flowers in early spring are a real joy. It needs very well-drained soil with plenty of organic matter and, though it's known not to be crazy about chalk, in practice, it tolerates a slightly alkaline soil as long as everything else is to it's liking.

Putting it all together

Sprinkling seasonal colour all around a garden doesn't make much impact, especially if it's a big garden and you only use a few flowers. What works much better is grouping plants together to make seasonal 'hot spots'; they show up well from a distance and will entice you outside for a better look. A tree, a shrub and a clump of perennials are a good 'recipe' for a mini-feature, especially if you add a little sculptural something – a big pot, or a large, round cobblestone. To brighten up an otherwise out-of-season border, use carpets of spring-flowering bulbs, winter bedding or low, spreading perennials to create islands of colour beneath shrubs and roses.

Key Jobs for Spring

This is the busiest time in the garden. Try to allocate some regular gardening time each weekend, making weeding and planting top priorities; if you fall behind now, you'll struggle to get back under control later. Stay on top now and your efforts will be rewarded.

Early spring (March)
- Spring-clean borders – hand weed or hoe and mulch with well-rotted organic matter. Fork over vegetable beds.
- Prune roses.
- Plant shallots and onion sets, sow early crops under cloches.

Mid-spring (April)
- Begin mowing the lawn regularly. Apply lawn feed and treat weeds or moss. Prepare soil and sow grass seed or lay turf.
- Feed beds and borders, specimen trees, roses, shrubs and hedges with general fertilizer.
- Plant roses, trees, shrubs and perennials. Move evergreens or conifers. Plant spring bedding in containers and gaps round the garden. Plant dormant dahlia tubers and gladiolus corms.
- In the greenhouse, prick out seedlings, or pot up if they're ready.
- Plant sprouted potato tubers. Most maincrop vegetables, other than frost-tender ones, can be sown now.

Late spring (May)
- Plant tomatoes in an unheated greenhouse and plant late vegetables, e.g. leeks, Brussels sprouts and cauliflowers outside.
- Prune spring-flowering shrubs after flowering and clip hedges.
- Move or divide spring-flowering bulbs after flowering.
After the last frost:
- Plant half-hardy bedding, dahlias, tender exotics and frost-tender vegetables, e.g. French beans, courgettes, sweet corn and pumpkins.

Start garden jobs early in spring. Put seed potato tubers in a bright, frost-free place (*left*) to get them to sprout, ready to plant out – sprouted tubers produce larger yields; (*centre*) dig up overcrowded snowdrop clumps as the flowers fade, and divide and replant them to make more colonies; (*right*) if you're short of colour in spring, you can get it instantly by planting out early-flowering pansies.

Summer

Flowers are the real stars of summer, whether it's bedding plants in pots and hanging baskets on the patio, perennials in the borders, or those old stalwarts, the roses. This is the time for being a bit more co-ordinated with your colours, now there's so much to choose from.

Bedding

Old favourites like pelargoniums and fuchsias still rate top of the pots, but now that everyone goes so mad on container gardening, demand has given rise to a heck of a lot of new and different patio plants such as scaevola – the pendent beauty with fan-shaped blue flowers. Modern strains of petunias put on some of the best and most long-lasting shows possible in hanging baskets; choose the 'Million Bells' type, with trillions of small flowers, or the popular 'Surfinia series', which have a wonderful scent if you grow them in a sheltered spot. The equivalent flower-power among the pelargoniums is to be found among the continental 'Cascade' type; they are a big improvement on the trailing, ivy-leaved pelargoniums. The plants are completely covered in narrow-petalled flowers all summer – like the old favourites seen in those spectacular window-boxes on Swiss chalet balconies, but with a modern twist.

The summer border that you dream about in winter. But it will be like this again – honest!

Perennials

You don't need to have a traditional herbaceous border to be aware of the welter of perennials in flower during summer, from old favourites like delphiniums, lupins and bearded irises, to loud red-hot pokers (*Kniphofia*), drought-tolerant pinks (*Dianthus*) and penstemons, or trendy euphorbias and alstroemerias – which are both pretty drought tolerant too.

For damp borders or watersides, you could pick tall rodgersias, with horse-chestnut-like leaves, pink-spired loosestrifes (*Lythrum*), and the plant that looks like chains of gold coins, the golden version of creeping Jenny (*Lysimachia nummularia*) 'Aurea'.

But in any situation, don't forget the foliage; plants like heucheras and hostas are handy for separating colours that 'fight', or for making individual flowers stand out from the horde.

A summer border awash with colour from *Geranium* 'Johnson's Blue' (left foreground), *Lavandula stoechas* (centre foreground), aquilegias (the pink columbines), bearded irises (centre) and purple sage (right).

Roses

Nine out of ten gardens grow roses, even though very few feature traditional formal rose beds now – the sort with bare soil beneath the plants. Nowadays, you'll more often see shrub roses grown in mixed borders, or prickly species roses, such as *Rosa rugosa*, grown as a hedge. Among the new developments of the past few years have been the compact patio roses, which are brilliant for pots. They have all the long flowering season of bedding, but without the need to replant every season, as you can leave them in the same pots outside all year round. Ground-cover roses are similar but, instead of being neat and bushy, they are low and spreading – perfect for covering a bank, or the front of a border. Standard roses are ideal if you want a bit of height and formality in a border. They look pretty good rising above a carpet of ground-cover roses, or a bed of knee-high perennials, but use them carefully if you want to avoid that retro 1950s look.

Key Jobs for Summer

Feeding, watering, deadheading bedding plants and keeping the grass mown are major priorities in summer. Perennials and vegetables by now shade the ground, so most annual weeds will be 'smothered' out, but watch out for nasties, such as bindweed.

Early summer (June)
- Paint liquid shading on to the outside of the greenhouse.
- Feed and deadhead roses after the first flush of flowers.
- Use netting to protect soft fruit from birds.
- Clear early vegetables and salads and replant beds.
- Feed and water tomatoes, peppers, aubergines, cucumbers and melon plants regularly.
- Sow seeds of perennial plants and winter bedding outdoors.

Mid-summer (July)
- Pick soft fruit.
- Water containers regularly and feed once a week.
- Keep up the feeding and deadheading of bedding plants.
- If the weather is dry, raise the lawn mower blades slightly; grass will stay greener if allowed to grow a little longer.

Late summer (August)
- Water rhododendrons in dry weather, to help initiate their flower buds.
- Summer-prune soft fruit and trained apple trees.
- Clip slow-growing hedges such as beech and yew.
- Pick open flowers from patio plants before going on holiday, so you come home to fresh new blooms instead of deadheads.

Close-weave netting (*left*) is a good shading material for a greenhouse. It can be rolled up on dull days. Picking gooseberries (*right*) is a satisfying sort of job – and you can dream of pies and gooseberry fool!

Autumn

Autumn is the fruiting season in the garden, when berries and seed heads are at their best, and the brilliant colours of autumn leaves change the character of the garden within a matter of days.

It isn't just fading leaves that provide autumn colour; flowers like these *Anemone x hybrida* 'Honorine Jobert' start coming into their own from late summer onwards.

Autumn foliage

In grand gardens noted for their fiery autumn colours, it's the big trees, like oaks and maples in the park, and the giant vines, like Virginia creeper covering the west wing, that make a splash as autumn comes around, but at home you can still create quite a ripple. Medium-sized trees, such as the paperbark maple (*Acer griseum*), the maidenhair tree (*Ginkgo biloba*) and the ornamental thorn, *Crataegus persimilis* 'Prunifolia', are just as good. If the soil is acid, then go for flame-tinted liquidambar and Persian ironwood (*Parrotia persica*) – one of my favourites. For something more unusual, there's the spectacular Katsura tree (*Cercidiphyllum japonicum*), with heart-shaped, smoky pink and yellow autumn leaves that smell of toffee apples when they fall. Pure fairground!

If you have less room to play with, the deciduous azaleas and Japanese maples (cultivars of *Acer palmatum*) are brilliant; those that change from green to red in autumn, such as *Acer palmatum*

'Ôsakazuki', are especially stunning. Some berberis and viburnums colour well too, among them *Berberis* 'Pirate King' and 'Buccaneer'. The leaves of the wayfaring tree (*Viburnum lantana*) turn bright cherry-red. There are even a few smallish trees that colour up well in autumn – the *Amelanchier* mentioned earlier (see page 125); birches (*Betula*) with leaves that turn a buttery yellow, and a few of the ornamental cherries, such as *Prunus* 'Spire', with orange and scarlet tints.

Berries and fruit

Colourful fruit, berries and hips show up well against green foliage, but combine them with autumn colours and they make the garden look as if someone has gone round turning the lights on – at least, until the birds get stuck in for a feed. Unless the weather is very cold, you should get a couple of months of enjoyment out of them first.

Species roses, such as *Rosa rugosa* and *Rosa moyesii* 'Geranium', are some of the very best for hips, and crab apples (*Malus*) can always be relied on for colourful fruit; cultivars such as 'John Downie', 'Profusion' and 'Golden Hornet' are among the heaviest croppers of the lot. Both edible and ornamental quinces have big, knobbly fruits but, while those of the ornamental quince (*Chaenomeles*) are long-persistent, those of the edible quince (*Cydonia oblonga*) fall from the tree long before they're ripe if it's windy.

Cotoneasters and pyracanthas are reliable old favourites for berries, but if you fancy something a bit different, try the spindle bush (*Euonymus europaeus* 'Red Cascade'), with fiery red autumn leaves and vivid pink capsules that split open to show bright orange seeds inside.

Seed heads

Setting seed is what flowers are all about and, by early autumn, the plumes of ornamental grasses, such as *Miscanthus*, *Pennisetum* and *Stipa gigantea*, are at their best. You'll also find that some of the species clematis, such as *Clematis tangutica*, are covered with Beatle-like wigs of feathery seeds. Then there are the teasels and honesty heads down in the wild garden.

A great autumn plant you don't see so much of these days is the Chinese lantern (*Physalis alkekengi* var. *franchetii*). It's a perennial with upright stems bearing papery, orange lanterns that look good running through a natural-style shrub bed, or a wilder mixed border. A good many perennials produce seed heads worth leaving through the winter, including bronze fennel (*Foeniculum vulgare* 'Purpureum'), bear's breech (*Acanthus*), and sea hollies (*Eryngium*). The seed heads look particularly good when rimed with frost, so don't be in a hurry to cut them down.

Key Jobs for Autumn

Bringing tender plants under cover before the frost is the first priority. When an autumn is mild, it's the best time for planting new trees, shrubs and woody climbers; their roots establish well if the soil is still warm and moist.

Early autumn (September)
- Clean the greenhouse; wash the glass, remove shading and check the heater. Remove old tomatoes and other fruits after harvesting.
- Bring in frost-tender plants, such as fuchsias and pelargoniums; cut them back, pot them up and keep them frost-free and in good light.
- Remove summer bedding when it has finished flowering and replace with winter pansies and ornamental cabbages.
- Plant spring bulbs and spring bedding, e.g. wallflowers, polyanthus and primulas.
- Prepare soil for new lawns; sow grass seed.
- Harvest pumpkins.

Mid-autumn (October)
- Plant deciduous trees, shrubs or climbers.
- Lift tender summer bulbs, such as gladiolus, and dahlia tubers (allow frosts to blacken dahlia foliage before lifting); store in a frost-free shed.
- Dig up potatoes and store in paper sacks in a frost-free shed.
- Pick apples before the autumn gales. Store in a shed or the bottom of the fridge.
- Lag the crowns of tree ferns with straw tied loosely with string.
- Tidy perennials; cut back dead stems, but leave ornamental seed heads, for winter interest and to feed birds.
- Lay new turf any time between now and April.
- Rake lawn to remove 'thatch' and apply autumn lawn fertilizer.
- Start compost heap.
- Clear fallen leaves from lawn and rock garden.
- Put net over fish pond.

Late autumn (November)
- Plant tulips and hyacinths.
- Clear fallen leaves from lawns, paths, flowerbeds and rock gardens.
- Plant hedging or roses sold with bare roots.
- After leaf fall, move any deciduous trees and shrubs that need it, provided they are not too big.

Store potatoes in the dark in a thick paper sack, and they are less likely to sprout than if exposed to daylight.

Winter

You'd be wrong to think of winter as a bit of a wash-out in the garden, because it's the time when evergreens and coloured bark and stems come to the fore. Combine them with what's around in the way of winter flowers, and you have yet another set of new views at your fingertips.

Evergreens

Evergreens are the backbone of the all-year-round garden, and there is an enormous range of golden, variegated, grey, blue and even russet-coloured conifers and evergreens available. I use as many different shapes as possible – bamboos, small trees and compact shrubs – to bring contrast and variety to the more predictable, wintery outlines of deciduous plants. A varied evergreen framework is a good background for spring and summer flowers, and autumn fruits and leaves, too, but in winter, it helps to make the best display of what's around in the way of coloured stems, trunks and flowers.

Bark and stems

Bare bark and coloured stems make the best possible contrast to a background of bushy evergreen shapes. Red-stemmed dogwood (*Cornus alba*) is the winter-effect shrub that first springs to mind, but there is also a yellow-green version called *Cornus stolonifera* 'Flaviramea'.

Just when you had given up all hope of another spring the snowdrops appear (here beneath the red stems of a cornus), to mark the end of winter and cheer you up.

You can chose from several shades with the shrubby willows; there's the scarlet willow (*Salix alba* subsp. *vitellina* 'Britzensis'), which is bright orange-red, or the pewtery-purple stems of the violet willow (*Salix daphnoides*). All are pruned hard back in early spring to produce more new stems for the following winter's pleasures.

There are birch trunks in shining white, such as those of *Betula utilis* var. *jacquemontii*; the jade-green-striped stems of snake-bark maple (*Acer capillipes*); the shaggy, rust-red coats of the paper-bark maple (*Acer griseum*), or the polished, conker-coloured bark of the Tibetan cherry (*Prunus serrula*). Or how about curls? Contorted hazel (*Corylus avellana* 'Contorta') has twigs that are coiled like springs and, in late winter, they jangle with long, sulphur-yellow catkins.

Iris 'Katharine Hodgkin' is a staggeringly beautiful winter-flowering iris, most easily admired when grown in a pot.

Winter flowers

Winter heathers and Universal pansies are the obvious choice for bulk colour anywhere that the ground is reasonably well drained, but don't overlook bold ornamental cabbages and kales for containers – and towards the end of winter, there are the first coloured primroses coming on.

Witch hazels (*Hamamelis*) are well worth having – their red or gold autumn leaves are followed by the first spidery, winter flowers almost straight away. Several mahonias – *Mahonia japonica* cultivars in particular – bloom from mid-winter into spring, with their delicious, lily-of-the-valley scented flowers. But the winter-flowering shrub everyone knows is the old favourite, winter jasmine (*Jasminum nudiflorum*), which is one of those invaluable plants for a north-facing wall.

Key Jobs for Winter

Now that the routine chores are finished for the year, this is your big chance to get on with any garden planning or redesigning, and to do any building jobs… but don't undertake concreting if it's likely to freeze.

December, January and February

- Continue cutting the grass if it is still growing in spells of mild weather – but don't cut it too short.
- Prune fruit trees, figs and grape vines when they are fully dormant.
- Protect containers planted with winter bedding, or all-year-round shrubs, from freezing solid. (Even totally hardy plants suffer when all the water in the potting compost freezes.) Stand them in a shed, garage or sun room, or lag the pots with bubble wrap, or plunge them to their rims in an empty bit of ground for insulation – before they freeze.
- Sprinkle sand or grit on icy paths, but not salt, which harms nearby plants.
- Take the opportunity to treat timber with wood preservative.
- Erect trellis, posts or arches.
- Order seeds from seed catalogues ready for spring.
- Float a child's ball on a pond so that hot water can be poured over it in icy weather and a hole created to allow fish to breathe.
- Put your feet up!

People think I'm nuts for washing the trunks of my silver birches in winter, but it removes green algae and makes them stand out in dull winter light.

Floating a ball on the surface of a garden pond will allow you to make a hole in the ice to let fish breathe in the depths of winter. Just pour hot water over it and then lift it out.

5 WHO'S IN CHARGE?

Weed wars

Weeds want to take over, make no mistake. They are the native inhabitants of the soil, so they can outgrow any foreign imports or man-made hybrids who aren't on home territory. Weeds live to breed, and they want to swamp your garden. So what's stopping them? You are!

The snakeshead fritillary (*Fritillaria meleagris*) a weed? No, it's a wild flower, simply because it's welcome.

What is a weed?

'A weed is any plant growing in the wrong place'. This is an old garden saying that should be tattooed on trowels. Weeds are not just old faithfuls like daisies in the lawn and greater bindweed in the borders (see pages 143 and 145); there are also some very invasive garden plants that come into the weed category when they come up where they aren't wanted. If you don't believe me, just see how fast the very pretty snow-in-summer (*Cerastium tomentosum*) takes over your rock garden.

The term you'll hear gardeners use for over-active cultivated plants is 'thugs', which perfectly describes their unsocial behaviour. You can't always spot a 'thug' until you've let it loose in your own garden, because some will display perfect manners on certain soils, but go berserk on others.

There are other plants that need watching because of their family connections. In my garden at Barleywood, I grow a stunning variegated form of that well-known nightmare, Japanese knotweed (see page 149), and I can say that – hand on heart – in 15 years, it's never gone as mad as its green-leaved relative, and its chest-high stems have such pretty pink, cream and green leaves that I don't intend to start worrying about it. Mind you, I still take the precaution of planting it in a large pot that is plunged into the border soil to stop its roots spreading. The ornamental, variegated form of ground elder (see page 146), on the other hand, definitely has big ambitions, especially when it is grown on moist clay soil.

Contrary to what you might think, wildflowers aren't the same thing as weeds at all. Respectable wildflowers are grown deliberately in wild gardens, or in wildflower meadows, and if they spread or self-seed, they do it in a dignified way that inspires respect and needs encouragement – they don't try and take over. Weeds are plants that do try to gain the upper hand and they'll succeed if you let them.

Weeds are great travellers and seeds often arrive on the wind, especially if you live near wasteland, untended gardens or allotments. Sycamore seedlings will certainly drop in this way if you have a big mature tree close by. Spreading, perennial weeds can creep under the fence from your neighbour's patch, or from fields. But you can also buy in weeds, as they can stow away in manure, topsoil or the potting compost of your bought container-grown plants.

Weed tactics
The trouble with weeds is that they compete with garden plants for food, water and, most of all, light. They grow faster than cultivated plants and, by burying your treasures in foliage, cut out the light from them. This either 'starves' them, or stresses them so much that they succumb to disease. It also leaves them at the mercy of slugs and snails, that find life under a nice weedy canopy most enjoyable, thank you very much. There are two basic types of weed, each with its own means of attack. Both need different treatment.

Annual weeds are the ones that grow each year from seed and live for one growing season. They germinate at lower temperatures than most garden plants and, since they grow from seed that sprouts wherever it falls, they don't suffer the setback of transplanting, unlike garden plants. This, again, gives them a great leg-up in the survival stakes. Some annual weeds, such as groundsel (see page 141), produce several generations of seedlings each year and spread even faster.

Perennial weeds have underground reserves in the form of over-wintering roots or rhizomes that enable them to spring into action fast at the start of the season. Their speciality is embedding their roots in those of shrubs or garden perennials, so they aren't easy to get out. Even when they grow where you can get at them, some have a very tenacious grip on life. Some, such as dandelions and docks (see pages 144–45), can be dug out without too much difficulty. The ones to worry about are those that spread by means of a pervasive network of roots or rhizomes. That's what makes bindweed, ground elder, couch grass and Japanese knotweed seem so unstoppable (see pages 145–49).

In the bag

Hairy bitter cress (Cardamine hirsuta), *which is now so widespread in gardens, originally grew wild on peat moorlands, and the seeds hitched a lift in peaty potting composts. Roots from perennial weeds can even penetrate bags of compost that have been stored on weedy ground – they penetrate the drainage holes in the packaging. Oh yes, it always pays to look before you buy.*

Well-known weeds

It's not absolutely essential to be able to put a name to each individual kind of weed you meet while you're working your way through the shrubbery on your hands and knees; you just need to be able to distinguish the villains from the tolerables. But knowledge is power, especially in the battle against the bullies.

Everyday weeds

These are the sort of weeds everyone has – mainly annual ones that appear in any exposed soil in spring and pop up almost at once on freshly dug soil.

Take prompt action

Don't wait until weeds flower to find out what they are. Learn to recognize them as seedlings, so you can remove them as soon as they appear in the garden, without accidentally eliminating flower or vegetable seedlings. Unlike perennial weeds, most annuals pull out easily even if they reach a good size. Put them on the compost heap only *before* they seed – otherwise you'll just be helping to spread them around.

Keeping a hoe going in spring and summer stops weeds getting out of hand – but keep it sharp, keep it shallow, and aim well!

Chickweed (*Stellaria media*) (**1**) One of the first to appear in newly turned soil, with masses of tiny seedlings that, at first, resemble a fine green mist. Plants eventually form a low carpet that roots as it spreads.

Red dead nettle (*Lamium purpureum*) (**2**) The leaves are deceptively similar to tiny stinging nettles, but the plant doesn't sting, it is low and creeping, not tall and upright, and the flowers are mauve. Most reach 10cm (4in) high by 15cm (6in) across by the time flowering begins.

Groundsel (*Senecio vulgaris*) (**3**) A fast colonizer of bare soil, with small clusters of yellow flowers without petals that develop into fluffy seed heads like small dandelion clocks. Expect several generations each year. Plants reach about 20cm (8in) tall and 15cm (6in) across.

Annual nettle (*Urtica urens*) (**4**) Short, bushy nettles with small leaves and vicious stings. Unlike the taller, more upright perennial nettle, it's easy to pull out, but don't imagine that its sting is any less painful than that of its big relation!

Everyday weeds:
1 (a) Chickweed (*Stellaria media*) seedling and (b) the full-grown plant.
2 (a) Red dead nettle (*Lamium purpureum*) seedling and (b) the full-grown plant.
3 (a) Groundsel (*Senecio vulgaris*) seedling and (b) the full-grown plant.
4 (a) Annual nettle (*Urtica urens*) seedling and (b) the full-grown plant.

Fat hen (*Chenopodium album*) (**5**) A fast-growing, upright weed reaching up to 2.2m (6ft) tall. It has greenish, plume-like flower heads that produce and shed masses of seeds and spread like… weeds.

Opium poppy (*Papaver somniferum*) (**6**) Smooth, grey-blue leaves and large, mauve poppy flowers followed by pepper-pot seed heads. Plants reach 75cm (30in) tall and 30–45cm (12–18in) across. A weed that's pretty enough to leave in the garden, if it comes up in a suitable spot.

Hairy bitter cress (*Cardamine hirsuta*) (**7**) Although only a short-lived annual, 2.5–5cm (1–2in) high by as much across, it flowers and seeds incredibly quickly and can spread a lot of seeds in its brief life. Pea-like seed pods pop open flinging their contents far and wide. A real pest.

Goosegrass (*Galium aparine*) (**8**) Also known as cleavers, it is easily recognized by its hooked, scrambling, 5–7.5-cm (2–3-in) long stems that 'stick' to everything they touch. So do the seeds – it's their way of spreading about.

Everyday weeds continued:
5 (a) Fat hen (*Chenopodium album*) seedling and (b) the full-grown plant.
6 (a) Opium poppy (*Papaver somniferum*) seedling and (b) the full-grown plant.
7 (a) Hairy bitter cress (*Cardamine hirsuta*) seedling and (b) the full-grown plant.
8 (a) Goosegrass (*Galium aparine*) seedling and (b) the full-grown plant.

5a   6a   7a   8a

5b   6b   7b   8b

Annual meadow grass (*Poa annua*) (**9**) The tiny blades of grass quickly colonize bare soil and develop into small clumps. It flowers while still tiny and, if left, plants knit together to form rough, shaggy 'turf' that covers large areas, when it takes a fair bit of digging out.

Germander speedwell (*Veronica chamaedrys*) (**10**) These blue-flowered, creeping plants form low, spreading mats that root as they run. A common weed in lawns, but seedlings often appear in borders too.

Yellow oxalis (*Oxalis corniculata*) (**11**) A frequent hitchhiker on container-grown plants, making low, loose mats of small, shamrock-shaped leaves that often turn purplish red in a dry or sunny spot. The tiny yellow flowers soon form explosive seed pods that shoot seeds everywhere. Another real pest.

Daisy (*Bellis perennis*) (**12**) A common weed of lawns because it manages to stay squat – even its flower stalks are shortened so that they can sneak under the mower. The leaf rosettes can be prised out with a 'daisy grubber'.

9 (a) Annual meadow grass *(Poa annua)* seedling and (b) the full-grown plant.
10 (a) Germander speedwell (*Veronica chamaedrys*) seedling and (b) the full-grown plant.
11 (a) Yellow oxalis (*Oxalis corniculata*) seedling and (b) the full-grown plant.
12 (a) Daisy (*Bellis perennis*) seedling and (b) the full-grown plant.

9a 10a 11a 12a

9b 10b 11b 12b

Nuisance weeds

These are the regular perennial weeds that'll often put in an appearance, especially if you leave an area of ground uncultivated for some time, and they are the sort you'll often inherit if you take over a neglected garden.

Clean and clear

Once you have them in the ground, these weeds can take a bit of shifting, especially if they've tangled themselves up with cultivated plants, so it's worth clearing your borders properly before planting if you discover any of these in the ground. Don't put the roots of these weeds on to your compost heap, or you'll just spread them everywhere when you use the compost. But even 'problem' perennial weeds can't survive regular hoeing. Catch them while they are small and hoe each time new shoots show their heads above ground. Hard work, I know. But, in time, you will wear them out!

Top tips for weed prevention

- Check topsoil, compost and manure before you buy to ensure it hasn't been infested with weeds, roots or seeds, because it is too old or has been badly stored.
- Inspect the surface of the potting compost on any plants you buy for signs of weeds and remove before planting.
- Learn to recognize weed seedlings (see pages 140–50) and act quickly, removing them early before they can get too established and especially before they can grow and produce seed.
- Don't put perennial weeds on the compost heap, or you will spread them around the garden next year.
- Use any of the following techniques, according to the size and severity of your weed problems: flaming, hand weeding, hoeing or chemicals (see pages 151–54).
- Consider root-proof barriers to prevent invasive weeds spreading from next door (see page 157).
- Mulch clean ground with organic matter to prevent infestation (see page 154).

Dandelion (*Taraxacum officinale*) (**1**) A perennial weed with a rosette of indented leaves about 20cm (8in) across, yellow 'double-daisy' flowers and characteristic seed head 'clocks' that distribute masses of seeds, which float off on 'parachutes'. Though seed is the main means of spread, established dandelions have thick tap roots and new plants will grow quickly from any fragments you leave behind in the ground. It's easily done; they snap off instead of coming out cleanly when you pull.

Greater bindweed (*Calystegia silvatica*) (**2**) Public enemy number one for most gardeners. The fast-growing, climbing stems twine tightly around flower and shrub stems. They can uproot perennials entirely when you try to pull the weed up. Left alone, bindweed can soon smother even large shrubs. The thick white roots (known in the country as 'devil's guts') spread quickly and, being brittle, any attempt to dig them out just turns them into root cuttings, which propagate the beast even faster. Bindweed needs to be caught just as the shoots first show through the ground, when they briefly form rosettes that can be hoed out or spot-treated with weedkiller – one of the few cases where it's justified, if you have a bad invasion. Bindweed is definitely best cleared from ground before planting it up, as you'll have a hard job keeping it under control if it grows up through cultivated plants.

Dock (*Rumex obtusifolius*) (**3**) The familiar broad leaved weed that you rub on nettle stings, with rusty red spikes of flowers that grow 60–90cm (2–3ft) high later in the year. They have deep tap roots that are inclined to snap off if you pull them out, leaving behind little bits that grow back. It's best to dig them out carefully.

Nuisance weeds:
1 (a) Dandelion (*Taraxacum officinale*) seedling and (b) the full-grown plant.
2 (a) Greater bindweed (*Calystegia silvatica*) seedling and (b) the full-grown plant.
3 (a) Dock (*Rumex obtusifolius*) youngster and (b) the full-grown plant.

1a 2a 3a

1b 2b 3b

Stinging nettle (*Urtica dioica*) (**4**) Small clumps are not too much of a problem, as you can dig them out quite easily but, once established, the roots spread quite a distance to form satellite colonies, and the stems can grow 2.2m (6ft) tall.

Creeping thistle (*Cirsium arvense*) (**5**) The standard prickly job with tough, spiky leaves. The flowers, like tiny pineapples with a tuft of purple threads poking out of the top, produce a mass of thistle-down seeds that blow away on the wind. In gardens, it spreads mainly by thick underground stems but, if pulled up while small, it isn't too difficult to deal with. Don't let them seed, or you'll have thistles forever. The saying 'one year's seed, seven year's weed' is especially pertinent to thistles.

Ground elder (*Aegopodium podagraria*) (**6**) Another real menace if you have it. The leaves and flowers are similar to those of elder bushes (*Sambucus nigra*), but they grow on a short perennial plant about 30cm (12in) high. Ground elder spreads from underground roots to form dense, knee-high carpets that are almost impossible to dig up if allowed to become established. Even small clumps take a lot of shifting, as bits of root left in the ground grow into new plants.

Nuisance weeds continued:

4 (a) Stinging nettle (*Urtica dioica*) young shoot and (b) the full-grown plant.

5 (a) Creeping thistle (*Cirsium arvense*) seedling and (b) the full-grown plant.

6 (a) Ground elder (*Aegopodium podagraria*) young shoot and (b) the flower.

4a

5a

6a

4b

5b

6b

Mind-your-own-business or helxine (*Soleirolia soleirolii*) (**7**) Helxine forms low, mossy-looking mats that root as they go, and any little piece left behind will re-grow. Regular hoeing and raking up the bits eventually gets rid of it from a border. In lawns, treat it with a lawn weedkiller formulated for small-leaved weeds, at regular intervals from spring onwards until it's all gone, or just keep raking it out.

Couch grass (*Elytrigia repens* syn. *Agropyron repens*) (**8**) This spreading grass with thin, wiry stems grows from the creeping, white, underground rhizomes that distinguish it from lawn-type grasses. Small clumps can be dug out, but if it invades perennial plants or bushy shrubs, the best answer is to dig up both weed and plant, so you can tease out weed roots from those of the ornamental plant you want to keep.

Creeping buttercup (*Ranunculus repens*) (**9**) These short, squat plants have rosettes of regulation buttercup leaves growing from a crown at, or just above, soil level. This makes them difficult to pull up and a new plant soon grows from the roots you leave behind. Creeping butter-cups spread by runners, rather like strawberry plants, but are more determined, so dig them out with patient perseverance and a small fork.

7 (a) Helxine (*Soleirolia soleirolii*) young growth and (b) the full-grown plant.

8 (a) Couch grass (*Agropyron repens*) young growth and (b) the full-grown plant.

9 (a) Creeping buttercup (*Ranunculus repens*) young growth and (b) the full-grown plant.

7a
8a
9a
7b
8b
9b

Rogues' gallery

These are some serious problem weeds that either don't respond to 'normal' methods, or which need handling with care.

Brambles (*Rubus fruticosus*) (**1**) These have deep roots and a habit of rooting wherever their stems touch the ground. Reduce the size of a large bramble by cutting the stems into manageable lengths with secateurs. Pile them up around the stump, leave them to dry out for a week or so and then use a flame gun to burn the lot. Flame any new shoots emerging from the stump as soon as they appear.

Giant hogweed (*Heracleum mantegazzianum*) (**2**) A gigantic and strikingly architectural plant whose sap, on contact with the skin in sunlight, produces a very unpleasant reaction and huge blisters. If it grows on your land, you must prevent it from setting seed. To dispose of live plants, wear protective clothing and a visor over your eyes, leaving no exposed skin, but rather than cut it down while it's growing, which makes it 'bleed' sap, I'd wait until it goes woody in winter. Use a flame gun to destroy seedlings while they're small.

Tougher, rogue weeds:
1 (a) Brambles (*Rubus fruticosus*) young plant and (b) flowers on a grown plant.
2 (a) Giant hogweed (*Heracleum mantegazzianum*) young plant and (b) in flower.

1a 2a

1b 2b

Japanese knotweed (*Fallopia japonica*) (**3**) A plant thought to have been introduced by a Victorian botanist who imagined it would look good in his border. It has since escaped and turned into a monster capable of forming huge colonies. There's no easy remedy. If you have it, all you can do is to cut it down or use the flame gun each time new shoots appear, which is just as effective as using weedkiller. With luck and persistence, you will weaken it so much that it can't grow back. If you spot seedlings, or the first signs of a new clump appearing, tackle them at once before they get any bigger.

Horsetail (*Equisetum arvense*) (**4**) Horsetail has a very deep and far-ranging root system, is strongly resistant to weedkillers and is especially prolific on damp clay soils, though it can turn up anywhere. In borders, regular hoeing starves it out in time. If it comes up in wasteland or rough grass, mowing frequently will have the same effect but with much less effort. You can also smother it with old carpets but, because it has large, underground food stores, it takes an awfully long time to die. Put a root-proof barrier in around your garden if it looks like invading from adjacent fields (see page 157).

Brushwood killer

For those who need a quick fix and don't mind using weedkiller, woody weeds like brambles and ivy or really persistent weeds like sycamore seedlings are the sort for which brushwood killer was designed. You'll find specific instructions for treating the different problem weeds on the pack, but the only thing I'd say is be extremely careful. Follow the instructions to the letter, wear rubber gloves and don't get the mixture on your skin. Never use brushwood killer close to plants you want to keep.

3 (a) Japanese knotweed (*Fallopia japonica*) young shoot and (b) the business end.

4 (a) Horsetail (*Equisetum arvense*) emerging shoot and (b) fully grown.

Ragwort (*Senecio jacobaea*) (**5**) This is fine in a wild garden, where its leaves can be a food source for orange-and-black-striped cinnabar moth caterpillars. In a paddock or grazing land, it should be pulled out and removed completely because it is very poisonous to livestock. If uprooted and left, the dead plant is even more attractive and dangerous to ponies and other mammals than the living one.

Wild ivy (*Hedera helix*) (**6**) Ivy makes a great wildlife habitat, so don't get rid of it unless you really need to. Ivy isn't parasitic and doesn't harm trees, although it may damage weak mortar and pebble-dash. To remove ivy, saw through the base of the plant close to the ground, then peel it off when it dries out and turns brown. Kill new growth by regular cutting, or treat the stump and new growth with brushwood killer.

Sycamore (*Acer pseudoplatanus*) (**7**) These are some of the fastest growing seedlings and, if ignored, can turn quickly into a junior sapling plantation. Dig the seedlings out while they are very small. Larger saplings, especially if they are coming up among garden plants where it is difficult to dig them out, are best sawn off close to the ground. Cut off all the new shoots each time they appear.

Tougher, rogue weeds continued:

5 (a) Ragwort (*Senecio jacobaea*) juvenile leaf rosette and (b) in flower.

6 (a) Wild ivy (Hedera helix) shoot tips and (b) mature leaves.

7 (a) Sycamore (*Acer pseudoplatanus*) innocent seedling and (b) full-grown leaf.

5a 6a 7a

5b 6b 7b

Eliminating weeds

Everyone wants a magic wand. If there were an easy, reliable way to get rid of weeds for good, someone would have made a fortune by now. There are various ways of tackling your weeds, from hand-weeding to more radical techniques such as applying chemicals or flaming them. Clearing weeds takes a bit of work but, if you know the right way to tackle each kind, even problem weeds don't turn out to be quite as bad as you thought.

Weed clearance on vacant ground

Suppose you want to make a new bed on rough grass or wasteland, or you've just taken over a neglected garden? The first job is to clear the weeds. You can make a good start just by chopping down everything close to ground level with a hand scythe; rake up and burn the 'hay' when it's dried. If you have a fair-sized patch to do, I'd hire an Allen scythe, which is a tough piece of kit specially designed for cutting down undergrowth. It looks something like a big motor-mower with a hedge-clipper blade along the front instead of normal blades underneath. It won't choke on brambles and the odd sapling, but instead scissors the whole lot off at ground level.

Once you've got rid of the luxuriant top-growth, dig the ground over and take out all the roots. This is where a lot of people go wrong. They rush out to hire a rotavator, which actually makes things much worse. Problem perennial weeds like greater bindweed, ground elder or horsetail (see pages 145–46 and 149) enjoy nothing better than having their roots chopped up small, because each piece re-roots. All you've done is to propagate the colony. Even nettles and docks will grow back in thickets, where once there were only clumps.

If digging out roots by hand doesn't appeal to you, there are several other options. One is to leave the cut-down weed stumps until they start throwing up new shoots, then blast them with a flame gun while they are still small. This is like 'hot hoeing' – you need only touch them with the flame, not wait for them to fry. If you repeat each time a new flush of shoots appears, you eventually kill weeds off completely by starving them out. The leaves don't last long enough to do any useful amount of photosynthesis, so the plants use up all the roots' food reserves; the roots eventually become too weak to throw up any more shoots. Then they die.

You can achieve the same result by covering vacant ground with old carpet or sheets of black plastic, so that emerging shoots can't reach the light (see pages 155 and 157). That eventually starves

A flame gun is fine for burning annual weeds off gravel drives, but its effect on perennials is temporary. Only frequent burning will eventually kill off these tough blighters.

them out, too. The trouble is that, though entirely organic, both methods take time to work. Persistent perennial weeds may take two years to die out completely. If you don't fancy looking out over a sea of plastic or old carpet for that long, the other alternative is to rake the area fairly level after clearing it, and sow grass seed to make a rough lawn. By cutting it regularly, you'll automatically keep the weeds chopped back, and a year or two of this treatment will work as well as the old carpet method or regular flame-gunning. It also looks better in the meantime.

Hand weeding

When weeds come up between cultivated plants in established gardens, hand weeding is the very best option. In a bed of trees and shrubs, where there's plenty of room between them, then a border fork is the best tool for getting out fair-sized weeds. It's just like a digging fork (see page 40) but about half the size; perfect for winkling out clumps and tussocks and for breaking the soil down to a reasonable tilth afterwards.

Between close-spaced perennials, use a hand fork (see page 43). It's easiest if you get down on your hands and knees rather than bending double; that's a quick recipe for a painful back. Around small plants, such as alpines, an even smaller weeding implement is called for. I find an old dinner fork is as good as anything. And for weeding cracks between paving, an old, short-handled kitchen knife with a pointed tip is just right.

Hand weeding, using a trowel or hand fork for stubborn perennials, is effective and pleasurable – provided you don't have to do too much of it!

Hoeing

There are lots of places around the garden where you can save yourself an enormous amount of time by using a hoe. It's perfect for clearing weeds from between rows in the vegetable garden and, if you are careful, you can use it in shrub beds and flower borders – anywhere that there's at least a hoe's-width of space between plants.

The trick with hoeing is to catch weeds early, while they are still seedlings. At that stage, they have very little root and all you need to do is disturb them by sliding a push hoe (see page 42) through the ground, barely below the surface. As long as the weed seedlings are small and you choose a hot, sunny day, hoeing is a doddle because the dislodged seedlings shrivel away to nothing; you don't even need to clear them up. Hoeing tiny seedlings is also incredibly quick – professional gardeners run round their borders with a hoe once a week, just disturbing the surface of the soil before there are any weed seedlings to see. It completely ruins a germinating weed's chances of growing.

The trouble is that it's very tempting to put the job off. Once weeds are big, you often need a draw or chop hoe to clear them (see page 42, the sort with a flat blade set at right angles to the handle). Hoeing is then more difficult, as you have to hack your way through the expanding foliage. That's not all, big weeds won't shrivel up on their own, so they need raking up and removing. If the weather is dull and damp they'll just take root again, so pick the right day. The other problem is that you can't see what you are doing for foliage, so it's easy to find you've cut into cultivated plants with the blade. You'll only do this a few times before you learn to be more careful, but if you remember to hoe sooner rather than later, you'll find it fun and incredibly satisfying – believe me.

The chemical alternative

If you are in a hurry and you don't want any hard work, then weedkiller is the answer, as long as you don't mind using chemicals. Choose a product containing glyphosate (sold as Round-up, Tumbleweed, etc) for this job, as it leaves the ground fit to plant as soon as the weeds are dead. Don't use path weedkiller or sodium chlorate; both persist for a long time in the soil.

Water the product on to the weeds – not the soil – using a fine rose on a watering can. (Keep a special can for weedkiller only.) The treatment works best when weeds are leafy and growing actively, so late spring is ideal. To tackle large, woody weeds, cut them down first and wait for soft new shoots to appear, then treat them. It takes three to four weeks for weeds to start dying – wait a few weeks and re-treat if new growth occurs, so the weeds don't

Paths and paving

If you're not averse to using weedkiller, then use a special path weedkiller to prevent weeds coming up between paving slabs, or on gravel paths and drives. Use a suitable product in spring; the effects last for the rest of the growing season. Don't use it on areas where you already have large weeds, as you'll have dead stems and leaves to look at for weeks once the stuff has worked. No, get the big ones out first.

In between paving slabs, the best alternative to weedkiller or weeding by hand is to fill the cracks with cement so that nothing can grow up through them. Old mortar between paving slabs often crumbles, so keep it in good repair to stop weeds growing.

have a chance to recover. A couple of applications are usually enough to kill most perennial weeds, except the real problem ones.

Glyphosate kills everything green that it touches, so protect the nearby plants that you want to keep and, to avoid spray drift, don't use it on windy days. As soon as the weeds are dead, the ground is quite safe to plant. Although lots of people prefer not to use weedkiller, it does have one major advantage. If you have a mammoth crop of nasty weeds to eradicate, using glyphosate to clear the ground as a one-off treatment does give you a head start, and you can always stay chemical-free from then on.

Preventing weeds

You can save yourself a heck of a lot of work by stopping weeds from coming up in the first place, but, before you get too excited by the idea, it's worth saying that you can't use weed-prevention techniques everywhere.

Mulching
The method of weed prevention most people use as part of their normal gardening routine is to mulch beds and borders in spring. Mulching means spreading a 5–8-cm (2–3-in) deep layer of mulch, for example, garden compost or well-rotted manure (see pages 50–52 for a full list), on any exposed soil. It actually does three jobs in one: saves water, smothers seeds and improves soil. How does it work?

You'll often hear people say that a mulch helps to 'seal in' soil moisture. What actually happens is that soil behaves rather like a wick and draws water up to the surface, where it evaporates. If the ground is mulched, the loose material stops the 'wicking action', keeping the soil underneath cool and moist, which is very much better for roots in a warm summer.

They say that a mulch smothers weed seeds. Weed seeds need light to germinate, so what actually happens is that the weed seeds on the soil surface are plunged into darkness by the mulch, so they can't come up. But weed before you mulch, as it won't kill existing weeds.

People also talk about the 'no-dig' technique (see page 54), and mulching is basically what they mean. Instead of forking well-rotted organic matter into your beds and borders, you spread it on top and leave the worms to drag it down. It's just as effective, but leaves you much less work to do.

Mulching is blooming marvellous, but it can't work miracles. It needs the right conditions to work well, which is why mulching is normally carried out at the start of the gardening season, just after you've weeded the borders and while the soil is moist. If you mulch

Cocoa-shell mulch

Cocoa-shell is a waste product of chocolate manufacturing, and it looks like lots of small crispy husks which often still have a marvellous chocolate scent. It's sold as mulching material to spread on gardens and it's quite popular because it's lightweight, clean and pleasant to handle, though expensive compared to home-made garden compost. Spread it 2.5–5cm (1–2in) deep and, once it is wet, the 'shells' meld together over the soil. Some people find that neither cats nor snails like to cross this mulch, though whether it's due to the odd, slightly sticky texture, or the chocolate scent, I couldn't say. Unlike chipped bark, which looks a bit similar, cocoa-shell breaks down quite fast, so you'll need to renew it annually. Don't let dogs eat the dry mixture from the sack – chocolate can be toxic to dogs.

over dry soil, the mulch just makes a semi-waterproof layer so that rain can't soak in; it just stays on top and evaporates instead.

Mulching is not completely infallible. If you have perennial weeds in your soil, they'll grow through a mulch – just as ornamental perennials and bulbs will. If any weeds do grow through, pull them out by hand or spot treat them.

As soon as you start talking about mulching, someone always points out the obvious drawback, which is that wind-blown weed seeds soon arrive on top of an organic mulch and start to grow. This certainly happens, but not for a while and, in practice, the mulching material is so loose and fluffy that weeds in mulch are very much easier to hoe or pull out than weeds growing in unimproved soil. But because mulching combines so many attributes that are good for the soil, it's well worth doing, even if it's not the ultimate weed-prevention technique.

Long-lasting mulches

In a shrub border where it's practical to plant and leave well alone, a mulch of gravel or bark chippings lasts a lot longer than compost or manure. Even these mulches need topping up every other year in spring, as they slowly sink into the soil as a result of worm action. It's still much less effort, though, than replacing mulch every spring, which is what you have to do with compost and manure. The bigger the bits, the longer the mulch lasts. A surface of gravel or bark shows plants off well, too. Use fine stone chippings or grit to 'mulch' a rock garden, and chipped bark for woodland or wildlife areas for a look that is in keeping with its surroundings.

Weed-proof membranes

You can take mulching one step further by using a weed-proof membrane beneath gravel or bark. Black polythene, woven polypropylene and similar 'landscape fabrics' are specially made for this job. They keep weed seeds permanently in the dark, where they can't germinate and, because the fabrics are tough, the shoots of perennial weeds can't grow through them. They should, however, let water through. If you're using black polythene, make sure it is the pre-slitted sort designed for the purpose.

The only drawbacks with weed-proof membranes are that because they are permanent, there's no further opportunity for adding organic matter to the soil once they're in place and, since they're difficult to fit around existing plants, their use is really only practicable before you plant a new bed.

Gravel or coarse grit makes the perfect mulch for alpines and dwarf bulbs, showing them off well and preventing them from being splashed by mud.

Start by preparing the ground thoroughly. Dig and rake it level, then cover the whole bed completely with the fabric, securing the edges with special pins sold for the job. Work out where you want to put your plants, then cut two crosswise slits in the fabric at each place. Peel back the edges, so you can dig the hole and put the plant in, then tuck the corners back around the stem. When the whole bed has been planted, hide the membrane with an even 2.5-cm (1-in) layer of gravel or bark chippings.

Synthetic mulches (weed-proof membranes) are fine to use where you are growing trees, shrubs or roses, but perennials and bulbs obviously can't grow through them. It's also no good using an anti-weed membrane where you want to grow annuals. You would have to cut so many planting holes that the weeds would have no trouble getting in to ruin the effect.

Even though it takes time to set up, in large borders of trees, shrubs or roses, this technique can save hours of work in the years to come. My only reservation is that, where the membrane is allowed to show through the mulch, it looks vile. Personally, I'd rather take time ridding the soil of perennial weeds and then placing my mulch – be it gravel or bark – directly on to the soil. But that's just me.

You can also lay weed-proof membrane beneath a bark or gravel path to stop weeds growing through, as an alternative to using path weedkiller. You won't eliminate weeds entirely, as some will grow on tiny specks of mud that fall off your boots and vanish between the path material. I avoid using membranes on sloping paths, as both bark and gravel are easily washed down-hill in wet weather to end up in a pile by your back door… and I speak from bitter experience. No, it's far better to lay your bark or gravel straight over bare soil in that situation, as it seems to grip better.

Mulch options

Mulch type	Advantages	Disadvantages
Bark	Long lasting, good-looking and effective, especially in a shady or woodland setting	May need an occasional top-up, as it sinks into the soil; rots down in time
Gravel	Long lasting, effective and shows plants off well	May need an occasional top-up, as it sinks into the soil
Cocoa shell	Lightweight, clean and easy to handle (and smells wonderful)	Can be expensive and needs renewing annually, as it breaks down quickly
Compost/manure	Very good for soil conditioning and home-made, so very cheap	Needs annual replacement and can be smelly
Membrane	Very effective and permanent	Hard work to install and can look ugly when exposed. Not practical on slopes or for use with flowers

Root-proof barriers

Think of a weed-proof membrane standing up on edge – that's a root-proof barrier. A root-proof barrier is the answer if the roots of the huge tree next door come up in your patch and take all the water, or if there is an adjacent privet hedge with the appetite of an elephant. It's also effective as a barrier to next door's pernicious weeds that spread under your fence. Dig a trench 30cm (12in) or more deep along the base of your fence, or wherever you need it, and bury an upright layer of something that roots can't grow through. The very best material is damp-proof-course (DPC) membrane – a tough, bituminized material that you can buy from builders' merchants, but I've also known people use heavy duty polythene, or even old bits of corrugated iron. In our first garden, which was very small and narrow, we had a privet hedge running down one side, the bottom of which was full of ground elder. I cut alongside the hedge with a spade, severing both the privet and ground elder roots, and inserted old roofing slates to act as a vertical barrier. It worked a treat and they are probably still there! Otherwise use the usual weed-proof membrane.

Another good use for root-proof barriers is to contain an outbreak of nasty perennial weeds while you treat it, or to protect the garden from invading nasties when there's wasteland next door, or wandering bootlaces of honey fungus (see page 221). I'm all for good-neighbourliness, but there are limits.

6 GARDEN MAINTENANCE

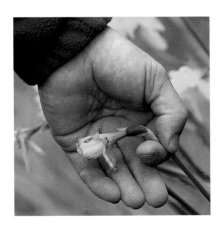

Garden routines

Gardening can be enormously creative – utilizing every ounce of your artistic talents in terms of landscape design and planting schemes. But, as anyone who's ever pulled on a welly knows, there's a deal of day-to-day upkeep to consider too.

Now I know that sounds dull, but once you know what you're doing and why, it needn't be dull at all. It can be enormously rewarding. Routine jobs, like weeding and watering, keep you close to the plants, the soil, and all the other living things, helping you get to know them better. Soon you develop a bond that makes the garden feel like part of the family. It's a bit like having a dog. After all the early excitement of buying a puppy, it's the everyday feeding, walking and spending time together that makes the relationship grow.

Gardening essentials

When you head out into the garden, it's a good idea to take along a few essentials. That way, when you spot a job that needs doing, you'll have some equipment to hand and it will save you a trek back to the shed. My essentials are the following:

- Hand trowel (see page 43)
- Hand fork (see page 43)
- Secateurs (see page 44)
- Sharp knife
- String, plant ties or garden wire
- Spare plant labels and a pencil
- Gloves
- Basket or garden humper to put all these in, that can also be used to carry weeds, etc, away

Learning the language

Just when you thought you understood plain English, along comes gardening with it's specialist vocabulary giving 'everyday' words a totally new meaning.

It isn't done to confuse – quite the reverse. If you know the right technical term, you often save a couple of sentences of explanation, and not just in conversation. In print and on TV, people often use 'gardening shorthand' for speed. There's no need to learn really specialist technical terms, but the well-used ones are worth knowing.

Bolting

A term usually applied to vegetable crops that have run to seed prematurely. It commonly happens to cauliflowers, lettuces and celery, if they are left too long in the ground once they are ready to eat, or if they experience a check in growth due to dryness at the roots, or extreme temperatures.

Check

A sudden slow-down in growth, usually due to cold, or hot, dry weather, lack of food or water, or serious attacks of pests or diseases.

Compost

When people say 'compost', there's often a bit of confusion as to exactly what they mean. There's the sort you make in a compost heap (see pages 204–7) and there are composts that are used as growing media – seed or potting composts. It's a little clearer in the USA, where they call growing media 'potting mixes' or 'growing mixes' – and garden compost just that.

Loam- or soil-based composts are formulated with loam as the main ingredient. Loam acts as a 'buffer' that holds nutrients, so you won't need to start feeding plants growing in loam-based compost until about three months after potting. The most commonly available are John Innes composts. Not a trade name, as most people think, but a standard 'recipe' for a series of loam-based composts made of sterilized loam (7 parts by bulk), peat (3 parts) and sharp sand (2 parts) with general fertilizer and a little lime. There are four potting composts: numbers 1, 2 and 3, often abbreviated to JIP1, JIP2 or JIP3, each containing increasing amounts of fertilizer and used for potting small, medium or large plants (or short-, medium- or long-term plants). The fourth is made without lime, an 'ericaceous mix' for lime-hating plants. John Innes seed compost is similar (2 parts loam: 1 part peat: 1 part sand), but with less fertilizer, and is used for seeds and cuttings.

Loamless or soilless composts are seed and potting composts based on peat, coir (coconut waste) or composted bark in place of loam. They include multi-purpose composts that can be used for seeds and cuttings and for potting. Loamless composts weigh less than loam-based ones, but tend to continue decomposing once in pots, so the texture gets progressively finer, and thus it does not 'last' as long. Due to their smaller nutrient-holding capacity, you'll need to start feeding after four weeks in the case of seed compost and six weeks in the case of potting. If allowed to dry out, soilless compost shrinks and is very difficult to re-wet; so it's best kept evenly moist at all times.

Lettuce often bolts (runs to seed) if it is left too long before picking, or if it has to endure extreme temperature conditions – whether heat or cold.

Garden compost is made in a compost heap. It is the product of the controlled decomposition of vegetable matter (garden rubbish or uncooked kitchen waste) in a compost heap or bin (see pages 51 and 204–7). It's for digging into the soil, or mulching the ground, not for potting plants.

Deadheading

Removing dead flowers (see pages 182–83). It's done for several reasons: to prevent fungal diseases, which often grow on dead plant material; to tidy the plant's appearance; or to encourage development of new flower buds by preventing the plant from expending energy on setting seed, thus extending the flowering season (see page 73).

Die-back

The death of a shoot, due to damage or disease that works it's way back from the shoot tip and down the stem.

Germination

The process whereby a seed develops into a young seedling given suitable moisture, air and temperature (see pages 60–63 and 68).

Hardening-off

Acclimatizing a plant gradually to cooler, more natural, conditions. It's mostly done with bedding plants to help them adjust from warm conditions in a propagator or greenhouse, before being planted out in the garden. They are moved to a cold frame, or stood outside on fine days and brought inside at night for two to three weeks before the date of the last expected frost.

A cold frame (an unheated, glazed structure) is ideal for hardening off greenhouse-raised plants, getting them used to lower temperatures before they are planted outdoors.

Pinching out
Removing the growing tip of sideshoots to encourage secondary branching. Also known as pinch pruning or finger pruning (see pages 180–81).

Potting
Putting a plant into a pot. Potting *up* refers to the first time a seedling or rooted cutting is potted; potting *on*, or repotting, is when a plant is transferred from an existing pot to a larger one.

Pricking out
Transplanting young, newly germinated seedlings to a wider spacing in seed trays of compost using a small, pointed stick called a dibber (see page 65).

Pruning
Cutting off selected parts of a plant in order to: encourage more fruit, flowers or stems; remove dead, damaged or diseased material in the interests of plant health; or develop a particular shape or restrict the size (see pages 179–92).

Setting
Seeds or fruit are said to have 'set' after the flower has been successfully fertilized, the petals have fallen, and a baby seed pod or fruit can be seen to start swelling.

Standard
A plant trained with a single, straight, branch-free stem or trunk, and a rounded or spreading 'head' of branches at the top (see page 184).

Stopping
Removing the growing tip of a plant to encourage the development of sideshoots (see page 181, see also pruning and pinching out above).

Top dressing
This can mean several things: an alternative to repotting by scraping away the top 2.5cm (1in) or so of old potting compost and replacing it with fresh mixture; the application of organic matter as a mulch or fertilizer (as a 'top dressing') to the surface of the soil around a plant or to lawns (see pages 50–53 and 248); the application of a mulch of stones or grit to the soil surface, for decoration, or to reduce evaporation of moisture from the surface.

Training
Making a plant grow into a particular shape, by pinching out, pruning, and/or tying in its stems to a supporting framework (see page 184).

A standard fuchsia – a plant grown on a tall, single stem, topped by a head of branches.

Organic gardening

To a chemist, organic compounds are those that contain carbon; they are found in, or derived from, living organisms – things like coal and oil, for instance. The term 'organic' has a slightly different meaning for gardeners, though the link with living things is still there.

Organic gardening is all about gardening in as environmentally-friendly a way as possible, which means using naturally-occurring materials rather than manufactured ones. It usually means using alternative (more thoughtful) techniques, or doing a job by hand, instead of using synthetic fertilizers, chemical weedkillers and pesticides.

Some people take organic gardening very seriously, and it's easy to get bogged down in the arguments about precisely what is and isn't acceptable. Real enthusiasts follow the guidelines of the Henry Doubleday Research Association (HDRA) whose HQ is at Ryton-on-Dunsmore, near Coventry.

It's quite possible to have a decent harvest of fruits, vegetables and flowers without resorting to chemical sprays and potions.

For most of us, it's enough to banish artificial fertilizers, chemical pesticides and weedkillers from our plots. At Barleywood, I reckon to be about 99 per cent organic – my one weakness is glyphosate-based weedkiller that I use once only to bring rough ground under cultivation. Glyphosate is inactivated on contact with soil and is non-persistent; as soon as the weeds have died away, I can perform all subsequent cultivations organically without fear of harmful residues. I like to think of my approach as common-sense organic gardening. For me, organic gardening is not the denial of science and a return to muck and magic; it is the utilization of our knowledge of biology and chemistry in a responsible, forward-looking way.

Organic products

Organic gardening hasn't changed much from the way our grandfathers gardened years ago, in some respects. They relied on manure or garden compost to improve the soil, and on fertilizers, such as hoof and horn, or bonemeal, based on animal remains. Strong plants growing in healthy soil have a natural ability to withstand minor problems, but, if needed, our forbears used natural products, like soft soap, pyrethrum, or derris, to tackle most common pests (see pages 224–25), and sulphur and copper compounds, such as Bordeaux mixture (see page 224), to treat fungal diseases.

These products and their modern alternatives (which are often specific in their action and less persistent in the environment) are now widely available in garden centres, although since the BSE crisis, many people prefer not to use animal-based fertilizers. Poultry-manure pellets are a good alternative, but 'vegetarian'

Making your own plant food

If you like to do-it-yourself, you can make your own liquid feed by dunking a sack of manure into a water tank for a few weeks. Draw off the 'manure tea' and dilute to about 1:5 with water; use it on your vegetable patch, or for anything around the garden in need of a quick boost. There's an even 'greener' alternative. Fill a tub with nettles or comfrey leaves, top it up with water and cover it with a lid, and a few weeks later you have a (rather smelly) brew ready to use. Dilute it in the same way as manure tea. The nettle version makes a high-nitrogen liquid feed that is good for vegetables and salads, while the comfrey 'flavour' is a high-potash feed that's especially good for tomatoes.

general-purpose feeds are available from specialist suppliers. Nowadays, a huge selection of organic supplies is available through mail order catalogues, even if your local garden centre doesn't stock them.

Me? I've settled on a system that allows a steady build-up of natural predators and which makes sure that there is no concentration of any one plant in any one place, so epidemics are less likely. I never spray with pesticides – organic or inorganic – and I have learned to live with the odd nibbled leaf and blemished apple. A garden that teems with all forms of wildlife seems to me preferable to one that is perfect but sterile.

Alternatives to peat

Although peat is a natural material, its extraction damages the natural habitat of a lot of specialized wildlife. Use a substitute wherever you can. Don't dig peat into the ground, use well-rotted manure or make garden compost instead; both are far more effective at improving soil, and garden compost doesn't cost a penny. Use loam-based John Innes seed and potting composts wherever you can (see page 161); it's true they contain a small proportion of peat but that's a lot less than a peat-based compost.

Soilless composts based on coir contain no peat at all – but against that you have to balance the environmental cost of transporting coconut waste halfway round the world using fossil fuels. I can't get on with them – too many are dusty and some produce plants that look distinctly unhappy.

Other types of soilless composts made from renewable resources are coming on stream all the time and steadily improving (see page 161), so see what's available and be prepared to adapt your growing technique to suit different materials. Those based on composted bark are among the most promising, but even these don't suit most seeds and seedlings. Carry out your own tests and see what works for you… that's exactly what I'm doing.

Organic techniques

You may think organic gardening is hard work, if you have to pick off pests and weed by hand or hoe and you can't use weedkillers or pesticides (but see pages 224–25). But so great is the gardening public's interest in cutting out chemicals, all sorts of techniques and gadgets have been designed to help.

Natural predators

In the natural scheme of things, nearly all pests have natural predators. Ladybirds and their larvae, for example, feed on aphids.

Mealybugs, red spider mites and scale insects all have natural predators, and several wasps are parasitic on the caterpillars of cabbage white butterflies. But nearly all pesticides are indiscriminate – they kill predators as well as pests. Give up chemicals and, to attract beneficial insects, grow old-fashioned hardy annuals that are naturally rich in nectar; poached egg plant (*Limnanthes douglasii*) and *Phacelia campanularia* are especially good for encouraging hoverflies (the adults and larvae consume aphids) and they look lovely, too. (See also Biological controls, pages 226–27; Beneficial insects, pages 230–31.)

Fly screens

Drape crop-protection mesh over carrots and members of the cabbage family from planting time onwards to exclude bugs, such as carrot fly or cabbage-white butterfly.

Fleece

Cover early vegetables with woven horticultural 'fleece' to protect them from wind, cold weather, and flying pests, such as pigeons. Remember to remove it to allow access for pollinating insects when the first flowers appear on plants such as dwarf French beans and courgettes. Don't leave fleece over plants in hot weather when they need a good circulation of air.

Horticultural fleece can provide valuable protection for early vegetables.

Small-flowered *Tagetes* planted among tomatoes will often keep whitefly at bay.

Unwanted compact discs strung on fishing line among lettuces, cabbages and other vegetables can help deter pigeons – it's the reflection, not the music, that does it.

Companion planting

It's claimed that planting small-flowered marigolds (*Tagetes*) between your tomatoes, garlic beneath your roses, and nasturtiums (*Tropaeolum majus*) around fruit trees and in the vegetable garden, will ward off pests. It may be that companion plants emit deterrent chemicals, or it may be that they attract lots of predatory insects, but it works for some, so it's worth a try. Complete charts of companion plants are available from organic suppliers.

Barriers and traps

Create an impassable ring around tree trunks, the rims of pots and the legs of greenhouse staging (the shelves for the plants), by applying a layer of crop-protection 'glue' or grease bands to prevent the passage of caterpillars and harmful creeping insects. Use upturned half grapefruit skins or beer traps for slugs and snails, and pheromone (synthetic sex-hormone) traps for fruit moths to avoid maggoty apples and plums. Hang yellow sticky traps in the greenhouse to snare flying pests, such as whitefly and thrips. Protect soft fruit from birds by using a web of cellulose threads that won't entangle them and which biodegrades at the end of the season – it's much kinder than netting.

Scarers

Humming line, and strings of old tins, or strips of tinfoil, help to frighten off birds; old CDs suspended from fishing twine so that they glint in the light also have a deterrent effect. Electronic devices that emit a high-pitched sound are often effective at keeping other people's cats out of the garden, if the sensors are correctly set to 'patrol' the fence. Transparent plastic bottles filled with water and stood in beds and borders are also said to be good at repelling cats. It may be their own distorted reflections that scare them off.

Watering plants

An outdoor tap is essential for serious gardeners, because if there's one job that needs doing regularly, it's watering – especially in summer. Young and shallow-rooted plants are the top priorities, so plants in containers, the vegetable patch, annuals and any newly planted beds are the ones to watch. Even during quite long dry spells, you can leave well-established trees, shrubs and lawns to take care of themselves.

Do they need watering?

Novice gardeners can find it confusing trying to establish when their plants are in need of water, and there is no one answer. Use your senses and try any of the following – you'll soon build up experience (see also pages 169–70 and 221–22):

Look at the colour of the compost. Your plants need watering if the compost is quite pale. In containers you can see if the compost has shrunk away from the sides of the pot, or the plants are droopy and wilting, then that's a real sign they need water.

Touch the soil. It should feel like a wet flannel, moist but not soggy. If it's not, water the plants.

Listen for a hollow empty sound when you gently knock on the side of a clay pot and if you hear that, then the pot needs water.

Hand watering

Hand watering is best, because when you are going around with the hose or watering can, you can take a good look at everything you pass and nip problems, such as pests or diseases, in the bud.

With containers, don't wait until plants wilt before watering. Check them regularly; you can tell those that need watering by the colour of the compost – it's paler when it's dry – but, if you want to be certain, poke it gently with your finger and it will *feel* dry. How dry is dry? Well, think of a freshly wrung-out flannel. If the soil feels like that, it's damp enough and does not need watering. Whether you use a slow-running hosepipe or a watering can, the art of watering containers is to soak the compost *thoroughly* and then wait until it *just* starts to dry out before doing it again.

For those who aren't sure, or who just like gadgets, you can get a water meter with a probe that you stick in the soil to give

Using a hosepipe to water newly planted border plants and shrubs ensures that the water goes exactly where it is needed. Always apply sufficient to soak right into the soil.

Where water runs off too easily and you need to get it down to the roots of a plant, cut the bottom off an empty plastic lemonade bottle, remove the cap and sink the bottle into the ground alongside the plant to act as a funnel.

you an accurate reading. But if you want to be a proper gardener, throw it away; watering is a skill you need to learn. If you use clay pots, the old-fashioned way of tapping them with a bit of broom handle works a treat – a damp pot makes a dull clonk; a dry one a clear ringing tone. When potting, always remember to leave sufficient space between the surface of the compost and the pot rim to allow for watering – the larger the container, the deeper the gap. Allow 1cm (½in) of space in 7.5–12cm (3–5in) diameter pots; 2.5cm (1in) for pots 15–25cm (6–10in) in diameter, and 5cm (2in) for larger containers.

In open ground, the surface of the soil may look dry, but this is due to evaporation. Soil acts like a wick, drawing up moisture from deeper down, so you don't need to water until there is a danger of roots drying out. That's why shallow-rooted plants, like rhododendrons and bedding plants, need watering long before you need to bother with mature trees or shrubs. You'll now realize the value of a moisture-retentive mulch to shallow-rooted plants.

Watering little and often is actually counter-productive; a layer of dry soil acts as a 'dust mulch', that prevents surface evaporation. If you just dampen the surface, the wick starts working again, and more water is lost from the soil. If you *are* going to water plants growing in the open ground, give them a really good soaking and don't do it again until they really need it. And if you funnel water precisely to where it's wanted – say, by sinking an upturned, bottomless plastic bottle alongside the rootball of a newly planted shrub – you'll do much more good than if you sprinkle water about indiscriminately.

Irrigation systems

The time may come when you end up with more watering than you can do by hand, and that's when you find yourself irresistibly drawn to the idea of an irrigation system. There are many types, but if your water is metered and you pay for every drop, it's worth choosing an efficient system that delivers water precisely where you want it.

Sprinklers are not very efficient; they shower water over a wide area and much of it misses the target altogether. Originally designed for lawns – on which few people waste water nowadays – those with a circular spray pattern are especially wasteful; the watered circles rarely overlap, resulting in both over- and under-watered areas. If you must use a sprinkler, choose the oscillating type that swings from side-to-side to give a rectangular spray pattern and the most even distribution.

Perforated pipe is plastic tubing with stitches or tiny holes all the way along, through which water slowly leaks out. This is the sort of irrigation system to use in between rows of vegetables, since it's easily lifted when you want to run a hoe through the soil. The water spreads out to between 45–75cm (1½–2½ft) on either side of the tubing, depending on soil type. Leaky hose can also be snaked between newly planted annuals, and is easily cleared away once they are established.

Sprinklers are not the most efficient means of applying water, but the oscillating type, which moves back and forth over an area of ground, is far better than the circulating kind.

Hanging baskets really benefit from a drip irrigation system which can be turned on once or twice a day in dry summer.

Drip irrigation is the most sophisticated system, as it waters each plant or container individually. You can put the bits together yourself to suit any garden layout. It's also great in the greenhouse. The idea is to have a drip nozzle in every pot, maybe two or more for big containers or growing bags. Both this and perforated pipe can be used permanently out of doors to water beds and borders. Run the tubing between plants, then bury the lot under a bark or gravel mulch.

When to water

In hot weather, it's best to water in the evening so that plants have longer to drink before the heat of the sun makes surface water evaporate. In cold or dull weather, water in the morning, so that plants can dry out before night-time. This is especially important in the greenhouse in spring and autumn when damp plants are more at risk of fungal infections.

Should you water at midday? Yes, if you see that a plant is obviously wilting – leave it until evening and it may be too late. The old wives' tale that plants scorch if you water them in sunshine is only true of some hairy-leaved plants that hate being splashed whatever the time of day. Just water them carefully and avoid wetting the foliage, whenever you water them.

Timers are the last word if you want to automate an irrigation system. These gadgets can be fitted to your outdoor tap before connecting it to the hosepipe at the start of your irrigation system. You set the timer to switch on for a defined period of time each day, and can even specify the time of day; it can be a real life saver when you are on holiday.

Feeding plants

We enjoy three square meals a day, but plants prefer to 'graze'.
Little and often is what they like best. They don't take in food in
solid form; the fine root hairs 'suck' in nutrients that are dissolved
in water held in the soil.

Stored nutrition

When plants are growing in the open ground, finding their own
'food' is no problem; their roots spread a long way in search of it.
On well-prepared soils, you can easily get away with feeding beds
and borders just once or twice a year to 'top up' supplies.
Nutrients that aren't used straight away are held by clay particles
and humus (the residue of decayed organic matter), so it figures
that the more clay and humus there is in the soil, the more
nutrients it can hold. That's why clay and loam soils are so fertile
(see pages 90–92). On soils with little clay or humus (as on
unimproved sandy soils), excess fertilizer washes straight through
the soil with the rain.

A well-fed border soon fills out so
that no soil is visible and plants
seem to bristle with health.

Well-manured soil which contains plenty of organic matter is far more efficient at holding on to food than poor, thin soil.

Solid feeds

On outdoor beds and borders, solid fertilizer – the powdered or granular kind – is usually used (see page 52). It's cheap, easy to spread and, because it shows up against the soil, you can see where you've put it. The idea is to sprinkle solid fertilizer thinly over the soil and hoe or fork it in lightly, so that it mixes evenly into the soil instead of just sitting on top. But before plants can take it up, the feed needs to dissolve and percolate through the soil to root depth, so clearly the ground must be moist. If it's not, either give it a good watering first or wait until the ground is damp.

The best time to feed beds and borders with solid fertilizer is in early spring, just before plants start growing. A second dose in early or mid-summer will top up nutrients for the benefit of greedy plants, like clematis and roses, which need a lot of input to keep up their output.

It's a bad idea to feed in late summer; the last thing you want to do is to encourage a lot of lush, late growth that will be well and truly clobbered by frost. And there's no point at all in feeding in winter; plants aren't growing then, so they can't use it. Bonemeal was traditionally used when trees and shrubs were planted in winter because, being coarse and organic, it took so long to break down that nutrients only became available when plants were ready for them in spring. Nowadays, we know that most of the phosphates bonemeal contains are locked up by the soil anyway. There is more benefit to be obtained by working in well-rotted manure or garden compost at planting time; it improves soil structure and so coaxes out roots more effectively (see pages 49–55).

Liquid and soluble feeds

Containers call for a completely different technique in feeding. You wouldn't feed a baby on beefsteak and brandy, so it's no good expecting a plant in a pot to take kindly to great lumps of solid fertilizer. It needs liquid feed. That way, the nutrients are already properly dissolved and, by diluting the feed in the right amount of water, you'll be applying a 'nutrient soup' at just the right concentration.

If you do use solid feeds for plants in containers, remember that the roots are in a very restricted volume of compost, so there's only so much they can cope with at once. It's difficult to gauge the right dose of a concentrated fertilizer – overdo it and you end up with a strong salts solution around the roots that actually sucks water out of the plant instead of letting it in (reverse osmosis, if you want to be scientific). An overdose can also scorch the root hairs, stopping plants taking up water. In both cases plants literally die of thirst. Liquid feeds are definitely the answer. That way you know what you are getting, and how much to use – just follow the directions.

Very little and very often is the right way to use liquid feeds. Commercial growers often feed at quarter-strength each time they water; it's done automatically through an irrigation system. At home, that's not practical, so aim to liquid feed plants in pots once a week or whatever it says on the back of the bottle, as it varies from brand to brand. Give each pot as much of the diluted feed as you'd use if you were watering normally, then you'll automatically be using the right amount. Plants in pots need liquid feeding all the time they are growing, from spring to late summer. Plants that are growing all year (such as indoor plants in warm rooms) can use the occasional feed even in winter, though they don't need feed as much, or as often, as in spring and summer. High-nitrogen feeds are best for leafy plants, and high-potash ones – usually sold as tomato feed – are good for anything that flowers or fruits – just dilute them more for pot plants than tomatoes.

Slow-release feeds

If you tend to forget about liquid feeding, then use slow-release feed sticks or granules instead. They work by 'leaking' nutrients very gradually; some of the more sophisticated kinds only 'leak' when growing conditions are warm and moist, which is when plants need feeding most.

Mix slow-release feed granules with the compost when you are potting plants in spring, or add it to new compost if you are top-dressing established plants in tubs. Otherwise, just poke in feed sticks around the side of your containers in spring, or a few weeks after potting. And read the instructions – the bigger the container, the more feed sticks you need to achieve the right dose, and some brands last to the end of the season, others don't.

Running on empty

If you've used slow-release feed in your pots, don't assume they keep working all the while you can see the granules – old ones don't disappear once they are 'empty'. Make a point of reminding yourself when they'll need replacing. For indoor plants, use the sort that lasts three months and refresh each time the electricity bill arrives.

Fertilizer sticks can be used in hanging baskets and other plant containers, if you have no time for regular feeding.

Supporting plants

Most plants can stand up for themselves, but there are some that need a bit of help. They fall into two categories; climbers, which obviously need something to climb up, and floppy plants that just need a crutch in life.

Trellis
Trellis is ideal for supporting plants, such as clematis and honeysuckle, that grow naturally through trees; the close-spaced lattice is the next best thing to twiggy branches. It's good for supporting climbers on walls or fences. You can fix trellis to horizontal battens screwed to a wall or fence, and fit it with hinges and hooks; then you can lay the trellis and its plant down on the ground if you need to do any painting or maintenance. Battens can act as spacers between trellis and wall, allowing air circulation and space for plants to grow through.

Structures
Arches, pergolas, pillars and gazebos are particularly spectacular ways of supporting climbers. If you choose plants that don't cling naturally, you'll need to tie them into the structure. Large structures, such as gazebos, are best built with trellis panels for the sides – you can get arches of the same type of construction – so that climbers can really spread themselves out.

Bamboo canes
Canes are ideal for tall, straight-stemmed plants, like delphiniums, or for training plants to *be* straight, as you would for cordon-trained sweet peas – the ones grown for exhibition-quality blooms. Tie stems in at about 20-cm (8-in) intervals with soft garden twine to avoid bruising. Think of a cane as a splint, but one that's used to prevent breaks rather than mend them. Split canes, which are about 45cm (1½ft) long and dyed green, are a lightweight alternative to canes for supporting smaller plants in pots.

Stakes
Use stakes to hold up heavy-headed plants, such as dahlias. Knock four or five stakes into the ground all around the plant, and tie soft twine between them to make a vertical cradle. It keeps loose-growing, or top-heavy clumps upright, instead of allowing them to splay open. Use heavy duty stakes for trees that need long-term support, or use short stakes at 45 degrees for others needing only temporary help (see page 79).

Against a wall, trellis provides a practical, yet decorative, support for climbers and wall plants whose stems can be tied in as they extend.

Pea-sticks

An informal means of supporting scramblers, like peas, or perennials that are only slightly floppy. Just push a few twiggy hazel stems, or woody prunings around the clumps before they reach 30cm (1ft) high. Gauge the length of your sticks by the ultimate height of your flowers, and cut the sticks about 15cm (6in) shorter so that they will be hidden by foliage.

Plant frames

Frames are intended for seriously floppy, bushy perennials. One type looks like a short metal stool with a wire-weave seat; it is seated over a perennial plant while it's still very small, so that the stems grow through the wire-weave as they elongate. Another type – looking rather like a partially straightened wire coat hanger – has legs that you push in all around a plant; the right-angled top pieces link the individual units together. Another alternative is the wigwam type (see below). In all cases, you need to choose frames that are a good 15cm (6in) lower than the top of the main dome of foliage when fully grown, so that the support system will be hidden by flowering time.

Woven willow wigwams are great for sweet peas, but renew them annually – they become brittle after a single season.

How to... **put up wires**

What you need

- *pencil*
- *electric drill with masonry bit*
- *wall-plugs*
- *vine eyes, which look like long screws with circular hooks at the end*
- *strong gauge wire*
- *garden string or plant ties*

Wires fastened to a fence or wall are the traditional way of supporting wall-shrubs and climbing roses, both of which have a fairly rigid framework of stems. Wires are also good for really vigorous twiners, such as wisteria, that can wind around them as they grow. By using vine eyes, which have a long 'stem', the wires are held a little distance away from the wall and this gives twiners room to wind themselves around the vine-eye stems and let a bit of air circulate. Wall shrubs need to have their stems trained out along the wires and secured at intervals with plant ties.

1 Your aim is to fix wires in horizontal rows about 45cm (18in) apart, to fill the area to be covered with plants, with the lowest wire 30cm (1ft) above ground. So, mark the wall with a soft pencil at the points where you want each wire to start and finish. Position these points in the mortar between the bricks, rather than on the bricks themselves, as it is softer to drill into. Now drill your holes.

2 Insert wall-plugs into the holes and screw a vine eye into each. Line up the hoops of the eyes, so they all face left to right and not up and down. Then secure a length of fairly stiff gauge wire to the first vine eye and stretch it across to the second, pulling the wire as tight as you can and winding the end around the vine eye to keep it taut. Secure a length of wire between each pair of vine eyes to give you several horizonal wires covering your growing area.

3 Once all your wires are in place, gently tie in the stems of your plant. Use lengths of garden string or plant ties taking the string around the wire and crossing it over before securing it firmly with a knot around the plant. This 'figure-of-eight' knot needs to be tight enough to support the plant and prevent it from moving and rubbing, while at the same time not strangling it by being tied too tightly.

Pruning

If there's one thing gardeners really get their knickers in a twist about, it's pruning, but when you start breaking it down, it's not half as complicated as people make out. There are lots of plants that never need pruning at all, or only rarely, so it's always a good idea to stop and ask yourself why you think you need to prune in the first place.

Woody plants with a branching structure, like shrubs, roses and fruit trees, are the ones that are most likely to need pruning. You might want to encourage a wall-trained plant to keep it's shape, or prevent shrubs from becoming too big and unruly, or maybe you want roses and apple trees to produce more flowers and fruit. You will need to prune, too, to remove dead, damaged or diseased tissue.

On some shrubs pruning can be dramatic, as with this dogwood (*Cornus*), which is being hard pruned so that it produces plenty of new stems.

Fine topiary pruning, as with this spiral of box, is best accomplished with a pair of sheep shears sold especially for the job.

Trees shouldn't take much keeping in shape. When you buy them from a nursery, the initial shape-forming will already have been done, so little pruning will be needed subsequently. If you have older trees that cast too much shade, you can cut off the bottom branches to lift the crown, or thin out the top, but big jobs are best left to a tree surgeon.

A lot of minor pruning jobs are things you probably do every day in the summer without even realizing it. When you are forming the shape of young plants that you've raised from seed or cuttings, or when you are deadheading flowers, or even clipping your hedge, you're still pruning.

Finger pruning

Finger pruning, as the name suggests, is the sort that you do with your fingers, so you can only really do it on soft young growth. It's mostly carried out on young plants to make them branch and form a good, bushy shape. You'll sometimes meet keen gardeners who let the nails on their thumb and forefinger grow longer specially to use as 'nippers', but most people seem to manage without such refinements. Fingernails generally do a much better job than the tips of scissors, which can't get in as close to remove small sideshoots – the alternative is to rub them out with the side of a finger.

Stopping

Some plants have stems that want to grow straight up and, if you want them to be bushy, you'll need to 'stop' them. Think of the old-fashioned seaside landlady sort of pelargonium: one long, bare stem with a handful of leaves and a flower at the top. Now, if only that had been stopped when it was 5–7.5cm (2–3in) high, it would have branched from the base, giving it a better shape that would have been packed with leaves and flowers.

Under normal circumstances, plants whose stems display what botanists call 'apical dominance', have natural hormones that encourage the bud at the stem tip to keep growing, so that the stem elongates. At the same time, the hormones flow back down the stem to inhibit the development of dormant buds, at leaf joints lower down, into shoots.

When you stop a plant, by nipping out the very tip at the end of the stem, you automatically deflect the growth hormones to the next buds down, which are then triggered into growth and they develop into sideshoots. It's all part of the natural system for making sure that a damaged plant survives, and goes on to flower. All we are doing is harnessing it to our own ends.

People often ask when's the best time to stop plants. I always stop rooted cuttings when I pot them up; that way, I can catch them at just the right size to encourage branching right from the base. Some plants, such as fuchsias, need a second stopping. This encourages the first set of sideshoots to 'break' again and form a second set of sideshoots; so you can see how this helps to form a nice, bushy, well-branched plant.

Pinching out

Pinching out is exactly the same idea – you nip out the growing tip of the shoot – but here, the aim is more to maintain the shape of an older plant. If you had a lovely symmetrical fuchsia, with one long shoot heading out sideways beyond the rest, you'd pinch the tip out to make it branch at that point, so the plant would just thicken out instead of growing lopsided.

Or you might also want to pinch out the tip of a shoot that has been damaged by pests or disease, or perhaps killed by a late frost. It's dead easy to get rid of greenfly or blackfly clustering round the tip of a stem by 'pinching out' the affected part, pests and all. By removing the damaged part, you help the plant's own hormones ensure that a new shoot replaces the old one as soon as possible.

You'll often see keen gardeners 'pinching out' shoots here and there as they walk around their garden. It's not to be confused with pinching cuttings: that's usually called stealing, which is something quite different.

Leave a young penstemon cutting to grow and it forms a long, single shoot, but cut out that shoot fairly low down (*top*) and the plant will become bushy (*bottom*).

Deadheading

The idea of deadheading is to prevent plants setting seed. But they will keep trying and, to this end, will produce another crop of flowers in the process. Call it cheating if you like, but I prefer to think of it as improving on nature or, at least, persuading her to be even more generous.

Some people deadhead sooner than others. The very tidy like to get rid of deadheads when the flowers are barely over, but others wait until they actually go brown. Regular deadheading is a good habit to get into. In summer, go over your containers once a week and take off any bloom that is fading. If you are disciplined about it, and keep deadheading from the time the first flush of flowers goes over in early summer, until the time the plants stop producing new growth in early autumn, you can keep bedding and patio plants, and modern roses, flowering pretty well flat out for five or six months. It may seem fiddly, but it pays dividends.

The question often asked by beginners is 'how exactly do you deadhead?' Keen gardeners take it so much for granted that it's just one of those things that is seldom explained properly. The answer is, it all depends on the kind of dead flower you are dealing with.

Flowers like lupins will produce a second flush of bloom if their flower spikes are snipped off as soon as they fade.

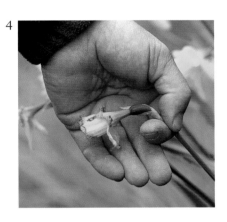

Deadheading techniques:
1 Faded pelargonium flowers should be removed by snapping off the entire stalk.
2 With fuchsias it is sufficient to remove individual faded flowers.
3 When an entire clustered head of roses has faded, the stem can be cut back 15–23cm (6–9in), but before then the faded blooms can be snipped off individually.
4 With bulbs, like daffodils, simply pinch off faded flowers to allow the food produced by the stalk to be transported back into the bulb.

One head of flowers (1) on the end of a longish stalk, as in pelargoniums. Remove the dead flower plus stalk. Snap it off cleanly at the point it grows out from the main stem of the plant.

Lots of short-stalked flowers (2), as in fuchsias and petunias. Nip the deadheads off with your fingers just behind the flower.

Roses (3): when it comes to roses, deadheading is like light pruning; use secateurs to remove 15–23cm (6–9in) of stem along with the dead flower or cluster of flowers. Cut just above a leaf joint. If you see a new shoot emerging lower down the stem, make your cut just above that; the next flower will appear a lot faster. If only one flower in a cluster has faded, as here, it can be removed individually.

Bulbs (4): pull the deadhead off leaving the stalk behind; nutrients in the dying stem will be drawn back into the bulb and will help to build it back up to flowering size ready for next year.

Masses of tiny flowers, like those of alyssum, are impossible to deadhead; don't bother unless you are really fussy. Fine scissors are a help, but please… there are more exciting things to do with your time!

Early deadheading

People growing plants for exhibition will remove unopened flower buds until so many weeks before a show so that a big crop of new blooms develops all in one go ready for the big day. You need to know what you are doing and most exhibitors experiment for years to get the timing right.

But if you are going on holiday, try removing all the open flowers from tubs and hanging baskets before you go. That way, instead of coming home to a sea of deadheads, everything will be coming back into full flower.

How to... **train a standard**

Training plants is a fascinating art. It's the process of taking a young plant and bending it to your will. Using a combination of stopping, pinching out and tying in, you can create shapes that plants wouldn't normally grow into – maybe flat, for growing against a wall, or as a standard (the classic lollipop shape), with a long bare stem topped by a rounded, bushy 'head' of leaves and flowers. Fast-growing plants, such as fuchsias, are the most fun to train because you see results quickly.

When you get round to more advanced training, you can create your own topiary, or fan-shaped fruit trees, starting from scratch, by combining pruning, or clipping, and tying in to the right sort of support, but that takes time and dedication.

What you need

- *unbranched rooted cutting of an upright variety of fuchsia*
- *10-cm (4-in) pot and a 15-cm (6-in) pot*
- *split cane plus a 1-m (3-ft) bamboo cane*
- *plant ties or raffia*

1 Remove all sideshoots from the rooted cutting, allowing only the central 'leading' shoot to grow and extend. Move the cutting into a 10-cm (4-in) pot, and push a split cane in alongside it. As the stem grows longer, tie it in to the cane at 10-cm (4-in) intervals to keep it straight.

2 When the plant reaches the top of the cane and fills the pot with roots, repot it into a 15-cm (6-in) pot and re-tie the stem to a bamboo cane 1m (3ft) long. When the shoot reaches just beyond the top of the cane, stop it by pinching out the growing tip. Allow the resulting sideshoots to grow to about 5cm (2in) and give them a second stopping. Remove any sideshoots that grow from further down the main stem.

3 Continue pinching out the very tips of the shoots at the top of the plant each time the new crop of sideshoots reaches about 5cm (2in) long, so that the head of branches will slowly grow larger and denser. When the head reaches the desired size, don't do any more stopping. After a few weeks, the plant will start flowering. The leaves on the standard's stem will naturally wither and die as the plant ages, or you can pick them off once the plant is in flower.

Clipping and trimming

Hedges, dwarf edgings and topiary are the garden's answers to poodles – good-natured, but they need regular clipping and trimming, which again are forms of pruning.

Whether you use trendy, single-handed sheep shears to shape up your lavender edging, a pair of shears to clip your topiary dome, or electric hedge-clippers to trim miles of Leylandii hedging (x *Cupressocyparis leylandii*), the operation has exactly the same effect as pinching out the tips of the shoots on your potted fuchsia – the stems below the cut will branch out. So, besides re-defining the shape, clipping also builds up a thicker hedge.

The great art of clipping is to know when to do it, so that you don't have to undertake the job more often than is necessary.

Hand shears allow you to clip hedges at a steady rate, and they are a darned sight quieter than electric trimmers!

Leafy formal hedges

Leafy, formal hedges, such as beech and conifers, need clipping twice a year if you like them to look perfect. Clip them in early summer and again at the end of summer, and they'll never look scruffy. If you want to cut down on clipping, you can get away with a single annual cut in late summer, though your hedges may look a bit fuzzy during the summer. Use the same timing for topiary. Formal edgings of dwarf box – used to outline borders or make knot gardens – are best clipped in late spring, but do the job in dull weather to prevent the cut leaf edges being badly scorched. I clip my yew hedges once a year, in late summer, or just at the very beginning of autumn. That way they stay crisp and clean-looking right through the winter.

Fast-growing formal hedges of hawthorn or privet are much more work, as they need cutting about every six weeks between late spring and early autumn. Don't make the last cut too late in the season, because clipping encourages a lot of soft young growth, which can suffer if it is hit by a late frost; the hedge won't really recover its good looks until next spring.

It can take ten years or more to encourage a hornbeam hedge to form an archway like this, but then not every job in the garden needs to be done at breakneck speed.

Lavender makes a wonderful informal hedge or kerb at knee height and associates well with other herbs and salad vegetables.

Dwarf herb edgings

These are an excellent way of edging flower beds. Clip rosemary after it has finished flowering, in spring. Santolina is good for edging and, if you don't want it to flower, clip it as soon as you see the buds starting to form in late spring – especially if the chrome-yellow flowers are going to clash with your colour scheme.

Dwarf hedges of lavender are clipped after they've flowered. All you are doing is snipping off the faded flower heads and lightly shaping the plants, so it's barely more than deadheading. With lavender, you mustn't cut back into thick, woody, old stems; they are reluctant to re-sprout. It's much better to give them a light hair-cut each year to keep them bushy.

Clipping technique

Clip a hedge so that its sides are sloping slightly inwards to the top. A 'batter', as it's called, looks better and it stops a hedge being top-heavy, so it's less likely to splay apart. Also, because the base receives more light, the hedge is less inclined to become bald at the bottom.

When clipping, start at the bottom of the hedge and slope your shears or hedge-clippers lightly inwards to get the angle of the slope right, and just follow the line upwards. If your hedge is taller than you can reach in comfort, then use a stepladder, or buy or hire a special platform. Make sure you are standing on something stable. And do plug power tools into an RCD (residual current device) or circuit breaker, designed to cut the power if you chop through a cable.

Informal hedges

Most flowering shrubs aren't particularly well suited to being formally clipped and things like shrub roses and flowering currant (Ribes sanguineum) are usually much better planted in a row and allowed to grow into their natural shape. But they still need keeping under control, and the way to do that is by pruning them just enough to keep them in shape. Do this in the same way as you'd prune free-standing shrubs, if you want to be correct about it.

Key pruning

You could go for years without really needing to do any serious pruning, but there are some things you simply must give a good going-over each year. So if you grow roses, some kinds of clematis, spring-flowering shrubs, and shrubs, such as dogwoods, that are grown for colourful winter stems... be prepared.

Where to cut

Always cut just above a leaf joint, a lateral stem (far left) or bud – about 5mm (¼in) away from it – even if you can't actually see a bud, as that is where the new shoot will grow out from.

Don't cut so close that you risk damaging the dormant bud on the stem, but, on the other hand, don't make your cut too high above it or you'll be left with a short stub or 'snag' (left) that will die back. Die-back may spread to the shoot that you're trying to encourage to grow.

Prune just above a bud that faces the direction you want the new shoot to grow in. In the case of a tightly packed bush, cut just above an outward-facing bud so that the new shoot grows away from the centre.

For single buds, make the cut at an angle that slopes gently away from the bud; it reduces the risk of rainwater carrying fungal spores into the wound. This isn't possible with paired buds; just cut them straight across, about 5mm (¼in) above the buds.

Tools of the trade

There are several different cutting tools for use in the garden. Each is specialized for the particular job it's designed to do. The main thing about cutting tools is to keep them well sharpened, as this will make the job much easier. These are the main types of tool that you will need for pruning:

Secateurs are essential. Use them for cutting through stems up to about 1.5–2cm (½–¾in) in diameter. Keen gardeners prefer the parrot-beak, bypass type that works with a scissor action (see page 44). Bypass secateurs give a cleaner cut; at least they do if you keep them sharp and wipe the sap off the blades each time you use them. If you don't want to spend so much, the anvil type (see page 44) is less costly and just as fine. Until you move into the rarefied world of specialist pruning, there isn't really all that much to choose between them, so buy whichever you feel most comfortable with.

Long-handled loppers are more powerful than secateurs; the long handles give you greater leverage for cutting through thicker stems. They are also good for reaching into the middle of dense shrubs.

Pruning saws are for branches. Always cut a branch off close to a trunk, or main stem. Don't leave a stump that will die back and don't cut flush with the stem. Leave the raised 'collar' at the base of the branch; it encourages bark to grow over the wound and it heals better.

Long-reach pruners are invaluable if you have tall trees to work on, as they save going up ladders. Keep them well oiled for a smooth action.

Loppers are useful for cutting branches between 2.5 and 4cm (1 and 1½in) thick, that secateurs would find too heavy-going.

How to... **prune spring-flowering shrubs**

Some spring- and early summer-flowering shrubs – *Philadelphus* (mock orange) and *Forsythia* in particular – can get very messy unless they are pruned every year. A neglected plant fills up with old stems that don't carry much flower. You can easily identify these stems, even outside the flowering season, because they have darker bark and look a tad gnarled. The way to prune these shrubs is to give them a glorified deadheading. As soon as the flowers are over, cut back all the stems carrying dead flowers. Follow the stem down until you reach a good strong bud or young sideshoot with no dead flowers on it, and cut just above the point where it grows out of the main branch. Do that regularly each year, and your spring shrubs will stay neater, and carry a lot more flowers.

The technique for most later flowering shrubs is pretty similar, but do it in winter. The rule of thumb is: if it flowers before mid-summer (say, mid-June), prune it immediately after flowering and, if it flowers later, prune it in late winter or early spring. You can apply that rule to almost any plant with woody stems.

1 Shrubs like *Philadelphus* (mock orange) and this *Ribes* (flowering currant) benefit from having a few older stems cut out each year. You can identify the older ones by their gnarled stems, and by the faded flowers carried on their sideshoots.

2 Use a pair of loppers to cut out the thickest of the stems, taking them as close to ground level as possible. Make your cuts just above a bud or a young sideshoot. Then use secateurs to remove any feeble or diseased stems you find.

3 As a result of this annual 'renewal' pruning, you will end up with a shapely and healthy bush, which produces masses of flowers on vigorous young wood each spring – rather than a tired old warhorse that looks ancient and tatty.

Pruning roses (1)

Large-flowered and cluster-flowered bush roses, the sort we used to call hybrid teas and floribundas, are the ones that are cut down hard every year between mid-winter and early spring. The latest theory is that they can be pruned with hedge trimmers, but unless you run a parks department with acres of the things, I wouldn't bother. Just prune all the stems back to about 15–23cm (6–9in) above ground level. Cut out all dead wood completely, and cut thin, weak stems back shorter than the strong, thick ones, as the harder you prune, the stronger the new shoots grow. Try to cut just above outward-facing buds. Shrub roses don't need hard pruning in spring, just deadhead them in summer instead, removing 10–15cm (4–6in) of stem along with each old flower.

Pruning clematis (2)

Some clematis need pruning, and some don't. The best way to tell is to keep the label when you buy a new plant, as it comes with in-structions. As a good rule of thumb, clematis species, such as *Clematis tangutica* and *Clematis orientalis*, as opposed to cultivated varieties, such as *Clematis* 'Barbara Jackman', don't normally need pruning. If you grow the large-flowered hybrids, wait to see when they flower. There are the late-flowering lot that start flowering in mid-summer (e.g. *Clematis* 'Jackmanii Superba') and keep going till early autumn, and it's these that need pruning hard. Cut them down to 30cm (12in) above ground level in winter, up to late February.

The other sort start flowering earlier, in early summer, then take a mid-summer break before a second flowering nearer the end of the summer (e.g. *Clematis* 'Nelly Moser'). Don't prune these quite so hard, or you'll be cutting off the later flowers and the stems that ought to flower early next year. Cut them back to silvery buds at around waist height in late winter. Varieties of *Clematis viticella* and *Clematis texensis* such as 'Princess of Wales' and 'Etoile Rose' can be cut back to ground level each spring.

Key pruning:
1 Always make pruning cuts on roses just above a bud or a young shoot.
2 In spring, clematis are pruned back to healthy emerging shoots – the height above ground depends on their season of flowering.

Key pruning continued:
3 It is only the young stems of plants, such as this *Salix alba* subsp. *vitellina* 'Britzensis', that give wonderful colour right through the winter, so prune them hard back each spring to encourage new growth.

Of course, if you reach the stage where any clematis gets too big, then you can prune it back hard in late winter and let it start all over again, or just tidy up the excess growth after flowering has finished. Either way, you'll probably miss out on a certain amount of flower next time round.

Pruning for winter stems (3)

Some shrubs benefit from a very hard and regular form of pruning known as stooling, which basically means cutting the whole plant down almost to ground level every year or two. It is commonly used on shrubs that are grown for their colourful winter stems, such as the red-barked dogwood (*Cornus alba*) and its cultivars, and shrubby willows, like the scarlet willow (*Salix alba* subsp. *vitellina* 'Britzensis').

The time to do the job is in late winter or early spring, just before the buds 'break' and the plants start growing. The idea is that, by removing all the old stems, which become less colourful as they grow woodier, you encourage a great flush of bright-barked new shoots. If you adopt this kind of pruning, you should mulch the plants well with manure (see pages 154–55) immediately afterwards to give them the wherewithal to produce new growth.

Alternatively, remove half the number of stems completely each year – taking the older ones – and allow half to remain. It's kinder and, provided it's the youngsters that are retained, you'll still have plenty of colourful bark.

Rejuvenating old shrubs

Most garden shrubs don't need regular pruning but, once they are approaching middle age, they may need a little cosmetic surgery to keep them looking good, and if you have really elderly or overgrown shrubs, then a drastic face-lift may be called for.

Mid-life tidy

The easiest way to maintain the shape of mature shrubs is to prune them lightly as soon as you first notice them starting to look a bit ragged. Winter or early spring is the best time to tidy shrubs that flower after mid-summer; prune earlier flowering kinds soon after flowering.

Whatever you do, don't clip flowering shrubs like berberis into the neat domes you sometimes see in neat and tidy gardens, as all you do is rob them of all character and you'll probably stop them flowering as well.

Don't snip bits off here and there, either. It's much better to take off a whole branch close to the base of the plant, or to cut it back close to the junction with a better-placed branch. That way you leave the shrub with a reasonably natural shape. Lopsided shrubs just need the offending branches cut back to restore their equilibrium, so prune just above the next well-placed branch emerging from lower down on the same main stem.

Very strong-growing shoots that push up through the middle of an otherwise bushy shrub can be cut back by half their length or more, in an effort to encourage them to branch out lower down – but if it's a grafted plant (see page 78–79), do check to see whether it's a sucker growing up from the rootstock underground and, if it is, dig it out.

You can avoid pruning by growing plants that need very little attention, such as Japanese maple (left centre) and fatsia, or false castor oil (right), growing here in a well-sculpted border with hostas and Japanese anemones.

How to... **restore old shrubs**

If you have geriatric shrubs that don't flower well, ask yourself whether it wouldn't be better to replace them, rather than try to restore them. Restoration takes time, whereas a new shrub will look better right away. But if you have something special, and it's not too far gone, or you're too mean or cash-strapped to lash out on a new one, then give it a go.

I know it's tempting to try and do the whole job at once, but be patient. If you cut an old shrub back too hard, it'll just fight back by growing lots of strong leafy, shoots that don't flower. If it's a grafted plant, you may end up with a thicket of suckers. It's much better to cut out one or two of the very oldest branches every year – they are the thicker ones with darker, more gnarled bark, the baldest branches and the ones with the fewest flowers. Winter or early spring is the best time to do the job on mid- to late-summer bloomers. Early-flowering shrubs can be given the chop after flowering. Don't remove more than one fifth of the plant's branches at a time.

1 Some shrubs, such as *Salix alba* cultivars, ornamental elders and dogwoods, grown mainly for their foliage and/or coloured stems, benefit from hard pruning every 2–3 years. Cut all the thick, dark-stemmed old branches down close to ground level with a pruning saw, in spring – just before the plant starts growing, but when the risk of severe frosts has passed.

2 Tidy up the small twiggy stems with secateurs. Strong young shoots will soon grow out from these 'stumps' to form a bushy new plant.

3 Later the same summer, you'll have exactly what looks like a brand new shrub, with large leaves and strong stems. This is *Cornus alba* 'Elegantissima', grown for its handsome variegated foliage and red stems, seen at their best in winter.

Restoring perennials

While shrubs are rejuvenated by cutting them back hard, the way to breathe new life into really old perennials is to dig them up and divide them.

Now if you look in a lot of the old gardening books, they'll tell you to divide one type in autumn and another in spring, and you'll end up feeling what you really need is a year-planner. Don't panic! The easiest way to go about rejuvenating perennials is just to divide everything in spring. By dividing them up just before they start growing – or even when there are some short new shoots showing – they will recover rapidly.

How do you tell when a plant needs dividing?

Unless you just want to propagate some more plants, there's no point in dividing perennials before they need it, because large clumps flower better than small ones and they make the garden look more mature. Whether a plant needs dividing or not depends on how it is growing. Perennials certainly need dividing if they are:

Dead in the middle i.e. if the middle of the clump has died out, or stopped flowering well – leaving a circle of young growth all around the edges – the plant's a prime candidate for rejuvenation.

Overgrown i.e. if the clump has outgrown its spot and started invading neighbouring plants, you'll need to divide it to keep the neighbours happy.

Taking leave of the soil i.e. if the clump has 'grown itself out of the ground', as heucheras sometimes do, then that's another good sign that your plant needs dividing.

How often do plants need dividing?

Some perennials take a long time to re-establish after being divided, so don't disturb things like the ice plant (*Sedum spectabile*), hostas, bearded iris and peony until you really have to. You can leave them for five years or more before they need splitting up, and even then they may go on happily for several years more.

Some of the very self-sufficient, cottage-garden perennials, such as hardy geraniums, can be left untouched almost indefinitely. But very vigorous perennials, like perennial asters and phlox, tend to run out of steam unless they are divided every two to three years.

What's wrong with autumn?

Autumn is okay for dividing up the tougher, fibrous-rooted plants, such as Michaelmas daisies (Aster novi-belgii), but try carving up the fleshy roots of sedum and hosta, and you leave big, open wounds that just rot when they're exposed to cold, wet soil all winter. If you garden on warm, light, fast-draining, sandy soil, you can probably get away with dividing in autumn, in most years, but on wet clay soils, stick to the springtime.

How to... **divide perennials**

You'll often be told that the way to divide perennials is to use two garden forks back to back. The idea is to dig the clump out of the ground, impale it on the two sets of prongs and lever the bits apart. All I can say is whoever came up with this knuckle-bruising wheeze has never tried to do it. It doesn't work! It's much better to chop the clump into pieces with a sharp spade. You can be quite rough about it.

What you need

- *secateurs*
- *sharp spade*
- *digging fork*
- *a good bucketful of manure or garden compost*
- *general fertilizer*

1 Some plants need dividing more regularly than others. Things like Michaelmas daisies can be divided every three years. Other plants, like this geranium, can wait rather longer. Use secateurs to cut off all the old, faded plant growth and reveal the healthy young shoots. Cut down the stems as low as possible, so that when you come to handle the plant the cut stems are less likely to get in the way or stab you. With a spade or fork, dig around the clump, then prise it out of the soil.

2 Divide up the decent, healthy young stuff into 12-cm (5-in) diameter clumps, by chopping into the main clump with a spade. Don't be too mean, as tiny clumps take ages to start flowering. You can pot smaller bits up and grow them on to give to friends, if you like. Discard the tired old central portion.

3 Improve the soil by forking in some good garden compost or manure and a handful of general fertilizer. Do this whether you're going to plant the perennials in the same spot, or take the opportunity to move them elsewhere. Re-plant the best bits at 30-cm (12-in) spacings.

Container gardening

Tubs, window boxes and hanging baskets are the easy way to personalize all sorts of 'special' places around the garden, from the patio and porch, to your rustic gazebo or designer tree house. They are also a very practical way of growing plants in places without soil, such as a paved courtyard or roof garden. Being portable, containers are ideal for anyone planning to move house and, if you are a compulsive re-arranger, containers allow you to reinvent your surroundings without the bother of digging everything up. All things considered, it's not surprising they've become so indispensable but remember, containers do need regular maintenance.

Seasonal colour

Think of hanging baskets and tubs, and you are immediately transported to a summery scene. But there are three distinct bedding 'seasons', and as long as you keep tipping out and replanting at the end of each one, you can keep your containers colourful for most of the year.

Summer is simple; in fact, you are spoilt for choice. You can't beat bedding plants like petunias and pelargoniums for a long, continuous flowering season, but anything with a compact, bushy, or trailing habit is ideal. 'Patio plants' is just a marketing term for

Almost any plant can be grown in a container. Here lavender planted in square pots adds to the formality of a flight of decking steps.

Experiment with containers for bedding – orange tulips look great in a galvanized miniature tin bath.

container-worthy, half-hardy perennials sold in little pots in spring. New kinds come into the fold all the time. These are planted after the last frost and, if properly cared for, should keep flowering until the first serious cold weather in autumn.

After the first nip of frost, autumn and winter bedding takes over. You can use ornamental cabbages and kales or Universal pansies, or make temporary arrangements of autumn-flowering heaths, winter heathers and berrying evergreens, such as skimmia and *Gaultheria procumbens*. Yes, I know they aren't annuals, but anything grown temporarily counts as bedding – and with these, you can always plant them in the garden when they are past their best in pots, so it's not nearly as extravagant as it sounds.

Once the worst of the weather is over, in spring, you can replace winter plants with primroses and polyanthus; the later you leave it, the bigger the selection of spring bedding you'll find in the shops. There'll be pots of ranunculus – those giant, turban-topped buttercups with jewel-coloured flowers – violas, forget-me-nots, and pots of dwarf spring bulbs just coming into flower. By the time they are past their peak, it's time to start on the summer stuff again.

Summer containers in my garden sport lilies, begonias, and the white bells of galtonia: I love a bright and vibrant mixture – subtlety can be so dull!

All-year-round planting

Year-round container gardens are stylish and practical for people who like the potted look but can't manage the regular make-overs of seasonal schemes. They want plants that can stay put for years on end without needing a lot of fuss. The sort of plants to go for must be hardy, of course, but they also need to look on top form all the time.

There are loads of suitable plants. Evergreens and naturally compact shrubs are brilliant, and dramatic architectural shapes can look superb. Yes, I know virtually everything you buy comes in pots, but that doesn't mean to say they'll be happy to stay restricted in the long term. If you want year-round container plants, don't bother pot-gardening with monsters like climbing roses, hybrid teas and blackberries.

Some of the very best year-round tub plants are natural show-offs, things like bamboo, dwarf rhododendrons and Japanese maples, or Chusan palm (*Trachycarpus fortunei*), yucca and phormium. Most of the smaller clematis are brilliant in tubs – grow them up posh obelisks or rustic tripods.

If you prefer a traditional look, then patio and miniature roses are the answer. I'd go so far as to say they are a better alternative than summer bedding for busy people, because they are just as colourful and flower for as long, but you don't have to throw them away at the end of the season. Just keep them in their pots for next year.

Vegetables and herbs

When you don't have much of a garden, it's smashing to have a few vegetables in pots, to bring the supermarket right up to your back door. Salad leaves, herbs, courgettes and climbing beans all grow perfectly well in containers and, provided you keep up to date with the feeding and watering, there's no reason why you shouldn't have crops just as good as you'd expect from a small, intensive garden bed. On a warm, sunny patio, you can add tomatoes and sweet peppers to the list.

Growing edibles in containers is only a little more labour-intensive, in terms of feeding and watering, than growing in open ground, but they can look infinitely more glamorous when growing in beautiful containers. Anyway, you'll enjoy looking at them almost as much as eating them, so they'll be good for you on both counts.

If you go for growing bags, you can hide the bright plastic covers under a piece of hessian, pile pebbles over the top, or stand them inside long wooden boxes. Besides looking better, this also helps insulate the compost, which keeps the roots cool in hot, sunny weather.

You can even grow herbs and salads in a hanging basket, provided you don't forget the watering.

Container-growing techniques

Gardening in containers is just like growing pot plants on your windowsill indoors; it's only the scale that is different.

But what is it about container gardening that brings out the Scrooge in some folk? I wish I had a pound for every time someone has asked me why they need to buy potting compost instead of using garden soil to fill their tubs.

Frankly it's not worth the saving. Potting compost is like giving plants a dinner party instead of asking them to survive on a bag of crisps. Potting compost is specially formulated to suit their requirements; with garden soil you just don't know what you are getting: it may contain soil pests or diseases; it might be short of basic nutrients; badly drained, or just poor quality. Since containers are showpieces, the plants in them need every opportunity to do their best. Sorry, lecture over, but you have to get these things off your chest!

Summer containers: jobs checklist

Planning	Watering	Feeding	Deadheading	Dismantling
Decide on shape and size of container, and position (sun or shade, etc). Choose plants accordingly (consider colour, shape – upright or trailing – etc). Get your compost, crocks and water retaining gel. Now plant up (see page 201).	Check regularly. Do not drown them in their early and late seasons, but they will need watering almost every day at the height of a hot summer. If you are unsure whether to water or not, check the 'Do they need watering?' chart on page 169.	Start feeding about four to six weeks after planting the container and follow the manufacturer's instructions on how frequently you should feed. Alternatively use slow-release feeding sticks or granules.	Do this regularly, at least once a week. The more you do it, the more flowers your plants will produce and the longer the flowering season will last.	When the last of the flowers has faded, clear the decks ready for next summer's planting up by putting the dead plants on the compost heap and washing and storing your containers, or plant up for winter colour.

How to... **plant a container**

If plants are going to stay in the same container for several years, loam-based compost is the answer as it lasts longest (see page 161). Look out for the ericaceous (lime-free) version of John Innes, for long-term lime haters, such as rhododendrons and camellias (see pages 93–95).

Soilless composts are fine for bedding plants that won't stay put for more than about five or six months (see page 161). They often hold more water, so they're especially good for small containers, hanging baskets and window boxes that are notorious for drying out quickly in summer.

You can get water-retaining gel to use in containers. It absorbs moisture every time you water, and retains this for the plants to use. It's a real help to container gardeners, but a word of warning, though, follow the instructions and don't overuse it – the gel expands and can push your plants and compost over the edge of the pot.

> ### What you need
>
> - *water-retaining gel*
> - *potting compost*
> - *slow-release fertilizer*
> - *container*
> - *crocks – bits of broken clay flower pot or coarse gravel, for drainage*

1 Mix water-retaining gel into the compost and wet it until the granules swell up, then mix in a little slow-release fertilizer (follow the instructions given about quantities on the box or packet).

Put a handful of crocks at the bottom of the container, to ensure good drainage, and part-fill it with potting compost.

2 Tip the plant out of its pot and tease out a few roots if it is pot-bound. Fill around the plant with more potting compost, so that the surface of the rootball sits flush with the surface level of the new compost. Don't fill the container right up to the top – leave a 2.5-cm (1-in) gap below the rim to allow for watering.

3 Firm the compost gently – don't press it down as though you were making bread – and water it well.

Feeding and watering

The first thing you notice when you take up container gardening is the way the chores change – you exchange weeding beds for feeding and watering pots. In beds, plants 'scavenge' for what they need; in pots, they need a delivery service… you.

The smaller the pot and the hotter the weather, the faster it will dry out. Be handy with the watering can – especially in summer when you might have to water twice a day.

Water with care early and late in the season when the weather is wet; it's easy to overdo it. But in high summer, the problem is usually keeping containers moist enough, particularly in hot, dry spells, or in breezy weather. Once containers fill up with roots, they dry out almost in front of your eyes. Hanging baskets often need watering morning and evening in summer, and large containers probably need watering every day. As a precaution, always use the finger test (see page 169) to see if watering really is needed.

By the time plants have been growing for four to six weeks in soilless compost, you'll need to start feeding; use liquid or soluble feed and dilute it exactly as advised by the makers (see page 175). If you know you aren't going to have time to liquid feed every week, don't let the job slide; mix slow-release fertilizer into the potting compost before you plant. If you give the occasional liquid feed as well, when the plants are in full bloom, they'll be as happy as Larry.

Care of all-year-round containers
Caring for all-year-round containers in summer is much the same as looking after tubs of petunias and fuchsias but, as the season comes to a close, you'll need to vary your potted gardening techniques to suit the changing weather.

Autumn is often lashed by gales, so it's worth moving containers of tall plants closer to the house for shelter and tying them up to trellis, or wedging them between bricks for stability. Not very pretty perhaps, but it takes a long time to re-grow a broken plant – and decent containers cost more than enough. As an added precaution, raise containers up on pot feet, or bricks, so that they don't stand in water. The last thing dormant plants need is wet feet, which encourages rotting, so you need to ensure that surplus water drains away quickly.

Winter brings weeks of freezing weather, so year-round containers need a spot of insulation. Even though the plants are perfectly hardy, their roots are less protected than they'd be in a border, and if the compost in containers freezes solid, the plants will almost certainly die. Well before they freeze, move containers into a greenhouse, car-port or porch – they won't come to harm in the shed or garage for a week or so. Otherwise, sink them up to their rims in a border, or push all your containers together in a sheltered spot and fill the gaps between them with bark chippings. Pile some more bark up over the top of the pots to act as a temporary 'quilt'.

Winter-proof containers

You can use any kind of container you like for summer schemes, provided it has drainage holes in the bottom, but if you want to keep it planted in winter, make sure it's up to the weather. Many ceramic or terracotta containers will crack if the compost inside them freezes, because water expands as it turns to ice. Wood, stone and plastic are naturally resistant. Don't be misled by 'frost-proof' terracotta – some people think it means that it protects tender plants from frost; it doesn't. It's just a better grade that is less likely to crack. But even so-called 'frost-proof' pots are not indestructible. 'Frost resistant' would be a more accurate term.

Spring is typically unpredictable and, if you have early-flowering shrubs, such as camellias, in tubs, don't stand them in an east-facing site; early morning sun shining on frozen flowers spoils them. Avoid a windy spot too, or flowers will go brown – especially white ones. If the weather is bad, move your pots into a porch or cold greenhouse for protection, which will have the side effect of bringing the flowers on early. If a late frost is forecast after the plants have produced new growth, or big fat flower buds, wrap them in horticultural 'fleece'. It only gives a few degrees of insulation but that's often all that's needed. Don't wrap plants in plastic because condensation builds up underneath, which might cause plants to rot; by contrast, fleece 'breathes'.

Making compost

People throw away a lot of stuff to clog landfill sites when it could be providing vital 'roughage' in their garden soil. There's no secret to perfect compost, just a few good tips on technique. Don't believe the old countrymen who'll kid you that the only way to get garden rubbish to rot down properly is to recycle ten pints of beer over it on the way back from the pub. There are other ways, even if they aren't quite so creative.

Compost heaps

Compost has to heat up to 'work' properly and one of the commonest reasons that compost fails to rot is that it's never been given the chance. Don't economize on the size of your heap; compost needs a certain critical mass to heat up properly, and a metre cube is just about right. To go bigger, extend the heap into an oblong shape, but a metre high (about 3ft) is probably about the most you can manage, as the ingredients must be stacked in layers, like a club sandwich.

If you have the sort of garden that generates lots of waste, the way to deal with it is by having two compost heaps. It's the same principle as having two gardening shirts, one on and one in the wash.

Start with heap number one, stack it up, cover it and leave it to rot down (see page 206) while you make up heap number two. By the time the second bin is full, the first is ready for use. By alternating between the two you can have a constant supply of compost.

You *can* make a free-standing compost heap, but you still need to build it rather than just piling rubbish up, and using a container makes it so much easier.

Every garden should have a proper compost heap. It need not be smelly and it recycles valuable organic material that feeds the soil.

How to... **make compost**

There are several ways to contain compost while it rots down; you can either buy a plastic compost bin, which suits a small garden (see page 206), buy a self-assembly wooden bin of the type shown here, or you can make your own container. You will need a level area of ground measuring 1 metre (3ft) square, with space enough to park a barrow alongside. Consolidate the ground and hammer in four posts, one at each corner, about a metre (3ft) apart. Tack wire netting all around the sides, or nail planks across to create solid or semi-slatted sides. Make the front section easily detachable by using galvanized hooks and eyes, so that you can remove the finished compost later. Now you can fill it up…

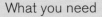

What you need

- *4 x 1.2m (4ft) high fence posts*
- *wire netting or planks for sides*
- *galvanized hooks and eyes*
- *coarse drainage material, garden waste, fresh manure and soil*
- *piece of carpet or tarpaulin*

1 If you decide to make your own compost bin, follow the instructions above, otherwise assemble your bought container. Then put a layer of coarse material, such as not-too-woody herbaceous plant stems, at the bottom, for drainage. Spread 15cm (6in) of garden waste evenly over the base. Firm it down by treading, and dampen it if it's dry. Firmness and dampness (not sogginess!) will help the rotting process. Avoid concentrations of any one ingredient. (See page 207 for a list of what you can and can't use to make compost.)

2 Top each new 15-cm (6-in) layer with a couple of spadefuls of fresh manure or soil, which provide beneficial bacteria and act as a 'compost starter'. Make sure that all your waste ingredients to be composted are mixed together before you add them, and remember to water the heap if it looks dry.

3 Each time you add more material, to keep heat and moisture in, cover with an old piece of carpet or tarpaulin. Keep building the heap up, sandwich-style, until it's a metre (3ft) high, and finish with a 2.5-cm (1-in) layer of soil on the top. Cover and leave for 6 months. Compost rots down faster in summer than in winter. A heap made in spring should have made good, brown, friable compost by autumn, but a heap made in autumn may not be ready until the following summer.

Getting a headstart

To rot down, compost materials need moisture, air and a supply of beneficial bacteria. You can add these by watering on a liquid 'compost starter' out of a bottle from the garden centre. Fresh, unrotted manure has a good 'bacteria count', too, and there are plenty in garden soil, so don't bother knocking too much of it off the roots when you are doing the weeding.

If you don't have space to build a compost heap, a smaller compost bin, like this one, is the solution.

Smaller bins

In a tiny garden, you might not have enough waste to make a large compost heap that works, and the answer is to go for a custom-made compost bin instead. Think of a plastic dustbin with the bottom missing.

Stand it somewhere convenient, and just pile all your rubbish in – no need to worry about layers, just mix everything together. Moisten it if it's dry and firm it with the back of a rake to avoid large air pockets. As long as there's some soil on the roots of weeds to provide the beneficial bacteria needed, you can even forget about adding the odd spadeful of manure or soil. Fill the bin to the top, and put the lid on. The compost should be ready to use in as little as two or three months, or maybe five in winter, when the weather is colder and compost doesn't 'work' so fast.

Troubleshooting

Most compost heap problems boil down to one or two simple things that are usually quite easily put right.

Slimy, smelly compost is often the result of an overdose of lawn clippings. Don't make mowings more than half the total bulk in your compost heap, and mix them well with other material. Alternatively, sandwich the clippings in 15-cm (6-in) layers between weeds and other waste, or use a compost rotter that is specifically designed to prevent grass mowings turning into dark green slime.

Mummified orange peel and other shrivelled but still-recognizable matter are signs that a heap is too dry – make sure that you dampen new materials each time you add them.

Slow rotting may be due to too-coarse, woody materials or thick stalks being used; cutting them up small, or passing them through a garden shredder first makes them rot faster. Remember, too, to keep your heap firm (by trampling it) and damp (by watering it in dry weather).

Rodents can be a nuisance sometimes, even if you don't put cooked food stuff in your heap. If you can, arrange to empty your compost bins in the autumn and put them away until spring, or look out for a metal compost bin with a small-mesh base that's rodent-proof.

Wormeries

If you only generate a fairly small amount of waste, especially if it's mostly from the kitchen, then you could consider using a wormery instead of a conventional compost bin to convert it. Worms are the modern answer to the traditional cottager's pig. You feed your scraps in one end and what comes out the other, incredibly quickly, is valuable plant food. Worm compost is good as it is and ready to use straight from the worm, whereas fresh manure gives off enough ammonia to 'burn' any plants it comes in contact with, so it needs stacking for six months until it is well rotted.

You can buy a kit containing the wormery, worms and everything you need to get started – the three-stage sort that looks like a pile of sieves is good if you are a bit squeamish about handling the little workers themselves. You can remove the bottom chamber, where the oldest material is ready to use, tip it out and return it to the top of the stack, for refilling. It's the closest thing you'll get to perpetual motion in the garden.

Use your rich, home-grown supply of worm compost – which is pure worm casts – to top dress plants in outdoor containers, or to enrich your vegetable and salad patch. Great for organic gardeners as it's 100 per cent natural.

A wormery can make efficient compost out of kitchen waste and will also provide liquid manure from a tap at the base.

The ingredients for good garden compost

What goes in...

- Annual weeds
- Tops of perennial weeds
- Spent bedding plants
- Uncooked vegetable trimmings and peelings, crushed eggshells and tea bags from the kitchen
- Lawn mowings (well mixed in with other materials)
- Soft hedge clippings, soft prunings and spent flowers
- Dead leaves
- Shredded woody stems
- Shredded paper, cotton and wool fabrics

And what doesn't...

- Cooked food scraps, meat or bones and bread should be avoided at all cost; they may attract vermin
- Diseased plant material and soil pests
- Dog or cat waste
- Weeds with seed heads
- Perennial roots, especially weed roots
- Woody material, such as prunings and Brussels sprout stems
- Synthetic fabrics and any other non-biodegradable matter

7 KNOW YOUR ENEMY

Prevent and detect

As you've probably realized by now, there are a lot of things that can go wrong with plants. Apart from being attacked by all sorts of insect pests, they also fall prey to diseases caused by microscopic fungi, bacteria and viruses. But not all problems can be blamed on pests or diseases.

Cultural problems come about when plants aren't given the right care or conditions (see wilting, page 221). They can suffer from physical damage, such as breakage or bruising, and the elements can cause trouble (see frost and wind damage, page 220), hence the well known gardening maxim 'blame it on the weather'.

But it's not all doom and gloom, because you can garden for years with only minor problems, if you're lucky, or if you take a few simple steps to keep plants healthy. I'm a firm believer in the idea that the best way to tackle plant problems is to prevent them from happening in the first place.

Avoidance tactics

Don't buy trouble. When you're choosing plants at the nursery or garden centre, check them for pests and diseases in all the obvious places: on or beneath tender young leaves and the tips of shoots. Spotty or pale leaves, holes, and wilting shoots can all be symptoms of problems you don't want to take home with you (see pages 144 and 212–19).

Once in the garden, there's a lot you can do to keep plants healthy by growing them well. It's a heck of a lot easier – even for the professionals – to keep a good plant healthy, than to rescue it after it has gone badly downhill. Healthy plants, well-cared for in healthy soil, have a tremendous ability to fend off all sorts of pest and disease problems, whereas frail specimens simply hang up their boots.

Do look plants over regularly. You can often nip a potential problem in the bud just by spotting it in time and doing something simple, such as picking off a mildewed leaf, or wiping off an insect, before you have a major outbreak on your hands. In containers or under glass, regular deadheading and dead-leaf-picking are easy ways to short-circuit many common problems. It's not difficult to tell there's something wrong with a plant once you start observing.

In the same way that you can tell that a person is out of sorts by their pasty complexion, so you can identify a troubled plant by it's lack-lustre appearance. What's not so easy is working out why it's not well. That's where the gentle art of gardening turns into something like a Sherlock Holmes plot – and some detective work is called for.

Scrubbing pots in winter might be a dreary chore, but it does make sure that pests are not transferred to plant roots right from the start.

Blow it up

You can get by without the deerstalker hat, but a magnifying glass is incredibly useful. Given a decent view, early symptoms are often all the clues you need to get on to the case. The best type of magnifying glass to use to detect plant problems is the sort that has it's own built-in light. Choose one with a large magnifying head, as those with small lenses are easy to slip into your pocket, but they don't give you a wide enough angle on the problem. You don't need huge magnification, about four times actual size is usually enough.

Odd spots on leaves may show themselves up to be clusters of baby bugs, or fluffy moulds, which are fungal diseases. Holes in fruit or vegetables, magnified to several times life size, often reveal themselves to be made by tiny rodent teeth, or boring insects. Holes in leaves may be revealed as damage caused by the rasping mouthparts of snails as opposed to the munchings of beetles.

Gather the facts

As the owner of the plant, you are in a much better position to know what might be wrong than an outside expert, to whom you describe the symptoms, or even send a sample. The reason is elementary, my dear Watson. Being on the spot, you know the plant's cultivation history, the garden situation and the local weather – especially transient occurrences, such as hailstones and late frosts; any of these may have had a bearing.

Keep your ears open. If other gardeners report early greenfly (aphids), or plagues of tomato blight, expect them to reach you, too. And if you've had trouble with blackspot, rust, clubroot or vine weevil in the past, the odds are you'll have them again. So be prepared for the worst and, who knows, you may be pleasantly surprised.

Know what to expect

Identifying plant problems is a bit like bird watching. You can safely assume that 99 per cent of what you see is quite common, so eliminate the obvious before thinking you have something unusual. It also helps to know which plants are prone to particular problems.

Roses, for instance, are martyrs to blackspot, mildew and rust (see page 218). All members of the cabbage family are affected by clubroot, and vine weevil larvae (see pages 216–17) are specially fond of cyclamen, tuberous begonias and primula roots. If you grow peaches and nectarines, you are sure to see peach leaf curl and, if you grow apples, you are bound to find the odd one with a codling moth maggot inside. There are some pests that attack almost anything, notably greenfly, slugs and snails, from which little is safe. Greenhouses are notorious as pest and disease hot-spots – the shelter offers them ideal conditions to multiply.

Don't over-react

Don't automatically rush for a spray every time you find a few pests in your garden. A small population can actually be quite a good thing, if it attracts beneficial insects or birds in to feed. When there is a healthy balance between friend and foe, natural predators build up each time pest numbers increase, so damage is kept within acceptable levels. Chemicals may solve the immediate problem, but wipe out the good bugs as well as the bad, leaving the way clear for pests to re-infest without competition. Try simple solutions, like picking pests off by hand, before you blast them with some noxious fluid.

Common foes

Sometimes you'll be able to see clearly what it is that's causing a problem with plants – a lot of snails and beetles can be caught red-handed by going out with a torch at night. But in some cases, the best way to identify the culprit, be it a pest, disease or cultural condition, is by recognizing the damage it does.

Pests

As far as a gardener is concerned, a pest is any member of the animal kingdom – from tiny eelworms to rabbits and deer – that likes to eat his plants. They can chomp, they can suck sap, they can nibble roots. And they are a real pain in the nether portions.

Snails (1)

Snails will also go for almost any soft, lush plant, though hairy or furry plants are usually fairly safe. Hostas are a particular favourite. Snails are surprisingly good at climbing, so if you see holey leaves on climbers or wall shrubs, or in containers like hanging baskets, it's probably snails; slime trails are a dead give-away. You can also tell snail damage by the way the soft green tissue of leaves is rasped away between the ribs, leaving a 'skeleton' behind – slugs eat the lot. Snails also work fast – a lot of people can't believe their eyes as new bedding plants disappear overnight.

Apart from collecting them up by hand, you can put out saucers of beer to trap them, or spray at-risk plants with yucca extract (sold in garden centres). Prickly leaves or very sharp grit can be piled around susceptible plants, but few methods are really effective. In autumn, set out empty clay flower pots under hedges for snails to hibernate in, then you can easily collect up large numbers in winter. Snails need calcium to build their shells, so they are less of a problem on acid soil – but on chalky soil, watch out. Oh, and if you remove snails from the garden, remember that they have a homing instinct. They'll travel a couple of miles in search of Chez Nous.

Slugs (2)

Slugs attack almost anything soft and lush and symptoms are similar to those of snail damage, but lower down on the plant. They are mostly found under leaves that touch the ground, or inside lettuces. Slugs are easily found by natural predators, such as frogs and toads, and they are very successfully dealt with using biological control (see pages 226–27). You can also lay down half grapefruit skins, which slugs will crawl into, and then you can throw them away.

1

Common garden pests:
1 Snails can wreak havoc in a garden, and they are adept at crossing all kinds of barriers, as my experiments have shown. Gravel, crushed eggshells, oatmeal and holly-leaf barriers will all be crossed by a snail intent on eating a tasty delphinium!

Caterpillars (3)

Caterpillars munch similar holes in leaves to those caused by slugs and snails, but caterpillars don't leave a slime trail and don't hide away so much during the day. They also leave black excrement – the polite term is frass – behind them that makes identification easier. You'll spot them quite easily, especially the tent-forming types that make dense webs around the tips of shoots, or those that live in colonies, like cabbage white caterpillars. Blackbirds eat small green caterpillars, but few birds eat large or vividly coloured caterpillars. Picking caterpillars off by hand is one of the best remedies for nuisance species like cabbage whites. But for solitary ones that don't do much harm, such as the mullein moth caterpillar, which lives on verbascum and buddleja, leave them alone and enjoy them… Oh, come on; there's more to life than worrying about a hole or two in a leaf. Moths and butterflies have just as much right to be here as we do. Take an interest in them!

Red spider mites (4)

Mainly a problem in greenhouses, or on pot plants indoors, red spider mites (usually referred to simply as 'red spider') are so tiny that you'll need a magnifying glass to see them properly. They look like animated specks of dust and they are only red in winter – the rest of the time they are buff-coloured. At first you'll see pale speckled patterns on the leaves that show where red spider has been feeding; in a bad infestation, you'll also see fine, silky webs at the tips of the shoots and on young leaves. In a very bad case, plants drop their leaves, which dry out and turn brown; 'just like autumn'. Red spider is very difficult to deal with, even when using chemicals. It's best avoided by keeping the air humid (red spider thrives in a dry atmosphere). Pick off affected leaves, or nip out shoots showing signs of webbing. Standing conservatory plants out in the garden for the summer often helps to avoid red spider mite attacks (see pages 227).

2 A grey field slug chomping his way through a pea leaf.
3 The caterpillar of the mullein moth is best tolerated; it only attacks the plants in their second year – very considerate.
4 Bleached leaves and fine webbing indicate the presence of red spider mite, which is not to be tolerated.

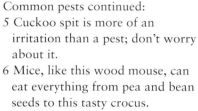

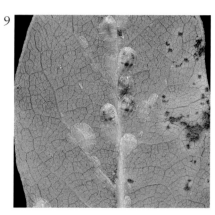

Common pests continued:

5 Cuckoo spit is more of an irritation than a pest; don't worry about it.

6 Mice, like this wood mouse, can eat everything from pea and bean seeds to this tasty crocus.

7 Ants, here in their red variety, farm greenfly and burrow under plants, sometimes causing roots to dry out.

8 The cutworm is the larva of a moth and eats plant roots, especially on the vegetable plot.

9 Scale insects are sap-suckers and cling beneath leaves, usually favouring the thicker-leaved plants that greenfly don't like.

Cuckoo spit (5)

The frothy white spittle you sometimes find on plants in early summer is a lot less sinister than it looks. It conceals the nymphs of the froghopper, which do very little harm to plants. Wash the 'spit' away with a hose if you must, but there's really no need. The adult is a positively friendly creature that'll happily walk onto your hand – it looks something like a cross between a giant aphid and a small grasshopper.

Mice (6)

The worst thing mice do in the garden is to steal big seeds, such as peas and beans – especially the early-sown ones. You'll often find a cache of stolen seeds hidden in the compost heap. They might also nibble tubers or vegetables that you've stored in your shed over winter, or newly planted bulbs, which makes them rot. It helps to sprinkle holly leaves in a row just over your pea and bean seeds, or on top of bulbs before burying them but, if you live in country areas with a big rodent population, it's a good idea to clear your compost heap away each autumn, so there's no cosy winter nesting site for them – or their larger cousins, the rats. And hang your fruit and vegetables (such as potato tubers) up in nets in the shed roof.

Ants (7)

Most of the time, ants do no harm at all apart from greenfly 'farming'; they like the sticky secretions (honeydew) that aphids leave behind, so they run a sort of protection racket. But in summer, ants make themselves unpopular with gardeners by nesting in dry soil in the lawn, in cracks between paving slabs, in rockeries, or in pots. They create conical mounds of what looks like sifted soil that's been excavated from around the roots. Though ants don't directly harm plants, their underground tunnels can leave roots dangling in thin air, so they dry out. That's what kills plants in ant-infested pots and rockeries if you don't react in time. If ants nest where there is nothing to harm, you can safely ignore them – they'll fly away after a couple of months. Otherwise, flood ants out with lots of water in early summer when they begin nesting, so they move elsewhere. Tip out ant-infested containers and wash all the larvae off the roots, then repot the plant in fresh potting compost. Better still, protect pots from ants before they start building by smearing crop-protection jelly around the sides (see page 225) – it will also deter snails, slugs and vine weevil too.

Soil pests (8)

Cutworms, leatherjackets and wireworms are the larvae of various moths, daddy-long-legs (crane fly) and click beetle respectively, and all feed on underground roots and tubers. Even if you don't see the grubs, you'll know you have them from the dead patches in the lawn, disappearing bulbs, newly planted bedding plants and vegetables suddenly separated from their roots, or holes in potatoes. Soil pests are most often found where grass has been dug up to make new beds, so if you don't want to use soil insecticide, turn the ground over several times in winter to bring pests up to the surface where birds can eat them. Or run your chickens over the patch for a few weeks first; they're a great natural way of eradicating pests, and weed seeds too. A flock of starlings pecking at the lawn is usually a sure sign of soil pests; let them finish what they are doing, then repair any damage.

Scale insects (9)

Yet another greenhouse and conservatory pest, scale insects look like tiny limpets clinging to stems or beneath leaves. They are sap-suckers but usually target the kind of plants greenfly don't like – the tougher ones with thick, waxy or evergreen leaves. Citrus plants are a special favourite. You can wipe scale insects away, then wash the leaves in tepid water to remove the sooty mould that often follows in the wake of an attack. Some species attack outdoor plants such as camellia and euonymus.

10

11

12

More common pests:

10 Blackfly are a kind of aphid – they suck sap, secrete sticky honeydew and transmit virus diseases.

11 Whitefly do the same but are more difficult to control than aphids because their young are tough little scales.

12 Vine weevil is the scourge of modern gardens. The adult weevils, with their 'elephant's trunk' mouthparts, chew the leaf edges of plants such as rhododendrons, and their larvae eat the roots of begonias, cyclamen and many other plants.

Blackfly (10)

These look like big, fat, black, greasy greenfly (see page 217), and are mostly found in summer as large, sap-sucking colonies clustered at the tips of shoots, often on elder (*Sambucus*) and bean plants – especially broad beans. As with all sap-suckers, extensive colonies weaken the plant; they'll also prevent bean pods from setting. Birds aren't very keen on them (who can blame them?), so the traditional way to shift them is to nip out the tips of broad beans once a good crop of pods has set, and as soon as you see the first blackfly. You can prune out colonies on elder without harming the plant.

Whitefly (11)

Whitefly are sap-sucking, greenhouse pests that look like minute, arrow-shaped white moths. They fly up from plants in clouds, if they are disturbed and are particularly fond of fuchsias and tomato plants. When at rest, they congregate beneath the leaves, out of the light, and it's here that you may also see the tiny, pinhead-like scales, from which the next generation hatch. One of the best ways to control whitefly is to hang yellow, sticky traps from the greenhouse roof (see biological control, pages 226–27), then shake the plants gently to get the pests flying. Or grow a tobacco plant (*Nicotiana*) in a hanging pot; the whitefly will home in on that and you can then pop it in a plastic bag to get rid of large numbers all at once. In a very hot summer, you may find greenhouse whitefly on fuchsias out in the garden, but whitefly on members of the cabbage family are a different species that only attacks brassicas (cabbage relatives).

Vine weevil (12)

Two pests for the price of one. The adult is a small, buff-brown beetle about 9mm (⅜in) long with Y-shaped antennae. It carves small notches around the edges of rhododendron leaves and other evergreens, but doesn't really do much harm; its larvae are the real problem. They are fat, white, legless grubs about 10mm (½in) long, that lie curled up in a C-shape in the soil, close to the roots of their favourite food plants. They are especially fond of primulas and cyclamen, but they'll attack other things and are very common in containers, especially on plants in soilless composts. The grubs stay safely underground, so the first thing you'll notice is a plant that quickly turns yellow and wilts – showing that it has suffered major root damage.

Once plants have been attacked, it's usually too late to do anything. To deter egg-laying adults, sprinkle a thick layer of grit around at-risk plants and destroy adult vine weevils if you see them. Repot or top dress all-year-round plants in outdoor containers each spring, and protect them with biological control (see page 227) if you've had problems with vine weevil before. A soil pesticide called Provado can be watered on to susceptible pot plants to prevent attack, and crop-protection compost containing 'Intercept' has the same effect. Both offer control for several months. Organic gardener that I am, I do occasionally use these chemicals because they are contained within pots in the greenhouse and so don't contaminate the wider environment of the garden. And vine weevils are such rotters!

Greenfly (aphids) (13)

Greenfly, or aphids, go for the softest parts of plants: the tips of shoots and the undersides of young leaves. Nearly all are female and, as they give birth to live young without being fertilized by a male (the ultimate in women's lib), one little aphid is all it takes to start a population explosion. Indoors and in heated greenhouses, greenfly are active all year round. Because they feed by sucking sap, they can spread viruses between plants by 'injecting' them with their mouthparts as they move from one plant to the next. Controlling greenfly does a lot to cut down on virus infections.

As greenfly feed, what comes out of their other end is sticky honeydew, upon which black, powdery-looking sooty mould often grows. This is a type of fungus that is not, in itself, harmful, but it is unsightly and prevents light from reaching the leaves. You can wipe greenfly off plants with your fingers (brace yourself) and wash sooty mould off with a damp cloth (and see biological control, page 227). Alternatively, let bluetits help themselves to greenfly and allow the rain to clean the plants up. But if you see sooty mould, suspect greenfly. Greenfly are often called 'blight', but are more correctly termed aphids. Aphids aren't always green, though – different species can be pink, cream, or brown, as well as grassy-green. There are other sorts as well, including blackfly, root aphids and the waxy-covered cabbage aphids.

13 Greenfly invariably attack the soft and succulent shoot tips of plants, sucking sap and spreading virus diseases.

Diseases

Diseases are plant problems caused by fungi, bacteria and viruses. The first two are especially encouraged by weather conditions – fungi love damp weather – and viruses can be transmitted by insect pests. Viruses seldom kill plants; fungi and bacteria do.

Blackspot (1)

One of the most regularly occurring fungal disease of roses, blackspot causes irregular, rounded black patches on leaves from mid-summer onwards. Other than spraying regularly with a specific fungicide all season, the best remedy is to replace badly affected roses with varieties that have some natural disease resistance. Even they will get a little blackspot in a summer that's warm, humid and overcast – ideal fungus weather – but pick up and burn dead leaves at the end of the season to reduce the risk.

Powdery mildew (2)

This is a very common fungal disease that looks like a light dusting of talcum powder over the upper sides of younger leaves. It affects all sorts of outdoor and greenhouse plants, particularly roses, and plants that are regularly short of water. You can help to avoid an outbreak of powdery mildew by mulching and feeding plants in spring, and by watering thoroughly in long, dry spells. In severe cases, pick off badly affected leaves and burn them.

Rust (3)

Rust looks like rust on ironwork – powdery reddish brown spots. Most rusts are specific to a particular species of plant, so if you have rust on your roses, it won't affect your leeks. Rose fungicides are fairly effective, especially if you opt for the latest kinds, but grow disease-resistant varieties if you want to avoid spraying. On plants like pelargonium, prune out affected stems, or burn and replace the plants; some rose fungicides are also suitable for use on other ornamental plants, so check the instructions. It's not worth spraying leeks – simply peel away the rusty outer leaves and eat the rest, but don't put rusted material on the compost heap. Hollyhocks are martyrs to rust, so they're best raised anew from seed each year.

Grey mould (botrytis) (4)

This is the fungal disease responsible for fluffy grey patches on dead or dying leaves and flowers in dull, damp weather, but also causes 'ghost-spotting' (small, round, translucent spots) on tomatoes. It's very common in humid greenhouses in winter, when light levels are low and there is little air circulation. Prevent grey

Expert diagnosis

If you have a pest or disease problem you can't identify, even with the help of a well-illustrated book, there are several places to find help. Members of your local horticultural club may know the answer; there may be an adviser at a large local garden centre, or, if you are going to a big gardening event, like the Chelsea Flower Show or Gardeners' World Live, it's worth taking a specimen with you to show to one of the experts at the gardening clinics held there.

mould by picking over pot and container plants regularly to remove dead leaves and flowers. Space plants out, so there's room for air to circulate, and ventilate the greenhouse whenever you can.

Brown rot (5)

A spectacular rot affecting fruit including plums, apples, pears and crab apples. It rapidly turns the whole fruit brown with concentric rings of raised white spots. Pick off infected fruits and burn them, or put them in the dustbin – not on the compost heap – and don't leave infected fruits lying around because they'll be a source of more fungal spores for next year.

Coral spot (6)

Virulent-looking, raised, coral-red spots on dead or dying wood. Avoid coral spot by pruning properly, just above a healthy bud or leaf joint, so you don't leave short stumps that die back and let fungal infections like this in. It can be a rampant spreader, so prune it out promptly – back to clean healthy wood – to avoid any spread back into living material. Burn infected prunings; don't put them on to the compost heap.

Common plant diseases:

1 Blackspot is a common disease of roses – especially those with thin leaves.
2 Mildew can attack all sorts of plants, especially those already under stress.
3 Rose rust is best avoided by growing disease-resistant varieties.
4 Grey mould loves a damp environment and will often attack damaged tissue.
5 Brown rot attacks fruits, displaying its tell-tale concentric rings of fungal pustules.
6 Coral spot is a fungus that attacks dead or dying wood.

Cultural conditions

If there's an advantage to pests and diseases, it's that you have something tangible to blame. But not all plant problems are a result of predatory organisms. Some of the cultural conditions that beset plants are what you might call 'acts of God' – late frosts, hurricanes and hailstorms – which are beyond your control. But most of the things that go wrong with plants that aren't pests or diseases normally boil down to a simple failure to provide the correct set of growing conditions, so if you can't find any other reason for plant problems, double check its soil and situation, as well as basic lapses in your tender loving care.

Frost damage

Young shoots that suddenly look like they've been hit by a flame thrower – shrivelled and turning black – are usually a symptom of a late frost. The damage is quite commonly seen in spring, if there's a sudden cold snap after the buds have burst and new leaves have started to open. If a late frost is forecast, drape plants in several layers of horticultural fleece to avoid damage. Otherwise, wait until you can see which bits of affected plants are dead and which are alive, then prune affected stems back to healthy growth. You'll know shoots are dead if they snap cleanly instead of bending, and, when cut, they will be brown or buff-coloured beneath the bark. Living, healthy shoots are flexible and are green beneath the bark.

Classic frost damage (*left*) on a rose. The unfurling leaf looks as though it has been burned, when, actually, the opposite is true – it has been frozen. Wind damage here on garrya (*right*), is similar in its effect – it causes drying out and browning of tissue.

Wind

Wind can also cause a scorched appearance, and young growth is most vulnerable, as it's soft. Wind-burn grows out in time, but if a delicate plant is grown in a windy location, it'll never be very happy. Make sure that wind-hating plants, such as Japanese maples, are grown in a sheltered spot.

Wilting

Most people rush to water a wilting plant, but dry soil is not always the problem. A waterlogged plant that has lost its tiny root hairs will also wilt, as it can't take up water, as will one that has lost its roots because of soil pests. Always investigate further before jumping to conclusions.

Toadstools

Mostly harmless, toadstools usually appear in mild, misty autumns and feed on rotting organic matter, often in lawns, or on soil that's recently been enriched with mushroom compost or manure. They disappear naturally after the first frost. Fairy rings in lawns are something you learn to live with, unless you're prepared to dig out the soil to a depth of 45cm (1½ft) to remove all the thread-like underground mycelium (the fungal equivalent of roots), then fill the hole with new topsoil before laying new turf or re-seeding.

Bracket fungi on trunks of old trees are often an early sign of a specimen that's on its way out. But the ones to watch out for are clumps of small, ochre-yellow toadstools on the ground close to dying trees or shrubs, especially if there are black 'bootlaces' present in nearby soil, or beneath the bark. Then it's worth suspecting honey fungus (*armillaria*), which can be a real killer. It needs expert diagnosis to confirm it for sure; but if it's in the area, your neighbours will probably know all about it. Dig up and burn infected plant roots and prevent attack by keeping plants growing well – feeding and regular manuring help to build up health and resistance.

Toadstools grow on rotting plant material – often old tree roots. I find that the best thing to do is (a) admire them or (b) sweep them off. They don't last long anyway.

Nursing sick plants

Faced with plants that are a bit under-the-weather, a lot of people find it easier to cut their losses and replace them. It's certainly the quick solution to the problem, but it can be expensive and, let's face it, if you love plants, there's a great sense of satisfaction in nursing casualties back to health.

Dealing with a dehydrated plant

One of the commonest plant disasters is the dried-out hanging basket, or the forgotten pot plant. You only spot it when the leaves are hanging down accusingly over the sides of the container. Often, normal watering doesn't hit the spot, because dried-out potting compost shrinks (especially the soilless types), leaving gaps at the sides of the container, so that water applied subsequently runs straight through without soaking in. The answer is to stand the container in 5cm (2in) or so of water for a couple of hours – no longer, or the plant can 'drown'. By then, the potting compost should have soaked up as much water as it can hold, and you can let the excess drain away. Never leave a plant standing in water, or you'll create a continuous cycle of waterlogging that gives the root hairs no chance of making a full recovery.

A light diet

The first thing most people want to do with a sickly plant is feed it, because the leaves look pale, but it's usually the worst thing you can do. The best remedy is a few weeks on an invalid diet. When a plant is under the weather, it isn't working properly; don't add to its stress by making it cope with fertilizer. No, not even liquid feed. And go easy on the watering, unless it's obvious that the only thing wrong with the plant is that it has dried out.

If your sick plant is in a pot and it has suffered root damage due to soil pests or waterlogging, then water it only sparingly for about four weeks. This gives new root hairs time to grow. If the plant normally likes moist air around it, increase the humidity by standing it in a loose plastic bag with a few holes punched in it, or put it in a propagating case; it's a good 'intensive care unit' that will help it to survive until new roots grow.

Otherwise, deal with the cause of the problem and give the plant time to recover naturally before resuming normal feeding and watering. If you really want to give a recovering plant a real shot in the arm, then spray it once a week with foliar feed. This is the quickest way of getting nutrients into it – especially if the roots are a bit suspect – and it usually regains a healthy colour quite rapidly. Don't be tempted to spray on any old feed – foliar feeds contain only nutrients that can be taken in through the leaves, and they are very dilute, so there's no risk of scorching.

You'll be able to tell when your nursing has done the trick, because the patient will start to look plumper and glossier and begin making new growth. In the case of a potted plant, you really know that you've won if you see healthy, white, young roots around the edge of the rootball when you gently tip the plant out of its pot.

The kindest cut

In some cases, a spot of surgery can be just what the doctor ordered. Reducing the size of a large plant can help its chances of survival when it's lost a lot of roots for any reason, because removing the leafy top means it's no longer losing water faster that it can take it up. It stands a better chance of recovering – and it'll soon make up the missing growth. As a rule of thumb, aim to cut back the top by a third or a half, if this can be done without wrecking the plant.

Pruning often makes a damaged plant look better in a hurry. If a bushy plant has been broken, or the young shoots have been distorted by a bad attack of greenfly, then cutting it back has the same effect as 'stopping' it (see pages 179–80 and 181), and encourages a rapid flush of sideshoots.

Plants that are well fed and watered are always much more likely to stay healthy in the face of pest and disease attack.

Non-chemical controls

In the past, spraying was seen as a magic wand for waving away any kind of plant problem but, today, there are all sorts of other controls that are often just as effective as chemicals and more environmentally responsible. The advantage of these techniques is that you don't eliminate the beneficial bugs along with the bad guys.

Organic alternatives

Organic gardeners prefer to avoid problems in the first place, so they'll screen vegetables from pests using barriers; they might trap pests, or pick them off by hand, or encourage natural predators by companion planting (see organic gardening, pages 164–68).

But use even 'organic' insecticides with care. Although many are non-persistent and environmentally friendly, some are simply 'organic hammers' which are non-selective in their action.

Insecticidal soap, or soft soap, isn't the kind you use in your bath, but a special soap based on fatty acids. It's sold as a liquid that you spray on to pests. Use it against aphids, red spider mites, and whitefly; it's one of the few really effective remedies for cabbage aphids, as it can 'soak in' through their natural waxy coating.

Beneficial bacteria, in concentrated form, are available in various products for different purposes. There are those that clear your pond, make your compost heap rot down faster, treat stored rain or bath water in a barrel so that it can be recycled on to the garden. Some products are used to increase the natural level of beneficial micro-organisms in the soil and they help make a healthier root environment; particularly useful when converting to organic gardening.

Bordeaux mixture contains slaked lime and copper sulphate made into a sprayable liquid. Use it for peach leaf curl, tomato and potato blight and various fungal diseases of soft fruit.

Green and yellow sulphur dust is good for powdering on stored bulbs to prevent rotting and can also be dusted on to the wound, if you have to cut out a rotten bit of bulb. It is also good for controlling powdery mildew on plants, but use a light puff – don't drench them in dust. Sprayable sulphur products are sometimes available, which are easier to use accurately on plants, and you can also buy sulphur candles to burn if you want to fumigate your greenhouse.

If you really must spray, then choose an environmentally friendly product and follow the manufacturer's directions precisely. Never add 'one for the pot'.

Crop-protection jelly, or barrier glue, is sticky gunge you apply round the rims of containers, the legs of greenhouse staging, or the bark of trees to protect against crawling pests, like snails, winter moth caterpillars, vine weevil adults, ants and woodlice, which don't like to cross it.

Derris is a natural product, in that it's active ingredient, rotenone, comes from tropical plants. But although it's pretty effective against aphids, caterpillars and thrips, it is non-specific in its action (killing the goodies as well as the baddies) and has recently been found to be far more toxic to humans than was originally thought. I'd avoid it.

Aluminium sulphate, while not acceptable to real organic purists, is a more environmentally acceptable alternative than using slug pellets to tackle slugs and snails – but look out for other, even greener, products such as aerosol sprays based on yucca extract, and copper barrier strips that give molluscs a minute 'electric shock'.

Liquid seaweed extract, used as an addition to liquid feeds or sprayed on as a foliar feed, is thought by many organic enthusiasts to act as a natural tonic by supplying trace elements. They often use it to treat sick plants, as well as to boost the natural defences of healthy ones.

Natural disinfectants are available that are made from citrus extracts, which are handy for cleaning up soil and pots or seed trays.

Pyrethrum is also derived from plants, in this case, the flowers of a type of chrysanthemum, and it's used against aphids.

Rape seed oil is the active ingredient of a natural insecticide that works by blocking up the breathing holes in the skin of small insects, such as aphids, leaving bigger beneficial kinds, such as ladybirds, hoverflies and lacewings, unharmed.

Crop protection jelly smeared around the rim of a pot will act as a barrier to slugs and snails and other crawling pests.

One plant will often distract pests from another. Aphids will home in on nasturtiums in preference to gooseberries – well it's worth a try!

Biological control

Biological control means really waging war on pests, because what you do is unleash a very powerful living enemy against them. Each biological control 'agent' tackles one particular pest and, although they aren't cheap, results are at least as good as using chemicals, and last longer.

The idea was originally developed for commercial glasshouses, where specially introduced insects can't fly away, but there are now several biological control agents, including beneficial nematodes (eelworms) that can be used very successfully in garden soil, or in containers outside.

At home, biological control is particularly worthwhile if you have a conservatory or greenhouse where you want to tackle all the common pests without using chemicals, or if you have a salad bed to protect from slugs, or containers that you want to protect from vine weevil.

Using biological control agents

Introduce biological controls under glass early in the season, as soon as the temperature is warm enough for them, as they can't overtake a major plague of pests. You'll need to send off for the relevant 'agent' by post. Various suppliers advertise in gardening magazines and some products can be ordered through garden centres. Use them within a few days of delivery because, being living organisms, they don't keep.

Glasshouse insects are usually delivered as eggs in phials of vermiculite, or as scales on cards to hang up among your plants – always place them near a group of pests, so that there's a fast food supply for the emerging biological control agents.

Beneficial nematodes are delivered freeze-dried, so you have to reconstitute them in water and apply them to the soil through a watering can at the correct rate. But they all come with full instructions and it's essential to read these first to get it right.

Caterpillars can be killed by introducing a caterpillar disease called *Bacillus thuringiensis* on to the foliage on which they are feeding. Treated caterpillars take a few days to die, but stop feeding very quickly. This bacterium is normally used outdoors, but only exactly where it's needed. It can kill caterpillars of desirable butterfly species too, so it's not a favourite of mine.

Scale insects, mealybugs and thrips under glass can also be wiped out with specific biological controls; they are available from a few specialist suppliers, so you'll need to seek them out.

Greenfly can be controlled under glass by introducing a parasitic 'fly' called *Aphidius*. It lays its eggs in young aphids, which turn into brown 'cases', from each of which a new aphidius hatches out. You can also buy lacewing and ladybird larvae to use in the greenhouse, or to let loose in the garden, to boost your natural population.

Red spider mite can be kept under control with the help of an aggressive predatory mite called *Phytosieulus persimilis*. A warmth-loving creature, it's no use introducing it unless the greenhouse temperature stays above 16°C (61°F) at night. Unless you're prepared to put on the heating, delay introduction until late spring.

Slugs are a real biological control success story. The slug parasite *Phasmarhabditis hermaphrodita*, is a nematode that commonly occurs in the wild, so, by increasing the numbers in your patch, you are simply fortifying natural defences. Use the parasite from mid-spring onwards, when the soil is warm (above 5°C/40°F) and moist. By wiping out your existing slugs, you also ensure there are no eggs in the soil to start up the next generation. Although the vendors claim that the product lasts six weeks or so, many people have found that it takes about a year before the slug population recovers fully in treated areas. It doesn't work on snails, because snails don't spend enough time on the ground, and it's not as effective on cold clay soil. Though not cheap, its often the answer when nothing else works. And if birds eat an affected slug, they aren't harmed by toxins which they pick up from slugs that have eaten slug pellets.

Vine weevil larvae are tracked down by a species of beneficial nematode, *Heterorhabditis*. Apply by watering the diluted nematode 'soup' onto soil or compost outdoors in late spring, early summer and early autumn, when larvae are most likely to be present. Use it under glass at any time; the pests have a longer breeding season in warmth. If no larvae are present at the time of application, the nematode will die out.

Whitefly are commonly controlled under glass by a tiny parasitic wasp called *Encarsia formosa*. It lays its eggs in the whitefly 'scales', so that instead of a young whitefly hatching, out pops another encarsia to keep up the good work. For best results, introduce three batches of encarsia at two-week intervals. There's also another whitefly predator called *Delphastus* that is a relative of the ladybird. This is claimed to be more efficient at tackling larger outbreaks.

Physical controls, like this sticky, yellow fly-catching paper, though not strictly biological, are an effective way of checking for whitefly in a greenhouse, and contain no chemical residues.

Gardeners' friends

There are plenty of creatures out there that'll be only too happy to make a meal of your garden pests for free. What's more, you don't have to do much to attract them. Stop using chemicals and create a reasonably undisturbed environment where there's food, water and somewhere to shelter – especially for the winter – and they'll find you all on their own.

Birds

Robins, I reckon, hatch out knowing that a gardener plus a spade equals lunch – they and blackbirds are the natural answer to soil grubs, but they'll also take caterpillars and all sorts of nuisances. The thrush's speciality is snails – thrushes use a handy stone as an anvil to smash the shells against, so they can get at the filling inside. Bluetits are like security patrols against greenfly; they'll do the rounds of your roses and fruit trees regularly in spring when they have chicks to feed. Wrens take lots of insects from hedges and are also very keen on the thunderflies and springtails that often live in and around compost heaps.

The way to attract birds to your garden is to feed them in winter with seeds, peanuts and fat, but make sure there are plenty of trees and shrubs to offer cover so that they can escape from predators. It's also a good idea to grow plants that provide seed heads and berries that birds can feed on in autumn. Provide a supply of clean water all the time, and some nest boxes, and you'll have the makings of a thriving resident bird population.

The wise gardener has more than a romantic attachment to the robin and other insect-eating garden birds, as they play an important part in pest control.

Mammals

Larger creatures play their part in the life of the garden, too, eating unwanted pests. Encourage wildlife by providing undisturbed areas for small mammals to take refuge in. Leave a few rotting logs in a patch of long grass among shrubs, and they might be persuaded to move in. Even if they don't, they are likely to at least pass through or wander around a quiet garden... if they are in the area.

Hedgehogs are good snail hunters, and their antics are fun to watch in the summer garden. If you put out a saucer of cat food for them, they'll learn to appear at the same place on time every evening, but don't give them bread and milk – it's not good for them because they can't digest it and so it upsets their stomachs.

Foxes are something gardeners don't always welcome, but when they are well fed, they rarely dig holes in the garden or do over the dustbin, and usually just pass through. Again they are fun to watch, and they'll eat snails and grubs as well as any scraps of pet food that you put out.

Friend or foe?

Some insects that gardeners traditionally treat as enemies turn out to have some beneficial tendencies as well.

- **Earwigs** are best-known for nibbling flower petals, but they also do a lot of good by feeding on greenfly and other small insects. Only among flowers like dahlias do they wreak real havoc. Encourage them to linger in places where they can do some good, by stuffing flowerpots with straw and perching them on top of short sticks.
- **Wasps** only go for sweet things at the peak of the plum season; the rest of the time they take aphids and small caterpillars for their larvae to feed on. As long as their nest isn't somewhere it's going to be a nuisance, then leave it alone.
- **Woodlice** have a bad reputation as eaters of seedlings, but it's debatable whether they damage strong healthy ones and, when you find them inside holes in fruit, it's unlikely that they did the initial damage – they are more likely to be using the hole, originally made by a slug, to shelter in.

Pond life

If you do nothing else to encourage wildlife, put in a pond – even if it's only a small one – as long as it has at least one shallow, sloping edge. Birds will visit to take a bath, and a whole range of wildlife will drop in for a drink. But you'll also attract frogs and toads, which are among the very best natural controls for slugs. The adults don't spend all their time in the water, they wander around between plants hunting for snacks.

A garden pond will encourage all manner of beneficial wildlife that will do its best to help with general pest control.

Beneficial insects

For many years, gardeners were brought up with the idea that the only good bug is a dead one, but attitudes have changed, which is good for the garden, as lots of insects help by hunting down plant pests. Attract the adults by growing nectar-rich hardy annuals, lavenders and flowering herbs. Poached egg plant (*Limnanthes douglasii*), *Phacelia campanularia* and *Convolvulus tricolor* are particularly good. And do learn to recognise the larvae as well; for years people went around bumping off ladybird larvae without realizing what they were.

Encourage beneficial insects to stay in the garden in winter. Don't clear your perennial beds properly until spring, so they have lots of safe hiding places. If you must tidy up, leave a fringe of long grass and plant stems around the edge of the garden, so that beneficial bugs are on the spot, ready to go to work when they emerge in spring.

How do you tell a good bug from a bad one? If it moves slowly, it eats plants; if it moves fast, it eats other insects. Obvious really!

Ground beetles (1), rove beetles, black beetles, call them what you will (there are several different types), are all well worth making friends with. They live in soil, under stones or logs and in debris under hedges, and feed on slugs, cabbage root fly, flea beetles, weevils and other soil pests. Their larvae have a similar diet, so the whole family does a lot of good. They're easily distinguished from vine weevils. Good beetles are generally black, shiny and move fast; they have two separate antennae on the front of their heads – bad vine weevils are smaller, buff-brown and have Y-shaped antennae. A black beetle with a purplish tinge is probably a violet ground beetle – another goody.

Ichneumon flies (2) lay their eggs in the caterpillars of the large white butterfly caterpillars (alias cabbage whites) – the ones that reduce members of the cabbage family and nasturtiums to lace – and parasitize them, which prevents them turning into new butterflies.

Lacewings (3) look like transparent-winged greenish moths. Both the adults and larvae eat aphids and other small pests. If you find them, leave them to hibernate in the shed in winter. To encourage them to stay in your garden all year, you can buy lacewing 'hotels' made of bundles of hollow cow parsley stems mounted in a frame.

Hoverflies (4) are those stripy jobs that look like slim-line wasps, except that they don't sting and they have a remarkable ability to hover on the spot. Both the adults and the larvae take huge numbers of aphids from early summer onwards, once the sunny weather sets in.

Spiders (5) are great hunters and trappers; the wolf spider is the one you sometimes see sunbathing on a leaf with its two pairs of front legs stretched out together – they run down insect prey. Web-forming spiders catch flying insects, and even tiny money spiders feed on aphids. Harvestmen, which look like small-bodied, long-legged spiders, take newly hatched caterpillars and woodlice. If you catch them indoors, put them out in the garden.

Ladybirds (6) come in red or yellow, and with varying numbers of spots; both the adults and larvae take huge numbers of aphids. Ladybird numbers are slow to build up in summer; in winter, they hibernate in large 'roosts' under hedges.

Velvet mites (7) look like minute, bright red money spiders; you sometimes see them scurrying around in hot, dry corners – they are a natural predator of many small insects, including red spider mite.

Centipedes (8) are the flattish, red-brown, fast-moving creatures that snake their way through moist leaf litter and debris, hunting for springtails, mites, slugs and other insects. The slow-moving, tubular black jobs, with waves of rippling legs, are millipedes which eat plants.

Beneficial insects:
1 Ground beetles polish off all manner of soil pests.
2 Ichneumon flies lay their eggs inside caterpillars – gruesome but very welcome.
3 Lacewings are aphid eaters.
4 Hoverflies eat large quantities of aphids.
5 Spiders feed on all kinds of insects, from greenfly to house flies.
6 Ladybirds eat aphids – very helpful.
7 Velvet mites feed on pests such as red spider mite.
8 Centipedes are fast movers who will demolish everything from slugs to mites.

Using chemicals

Chemicals are, to my mind, very much a last resort. I am very rarely persuaded to reach for a bottle if the only alternative is losing a good plant. If you feel the same, the one thing I'd say is don't use anything more powerful than you really need. If there's a product that tackles the specific problem, then use it. It will have less impact on the rest of the garden community than a broad spectrum product that kills lots of things. Only treat the affected plant – don't blitz the whole garden. In extreme circumstances, I think it's far more responsible to use a specific inorganic pesticide than a non-selective organic one.

Types of product

A glance at the chemicals department of a big garden centre can be daunting, as there are so many bottles, packets, pots and potions on sale. But they fall into several categories, so look out for key words:

Systemic products are taken up into the sap stream of the plant and move around inside it. Systemic weedkillers are taken in through the leaves and kill the roots as well as the leaves and stems. Systemic insecticides kill sap-sucking insects for some time after treatment, so one spray can protect plants from attack for two weeks or so.

Contact products work only on what they touch. They kill leaves but not roots. Contact insecticides only kill those pests that get sprayed. With these, it's vital to cover the whole plant thoroughly.

Stomach-acting insecticides work by being sprayed on to plants and then eaten by pests along with the leaves, so they are good for killing munching bugs like caterpillars.

Combined products contain a cocktail of ingredients. Path weedkillers, for example, usually contain one chemical to kill off existing weeds and another to kill emerging seedlings. Some rose fungicides contain several ingredients to treat different diseases, plus a greenfly killer or foliar feed. Combined weedkillers and fertilizers are available, usually as lawn 'feed and weed'.

Total weedkillers kill everything green that they touch.

Selective weedkillers 'choose' what they work on; the only example of this type of product is selective lawn weedkiller that kills broad-leaved weeds and leaves grasses unharmed.

Stay safe

The important thing when using any kind of chemical is to read, understand and follow the instructions. Safety must always come first, so I make no apologies for nagging.

Check the harvest interval before using a pesticide on edible crops. It tells you how many days have to elapse between spraying the product and eating treated fruit or vegetables. You can't put treated produce in the freezer to bring out after the harvest interval is up – that doesn't count.

Read the small print to see if the plants you want to spray are unsuitable for treatment with that product, to avoid damage. If you make a mistake, wash the plant off well and flush the compost or soil through with plenty of water.

Concentrated liquid products *must* be diluted for application, whether by sprayer or watering can. The directions often assume you need large amounts of the diluted product, so calculating the right dose for small areas can be tricky. If you know you're not a wizz at mental arithmetic, work it out on paper, or use a calculator. Once diluted, chemicals don't keep, so only make up as much as you need and dispose of any surplus safely (see below).

Stick to the dilution rates given in the instructions. Avoid using products at a stronger dilution than suggested – far from working better, they are usually less effective.

Avoid the use of weedkillers just before it rains; most need at least 12 hours in contact with the leaves to be absorbed properly.

Safety with chemicals

- **Do** wear rubber gloves and cover any exposed skin when applying garden chemicals.
- **Do** wear safety goggles or a visor when mixing liquids to avoid chemicals splashing into your eyes.
- **Don't** breathe in the spray.
- **Don't** spray in windy conditions, as droplets can reach plants you didn't mean to treat. Protect nearby plants if you're using weedkiller, even in still conditions.
- **Don't** decant products out of their original container, or use anything that's lost its label; you won't know what it is, or how to use it.
- **Don't** tip unwanted chemicals down the drain. Even if there's only a bit left, dilute it as per instructions and water it thinly over a patch of gravel or vacant ground. For advice on disposing of larger quantities, contact your local authority; they have arrangements for dealing with what they call hazardous household waste.

8 THE GREEN CARPET

Grass in gardens

To most people, grass is 'outdoor carpet', as indispensable in the garden as wall-to-wall Wilton in the living room. Yes, fashions change and hard surfaces – paving, gravel and decking – are on the increase outdoors, in much the same way as seagrass matting, or polished wood floors, are indoors. But there are very few gardens that don't have at least a small patch of lawn.

There's something about a striped lawn that brings out the Brit in me – it's afternoon tea on the lawn, the crack of the croquet ball and the evening song of the blackbird.

Grass is still the cheapest and most traditional outdoor floor covering, particularly for large areas, so it's easy to take it for granted. But don't think of it as a self-renewing carpet; see it instead as thousands of tiny individual plants growing tightly packed together in each square metre of soil. It is not maintenance-free. Although grass doesn't take quite so much time and effort as a border, it still needs looking after.

Which grass?

When I was a lad, you had two sorts of grass. In the back garden, you had your everyday stuff dotted with springy heads of ryegrass that popped up from under the mower instead of being chopped off – just like that lump of hair on the back of your head that wouldn't lie down. Out front was the posh lawn that you kept off; it was there to impress the neighbours. Both had the perfect stripes that were created by using a cylinder mower, and woe betide you if your lines were wavy.

Things have come a long way since then. Today's lawn is a much more natural style of grass that the family can use to the full for outdoor activities. Weeds are no longer a dirty word and, to some gardeners, are even classed as desirable wild flowers to be welcomed. Stripes have almost vanished now that so many of us have rotary mowers, and you'll sometimes find 'feature' lawns that don't contain any grass at all, but are covered with herbs or flowers instead (see pages 255–57).

Yet despite all the emphasis on contemporary design and trendy hard surfaces, people are still making new lawns. Modern strains of ornamental ryegrasses are bred for looks, compactness and hard-wearing qualities, so you have the best of both worlds, without the stiff seed heads that made 1950s lawns so uncomfortable to sit on. You'll find various grass seed mixtures: some suitable for damp, shady areas; others for dry, sunny spots; some slow-growing 'low maintenance' blends, and other mixtures with wildflower seed added. On the turf front, you can choose from several grades of cultivated turf, which are farmed as a crop, or you can use meadow turf, which is stripped from a pasture (see page 238).

Nowadays, many people have several types of lawn; they'll have distinct areas – perhaps a patch of 'best', with grassy paths, rough turf for the kids and dogs to play on, maybe a feature lawn or a wildflower meadow. At Barleywood, I have a bit of everything, but the greensward binds everything together in a kind of verdant unity.

Sports turf

Not many people would really want a lawn 'like a bowling green' if they knew what was involved. Proper sports turf needs colossal amounts of maintenance because it's trying to do two things: provide a hard, flat playing surface that stands lots of wear, while growing grass that is cut almost daily to keep it about 1cm (½in) high. That's why clubs employ groundsmen to do all the maintenance – the rolling, serious slashing of the lawn's surface and regular reseeding – none of which you'd want to do at home (and frankly you shouldn't need to).

What a lawn does better than any other surface is to bring together all the elements of the garden.

Lay turf as soon as possible after arrival and within a month or two you'll have a usable lawn.

Turf

Turf is pre-grown grass, which is cut from the ground ready for you to unroll as an instant lawn. Cultivated turf gives a good quality lawn, but meadow turf (possibly with weeds or bare patches) is cheaper. Once turf has rooted into your soil, you can treat it as a normal lawn. But, be prepared to water it, if the weather is dry. If you lay turf in early autumn, there should be plenty of rainfall to do the job for you.

You order turf by the square metre. It is delivered in strips measuring about 100 x 30cm (3 x 1ft), rolled up so that it's easier to handle. Arrange to have it delivered just before you want to lay it; if you can't get on with the job for two to three days, don't leave it rolled up. Unroll the turves and lay them flat, with the grass exposed to the light, and water them, if necessary. If you leave your turf rolled up, it will turn custard-yellow in a matter of days. It will look vile, be weakened as a result, and may die out in places.

How to... **make a lawn from turf**

The great advantage of laying turf is that one day you have what looks like a building site, and the next you have a lawn. You're not limited as to timing either. You can lay turf for eight months of the year; from early autumn to late spring, as long as the ground is in a fit state – not too dry, frozen solid, or boggy. Don't risk putting it down in summer, although you might get away with it if the weather is cool and wet and you keep it heavily watered. Busy folk tend to forget and, before they know it, their green carpet tiles have shrunk and turned brown at the edges.

Fast results come at a price. Turf is ten times more expensive than grass seed and, if you go for the cultivated sort, it costs about the same as good carpet. Turf is fast but, although it looks the part straight away, don't walk on it until it has rooted down into the soil and started to grow.

What you need

- *sharp spade and garden fork*
- *garden rake*
- *special lawn fertilizer or autumn lawn feed (without mosskiller or weedkiller)*
- *rolls of turf, enough to cover the area*
- *wooden plank*
- *sharp kitchen knife*

1 Dig or fork the ground over in the same way as if you were preparing a new flower bed (see page 66). Rake it roughly level, removing stones and roots as you go. Sprinkle on fertilizer at the recommended rate and rake it in. Tread the whole area over, sinking your weight well down into your heels to consolidate the soft patches. Rake again to cover the footprints, leaving a fine seed-sowing 'tilth'.

2 Without walking on the prepared ground, lay a line of turves in a straight row along one end of the area, butting their short sides up together. Pat down with the rake head, so that each turf makes contact with the soil beneath.

To avoid making footprints and dents, place your plank on the turf row you've just laid and walk along it as you lay the next row, staggering the joints between the turves like joints in brickwork. Repeat, patting each new row down with the rake.

3 When you've covered the whole area, trim the outer edge of the turfed area with a sharp kitchen knife, so the lawn edge follows the shape of your beds.

If it doesn't rain for several days after laying, turn the sprinkler on. Repeat every few days until the turf has knitted into the ground. To test, try to peel back the corner of a few random turves – if you can't lift them, then the grass has rooted down.

How to... **make a lawn from seed**

Growing grass from seed costs a lot less than using turf (see pages 238–39), but there are only a couple of windows of opportunity for successful sowing; mid-spring (April–May in the UK) and mid-autumn (September–early October). It takes 4–6 months before you have a usable lawn, so most people sow in autumn. It gives new grass a whole winter to turn into a proper lawn before heavy demands are made upon it. It also means natural rainfall keeps your grass seed watered – sowing just before the start of summer makes it much more likely that you'll need to use a sprinkler while the new lawn establishes. Weed seedlings are also less of a problem in autumn than in spring. On balance, although you have to wait longer for a lawn from seed, it's less arduous than laying turf.

What you need

- *digging spade and fork*
- *garden rake*
- *special pre-seeding lawn fertilizer or autumn lawn feed (without mosskiller or weedkiller)*
- *grass seed: allow 25–50g per 1sq.m (1–2oz per sq.yd)*
- *twiggy pea-sticks, if birds are a problem*

1 Prepare the ground in the same way as if you were laying turf (see page 239): dig or fork over, rake, spread fertilizer, rake, tread and rake some more. You are aiming to produce a level, evenly firmed seedbed, which will lead to a level lawn.

2 Divide the total amount of grass seed in half. Sprinkle one lot north-south, then repeat, this time spreading east-west. You don't have to take a compass to it, but the general idea is to make sure the seed is spread very thinly and evenly all over, with no bare patches.

3 Rake over the area again very lightly, starting at the far end of the 'lawn', scuffling the seed into the ground. You won't cover all of the seed – expect to see about half of it still showing when you've finished. Most grass seed is treated with bird repellent but, if you anticipate a problem, lay twiggy pea-sticks over the ground to prevent birds from taking dust baths.

And after?

It's quite exciting watching grass seed come up – in a rather Zen-like way. For days there's nothing but bare earth but, after a couple of weeks of mild weather, crouch down and look across the surface of the soil and you'll see a green haze over the ground that will rapidly turn into green stubble. Water, if you need to, and keep off the new grass while it's looking a bit thin and wispy. Don't worry about lots of weeds coming up – that's quite normal, and they won't stand a chance once you start cutting the grass.

As the lawn starts to thicken up and once the longest tufts are 5–8cm (2–3in) long, cut the grass very gently with a mower set high enough to take only the tips off the grass blades. Remember: all you are trying to do is take the tips off the grass, which helps it to root in more firmly and makes the grass seedlings bush out and develop into tiny clumps. Make sure your mower is sharp, or it will rip the young plants from the earth rather than scissoring off the ends of the leaves.

For the first proper cut, choose a day when the grass has dried out completely: if it's wet, the blades will, again, just tear and pull bits up instead of cutting cleanly. Adjust the mower so that the blades are at their highest setting, and leave the grass box on to catch the clippings.

Apart from essential cultivation, keep off the grass until it has been cut several times and starts to look like a proper lawn. Keep the blades set high for the first few cuts, then lower them gradually, but don't cut any shorter than 3cm (1¼in) to start with. The good news is that within the first few cuts virtually all the weeds will disappear as if by magic. If you find typical lawn weeds, such as daisies (see page 143) and plantains, pull them up by hand or wait for six months or more, then you can start to use normal lawn weedkillers, or combined fertilizer and weedkiller treatments – not before.

If you have a small lawn, make it an even shape that is easily mowed, then maintenance will not become a problem.

Under the surface

Lawns are a bit like swans – the top may look serene but, below the surface, there's a lot of frantic activity going on. Here's a worm's-eye view of the sort of situations your grass has to put up with as it grows older.

Thatch

Thatch is a build-up of dead bits of grass and tough horizontal stalks that knit together on the surface of the soil beneath the lawn like a fibrous underlay. You can check for it very easily by cutting a small square of grass out of your lawn and looking at it edgeways on – thatch is the straw-like layer between the roots and the green leaf blades. Thatch is quite natural in lawns that are getting on a bit, and a lot of people – mistakenly – think that the springy surface of a badly affected lawn is a sign of quality. It isn't. The trodden-down thatch acts like a spongy umbrella, preventing rain from soaking down to the grass roots, where it's needed, and keeping moisture at the soil surface, where it encourages moss.

You probably won't have any trouble with thatch until your lawn has been down for five years or more, but it builds up faster if you don't use a grass box on your mower. Once it's there, it needs raking out regularly. Autumn is the best time to do this, as part of a regular lawn-care programme (see page 251).

Surface compaction

This is another regular problem to expect once lawns have been in place for a few years. It's the frequent trampling that does the damage. When the ground is wet, it's softer than usual, so your feet sink in, and standing garden furniture on it, or running heavy barrows over it, squashes the lawn down badly. Then, as with any well-trodden patch of soil, plant roots have more of a struggle to push through the hard ground and in wet weather, puddles form.

Compacted soil has a lot of the air spaces squashed out of it, which is why it's a good idea to spike the lawn with a fork. Spiking alleviates compaction and, by making some airways, helps the grass grow. Again it's a job that's best done in autumn. On small-particled soils, like clay, follow up by brushing gritty sand into the vertical drainage channels (about a bucketful per square metre), so that the 'pores' aren't squashed shut again next time you walk over the area. You won't brush it all in, but the surplus 'treads in' to the surface over time, making it firmer to walk on, yet better drained in wet conditions.

A plastic or wire-toothed lawn rake is an efficient way of getting rid of 'thatch'. Powered lawn rakers make the job easier, but will do nothing for your stomach muscles.

Lawn pests

Even the best-kept lawns can suffer from the occasional attentions of unwanted visitors, but, if you're vigilant, and know what to look out for, you can nip problems in the bud before they reach epidemic proportions. It also pays to know the difference between problem pests and the creatures that you can happily live with.

Sweep off worm casts with a birch broom, or besom, on a dry day and they will add to the lawn's fertility.

Earthworms

Worms are actually beneficial in the garden – they make hundreds of tiny drainage channels in the soil. They also drag organic matter, such as dead leaves, into the ground, helping with soil enrichment. Of the 25 British species of earthworm, only two leave worm casts on the lawn's surface, and then mainly in spring and autumn, so don't over-react; earthworms are a sign of a healthy soil. Wait for a dry day and sweep worm casts off with a besom broom – the sort made out of a bundle of birch twigs – they will quickly disintegrate before you start to mow.

Ants

Ants like nesting in dry soil in lawns in summer, when they push up little volcano-like cones of fine soil. They will defend their nests, often giving you nasty nips if you sit down near them – red ants are the worst. Ants usually target patches where the grass is thin and bare soil is exposed, so a lush, well-maintained lawn is less likely to be bothered. Keep an eye open for nests in early summer. If you soak new nesting sites thoroughly with water, you can often drive ants away. If they are well entrenched, take heart; in late summer, the whole colony will fly away. Soak the area well when the ants vacate and you will wash a lot of the loosened soil back into place.

Moles

Moles burrow beneath lawns in search of their favourite food – earthworms. Years ago, pesticides were used to kill the worms in the hope that the moles would leave too, but those toxic products are no longer available, even if you wanted to use them. You can often deter moles by flooding new runs with water, by placing prickly holly leaves inside, or filling the runs with something smelly, such as the contents of the cat's litter tray. Don't connect the exhaust pipe of your car up to gas them out – it does more harm to the car. Some people swear by burying something noisy inside the run – a musical birthday card or a transistor radio, wrapped in a plastic bag, and tuned to one of the noisier pop channels. You can buy electronic mole repellents (which work better on clay soils than on sandy ones), or sink empty wine bottles into the runs, so that

Moles are a pain to get rid of, but their molehills are an excellent basic ingredient for home-made potting compost.

the wind makes an eerie howling noise when it blows across the bottlenecks. They usually work for a while if you 'plant' a row and keep moving them, so you 'sweep' your mole out of the lawn, but it pays to change your strategy regularly, because moles get used to anything in time.

Moles are quite territorial, so even if you persuade the current incumbent to leave, the vacant patch soon attracts a new tenant. If your garden is surrounded by farmland, you've little chance of winning, so it's probably best to learn to live with them. Just be sure to clear molehills away before mowing the lawn, or you just end up with big bare patches where the grass has been smothered. If possible, wash the soil back into the hole, so that you don't end up with a sunken lawn. Not very satisfactory, I know, but it's about the best we can do these days. Unless you want to call in the molecatcher...

Solitary bees

These creatures sometimes turn up in garden lawns, but they are quite shy and don't do any harm. You are most likely to see them if you have a wildlife garden where the lawn isn't cut very often, or – how shall I put this delicately – on a rather neglected lawn with a lot of bald patches. Each bee, which looks like a small bumble bee, excavates a round hole about as wide as a pencil, with a few honeycomb-like cells below ground in which she rears her family. All you'll see is the queen bee flying in and out of the hole. You may find several holes in the same area, but solitary bees don't make colonies. Frankly I'd leave well alone – they only nest in spring and by autumn they've moved on. You're unlikely to find them in a smart well-maintained lawn, because they don't like being disturbed.

If you do find them, consider it an honour and a privilege; you can also feel smug at doing your bit to conserve a self-sufficient little beauty.

Leatherjackets

If you see hordes of daddy-long-legs (crane fly) dancing over your lawn in autumn, be prepared for an invasion of their larvae, leatherjackets, the following year (see page 47). Leatherjackets eat grass roots, and the first thing you know about it is lots of little yellow patches, or flocks of starlings probing for grubs. Since the chemicals that were once recommended for use against lawn soil pests have now been withdrawn, your best bet is to let nature take its course. You can repair a pecked-up surface after the birds have done their bit. Alternatively, nip the problem in the bud by collecting up the craneflies when they congregate for an orgy.

Regard the arrival of a 'solitary bee' as a compliment and congratulate yourself on doing your bit for conservation.

Lawn maintenance

Rough grass can be left to look after itself for much of the time, but a proper lawn needs a little regular attention if you want to keep it looking its best. The amount of trouble you are prepared to go to depends on how much of a lawn perfectionist you are.

My rotary mower, with its heavy rear roller, has resulted in quite a decent lawn that even has stripes.

Mowing

Although it's more convenient to cut the grass at weekends, it really needs cutting every time it grows about 1cm (½in) longer than you want it. The time it takes to do that varies during the year, according to the growing conditions. I know that regular care isn't always possible, but it is the ideal to aim for. If you leave a lawn to grow long and shaggy and then cut it short, the odds are that it will look unhappy for a while, because you will have cut into the thick, brown or yellow stems at the base of the plants, instead of through lush green leaf blades. Regular mowing produces a greener, denser, harder-wearing lawn.

To keep a lawn looking really good, it helps to vary the height at which you cut it during the year. Start mowing in spring, as soon as the grass is dry enough, with the blades set high – maybe 4cm (1½in) – just to slice the top off. Lower the blades as the lawn gets used to being cut. Aim for a height of 2cm (¾in) for a fine lawn; 2.5cm (1in) for a family lawn and 4cm (1½in) for rough grass beneath trees, or in a wild garden. If the weather turns dry in summer, raise the blades again to reduce stress to the grass. Grass will remain greener if it's allowed to grow a little longer until the conditions for encouraging growth are better. As the weather turns colder in autumn, raise the mower blades back up to their spring level, but don't give up cutting the grass for the winter. It keeps growing unless it's really cold, so, if it is still growing, top it lightly whenever it dries out enough.

It's entirely up to you whether you prefer to use a grass-box or not; smart lawns look the better for it and, if you use a cylinder mower with a roller on the back you'll be able to make the traditional stripes. Rotary mowers with a heavy roller can produce stripes, too.

A rotary mower without a grass-box is much quicker to use because you don't have to keep emptying out clippings, but mow frequently so that the short clippings disappear quickly into the lawn and help to feed the grass. Otherwise, go for a 'mulch mower' that shreds the clippings and blasts them down into the lawn.

Using a mower without a grass-box once every two weeks is a recipe for disaster. Long grass, if left in clods on the surface, will kill out the lawn and make it patchy. Added to which, the freshly cut lawn looks a real mess. Nothing at all to laugh at.

Edging

After cutting the grass, trim around the edges with edging shears – the long-handled sort – to tidy up the tufts of grass that stick out sideways over the margins. But before you can use edging shears, you need a properly made lawn edge – a shallow, neat-edged gully all around your beds and borders with a vertical drop of 5–7.5cm (2–3in). Hold the blade of the shears against this flat surface as you cut.

Lawn edges need redefining each spring, as winter rain tends to wash the soil from the adjacent beds down to fill in the edges; this prevents you from using your shears properly. That's why, before your first lawn-mowing session each spring, you should go around all your lawn edges with the back of a spade to reshape them.

Edging shears will provide the finishing touch – a neat, clean rim to the lawn.

It doesn't take long, but it does make edging so much easier for the rest of the year, not to mention making the whole garden look neater. If the edges are badly broken, more heavy-duty maintenance may be needed (see pages 252–54). Some folk can't be doing with this sort of perfectionism. I find it worryingly therapeutic.

Feeding

A heck of a lot is asked of lawns – they are 'pruned' more regularly than any other plant in the garden and then they are walked all over. So they need feeding if they are to look good, especially if they have to stand up to heavy wear. The most important time to feed is in late spring, as that's the start of the growing season, but real lawn enthusiasts often keep feeding every six weeks until autumn to keep grass looking lush. When the soil is dry, the grass is already stressed and can 'scorch' if it's fed, so don't feed unless growing conditions have been favourable for a few weeks and the grass has recovered.

What to feed? Spring and summer grass feeds are high in nitrogen and so produce a rich green lawn but, as summer comes to an end, lawns need a different nutrient blend. Use an autumn formula that is low in nitrogen but high in phosphate and potash to toughen up the roots ready for winter. If that sounds too much like hard work, then try an organic lawn fertilizer once a month. It will not scorch the grass and it releases nutrients over a longer period of time than other lawn foods. It's always best to use a proper lawn fertilizer – either granular or liquid – for feeding grass. Some people economize and use a general-purpose fertilizer instead, but if you do, you won't get the same flush of lush green grass, and the large granules need a lot of watering in. If your aim is to improve the lawn without making it grow any faster (so it doesn't need so much mowing), simply use an autumn lawn feed during summer instead. Organic gardeners can now find organic lawn food with little difficulty.

Organic lawn food is easily applied by hand from a bucket, though for ease, and accuracy with inorganic kinds, a wheeled distributor is a safer bet.

Weeds

The sort of weeds that are a real pest in lawns are the ones that lie flat and pass safely under the mower instead of being chopped off. These are the rosette-forming weeds, such as daisies, plantains and dandelions, and the low-spreading sort, such as trefoils. The rosette-formers are known as broad-leaved weeds in chemical-company speak and they are easy to eradicate with selective lawn weedkillers.

You can either spot-treat individual weeds with a ready-to-use product that comes in a 'water-pistol' pack, or as a waxy, deodorant-style stick, or you can sprinkle a combined weed-and-feed treatment over the whole lawn.

For small-leaved weeds like trefoil, you'll need a liquid weedkiller that is specially designed for this type of weed. Dilute it and water it on with a can. It's always a good idea to feed the lawn around the time you kill the weeds. Dead weeds leave bald patches in the lawn that are quickly colonized by weed seeds and moss, unless you encourage the grass to thicken up and fill the gaps.

If you don't fancy lawn weedkiller, then use a daisy grubber to lift individual weeds out by hand. With trefoils, which grow out from a central root in the shape of a lace doily, find the middle, gather the doily in one hand and twist until the whole plant lifts out.

Organic gardeners cannot use lawn weedkillers, but there are several products on the market that will encourage grass at the same time as discouraging moss and weeds from colonizing. The basic premise is that if the grass is growing vigorously, there will be little room for invaders.

For best results

Use lawn weedkillers in late spring when weeds are growing fast, but before they start flowering; by the time they flower, weeds will have become too tough to respond well to treatment. Apply liquid lawn weedkiller on a dry day, so that it has at least 12 to 24 hours to be taken in through the leaves. If it's washed away too soon, it won't have a chance to work.

If you opt for a granular weed-and-feed treatment, you need to time the application carefully, because although the weedkiller needs the same 12 to 24 hours' absorption period, the fertilizer has to be washed in as soon as possible afterwards. Turn on the sprinkler, if it hasn't rained after 48 hours, to make sure that the treatment is effective.

Moss

I wish I had a pound for every time someone has told me that their lawn weedkiller didn't touch their moss. Well, it won't. You need a completely different product. Some moss killers also work on green lawn slime and on liverwort (that crusty green growth that looks like an alien invader), but not weeds.

The best time to treat moss is in spring, and you can buy liquid lawn mosskiller, or products that combine mosskiller with lawn

Regular spiking with a fork to improve surface drainage will help to discourage moss on lawns.

feed. You need to feed the lawn, so that it thickens up and fills gaps where moss has been, to stop weeds coming in.

Lawn sand is an old-fashioned, but effective, preparation that acts as a fertilizer, weed- and mosskiller, but it can scorch the lawn if applied too heavily. That said, some gardeners swear by it. Buy it or make it up yourself from 4 parts (by weight) sulphate of ammonia: 1 part sulphate of iron: and 20 parts fine silver sand. It has to be applied in dry weather, but when the soil is moist, at the rate of 115g per 1sq.m (4oz per sq.yd). It is used in spring and early summer, rather than in autumn.

Most mosskillers take a couple of weeks to work and you know when they have, because dead moss turns black. A light infestation may well vanish on its own after that, but it's usually recommended that you rake the dead stuff out. Frankly, I'd sooner rake the stuff out in the first place and save on the chemicals. It's hard work, so I use a powered lawn raker. On damp, shady lawns, moss will keep coming back whatever you do, so you'll probably need to treat it in spring and autumn to keep on top of it. Anything you can do to let in more light and improve the surface drainage – spiking and sanding – will also help.

Lawn-care calendar

Just as your car needs servicing, your lawn needs maintenance, too.

Spring
• Feed and apply weedkiller or mosskiller, if needed.
• Start cutting regularly.

Summer
• Raise your mower blades and mow regularly, even if the grass isn't growing rapidly, to control upright weeds.
• Don't use lawn feed or other treatments in hot, dry conditions.

Autumn
• Mow the lawn from top to bottom, then from side to side.
• Rake to remove thatch and moss, then spike with a fork to aerate.
• Apply autumn lawn fertilizer to prepare grass for winter.
• Top dress with gritty sand or turf dressing, if needed.
• Clear fallen leaves regularly.

Winter
• Keep off the grass as much as possible; lay a plank or 'portable path', if you have to use a barrow.
• Mow occasionally, as needed and when conditions allow.

It will all have been worth it in the end when the final result is a good-looking, hard-wearing lawn.

Renovating lawns

If you've taken over a badly neglected lawn, or the grass takes a battering because the family use it as an outdoor leisure centre, it needs more than just routine care. One dose of intensive restoration work should be enough to put a neglected lawn back on it's feet, but grass that receives regular hard wear will need a session once a year, in spring or autumn, whichever is the most convenient. The recipe sounds simple, but it means a lot of hard work, I'm afraid. The good news is that you'll notice a difference within a few weeks and the improvement will continue, as time goes by, if you keep up with normal, routine maintenance during the rest of the year.

Where to start

Begin by giving the lawn the annual autumn lawn treatment, as described on the previous page in the lawn-care calendar. If you are doing this as part of a programme of lawn restoration, it can be undertaken in spring or autumn. If a neglected lawn is in a really bad state, there's no reason why you shouldn't renovate it in summer, as long as the weather is cool and the soil is moist; but don't attempt it in a drought, or a heatwave. Since summer is the barbecue season, be aware that the treatment will make the lawn look worse before it gets better and it won't impress your guests!

After you've mowed, and mowed again at right angles to the first cut (to catch the bits that usually just get flattened by the mower), rake and spike the lawn, then use autumn lawn fertilizer – even if it's spring or summer. It's the best for thickening up the grass and stimulating the roots, which is what you want. Then, while the lawn is moving into top gear, see what other problems there are that need tackling.

Bald patches

Some bald patches are bald because that particular piece of lawn is in constant use by regular heavy foot traffic. If that's the case, you would be better off putting in a proper path, or at least sinking a series of paving slabs into the surface to use as stepping stones.

Some patches may look a bit thin because the grass isn't growing very well, and spiking and feeding may be all it needs. Other patches may simply be 'scalped' bumps; that happens when the mower 'grounds'. Levelling will put them right (see Peaks and hollows, page 254). But if there are bald patches where large rosette weeds have been removed, or because the lawn is in very poor condition, the quickest way to deal with them is to re-seed.

You can buy 'patch' kits that contain grass seed mixed with compost. Alternatively, you can buy the two separately, mix them in a bucket and sprinkle the mix thinly over bald areas, after spiking them well to loosen the soil surface. Rake the seed-and-compost mix in lightly and stick in some canes to prevent people walking on the area until the grass has come through. Autumn or spring are usually the best times to 'patch' lawns but, as long as it's only a few spots, you can do the job in summer, provided that the weather isn't too hot and you keep the areas watered.

Broken edges

Broken lawn edges don't just look untidy, they make mowing difficult and proper edging almost impossible, but they are very easily fixed. All you need to do is take a sharp spade and cut out a square of turf that has the broken edge along one side. Turn it around and fit it back into the gap, so that now there's a complete straight edge around the outside of the lawn and the broken piece is on the inside. This leaves a hole in the lawn. Fill the hole with topsoil and firm it down, so that it doesn't sink below the level of the rest of the lawn. Then re-seed it as if it were a bald patch (see page 252). If you do this in autumn, by spring, you'll have a complete lawn and you won't even see the joins.

Running repairs to lawn edges are easily carried out. Remove a square of turf (*top*), which includes the broken edge. Reverse it and pat it back into place (*bottom*), then re-seed the bald patch which is now within the lawn area.

Peaks and hollows

Long after a lawn has been laid, it's not uncommon to find that parts of it sink, so that you end up with a slightly uneven surface. In a wild garden, this looks very natural. It's not so good in a smart lawn that you keep closely cut, because the mower tends to scalp the peaks, leaving them permanently bald. That's bad enough if you want a good-looking lawn, but it's hopeless if you want to play croquet or boules; the ball shoots off in all directions.

Shallow dips on a lawn can gradually be filled in by raking topsoil or potting compost into them.

To flatten peaks, don't bash them down with the back of a spade, or take a garden roller to them. That just compacts the soil even more and the grass still won't grow. Instead, strip the turf off the peak, remove some of the soil beneath and level the spot before putting the turf back. Easier said than done, I know, but you'll be glad that you did it.

Hollows are treated in the same way, but in reverse. Remove the turf, add topsoil until the hollow is level and put the grass back. If the dip is very shallow, just fill the hollow in easy stages by top dressing. Use sieved topsoil or turf dressing, which you can buy in bags at the garden centre. Sprinkle it thinly and evenly over the area, and brush it into the grass. Don't put on more than about 1cm (½in) of dressing at a time, or you'll smother the grass and kill it. But if you top dress the dips two or three times a year, it's amazing how quickly they will even out.

Alternative lawns

If the traditional close-cropped lawn doesn't fit your style of garden, there are plenty of other kinds to choose from. Some contain grass along with other ingredients – wildflower lawns, for instance – but there are others that don't have any grass in them at all, such as herb or flower lawns.

Don't make the mistake of thinking that non-grass lawns are direct substitutes for grass. Grass is the *only* type of lawn that you can use for running around on – the rest don't stand up to very much wear at all. They are fine for small areas, where you don't need to walk all the time, and great for areas around a garden seat. My advice is, if you need somewhere for the family to play, stick to the traditional lawn at the back of the house, and save the other sort for quieter places, well out of harm's way. Treat the special lawn as an occasional walk-through flower bed.

Wildflower lawns

A wildflower lawn is just a patch of grass that isn't cut quite so short as usual – say 5cm (2in) instead of 2.5cm (1in) – where you encourage low-growing wild flowers, such as primroses, violets and cowslips. Some people also like to encourage Germander speedwell, trefoils and other plants, which, to traditional gardeners, are lawn weeds.

A wildflower meadow is wonderful in summer and a great butterfly attractant, but remember that you will still have to cut it a couple of times a year in early spring and autumn.

You can either let the wildlings come up naturally, and weed out the ones you don't want, or you can plant the wild flowers of your choice into the turf in spring; they'll self-seed once established. A wildflower lawn doesn't need feeding, but it does need mowing regularly, even though it's allowed to grow taller than usual. Don't confuse a wildflower lawn with a wildflower meadow; the latter is where tall wildflowers grow in long grass. Meadows are only cut twice a year and look completely different.

Clover lawns

Clover is the sort of 'weed' that traditional lawn fans spend years trying to eliminate from posh turf but, on it's own, white clover (*Trifolium repens*) makes a very good 'lawn'. Sow it in the same way as a normal grass lawn, using clover seeds that you can buy from specialist seed firms. It's much less trouble than grass – clover stays green in dry weather when grass looks like hay, and its full height is only about 5–8cm (2–3in), so it doesn't need regular mowing.

If you sow clover and grass seed together, you'll have a more conventional-looking lawn that needs mowing, but feeds itself; clover roots 'fix' nitrogen out of the air and enrich the soil. Clover is a mass of flower in summer and very attractive to bees, so if you want a 'play' lawn for children, simply mow down the flowerheads to prevent your kids from being stung by foraging bees.

Flower lawns

The classic flower lawn is chamomile, which, ironically, is usually made of the non-flowering form, *Chamaemelum nobile* 'Treneague'. You can also grow a lawn of creeping thymes; a mixture of mat-forming alpines; or one of the flowering chamomiles, such as the double-flowered Roman version, *Chamaemelum nobile* 'Flore Pleno'.

Good flowering lawns look superb and the idea is that they don't need mowing; just a clip over after flowering – a bit more often, in the case of non-flowering chamomile. You probably won't want an extensive area, because flower lawns have to be weeded by hand, but it's not quite as bad as weeding a flower bed. Once the plants cover the ground densely, the foliage smothers out a lot of weeds. Think of these lawns more as low-growing groundcover.

A lawn of chamomile, of other herbs, or alpines, is very fussy about its growing conditions. A sunny spot with first-class drainage is essential, so on 'normal' ground, dig plenty of grit or gravel into the area. Improve the drainage even more by spreading a 5-cm (2-in) layer of gravel over the area, with gravel board around the edge to stop the lawn from 'creeping'.

Put the plants in through the gravel, so they have a deep collar to protect them from damp, which can easily make them rot off at the 'neck'. You don't have to plant a continuous carpet of the same type of flower – you can mix different creeping herbs or alpines together, to create more of a Persian carpet effect. You could add pieces of paving, so you have somewhere to put a seat, or some containers with sun-loving plants. If drainage is a bit 'iffy', be prepared for such a lawn to need quite a bit of restoration work in spring. Yes, a herb-rich sward is lovely, but it's more fun if it's small.

Creeping thymes make a fragrant 'lawn', even though they don't take a lot of wear and tear.

Mossy glades

If you want a mossy green carpet for a damp, shady area, then you can't do better than real moss. It's sometimes sold in pots for creating Oriental-style gardens. In the right spot, moss will appear all on its own, so instead of fighting it, why not go with the flow? The odds are you won't get all that many weeds in a damp, shady corner, but if you don't want to weed by hand, then use a paraquat-based weedkiller, which doesn't harm moss. It is a rather nasty chemical, though, so take all the recommended precautions and follow the intructions to the letter when you use it.

Alternatively, you can achieve a good mossy effect with helxine or mind-your-own-business (*Soleirolia soleirolii*, see page 147). Several forms, including gold, silver-edged and green, are sold as houseplants, but the plain green is the hardiest one and the best to use as a 'lawn'. But be warned: once you have it, you'll never be rid of it, and it can be a terrible weed if it comes up where it's not wanted.

Epilogue

If you've just finished this book, you're probably feeling a mite punch drunk. There's so much to learn and so much to remember. Relax. If gardening becomes a worry, it is not worth the candle. It should be looked upon as a challenging pursuit, not as a chore. I know there are some dreary jobs to do, and that it always seems to be raining just when you need dry weather to mow, feed or whatever. But once you get in touch with your basic earthy self – and that, as much as anything, is what this book is about – then you'll start to become an instinctive gardener, who realizes that common sense is the most important attribute of any son or daughter of the soil.

The next book, *How to be a Gardener Book Two*, concentrates more on plants. Now that you've come to grips with the basics of cultivation, you can open your eyes to the real magic of it all and the reason for learning all this stuff in the first place – to grow flowers, fruits and vegetables better, whatever your situation, and to realize just how much variety there is to be had, wherever you garden, and whatever style appeals to you.

Whatever the weather… well, you know the rest.

Index

ACKNOWLEDGEMENTS

This book has been as much fun to prepare as the *How to be a Gardener* television series, and I have had the good fortune to work with two teams of people who are as passionate about getting over the feel and the soul of gardening as I am, and as keen to explore the 'why?', as much as the 'how?'.

To Sue Phillips, Nicky Copeland, Khadija Manjlai, Lin Hawthorne and Charlotte Lochhead, I owe a great debt of gratitude for making this book what I hope is a readable and reliable guide for the beginner and the experienced gardener alike. To Isobel Gillan, the designer, and Jonathan Buckley, the snapper, I can only apologise for the standard of my tea-making and thank them for their unquenchable good humour in the face of foul weather and muddy earth over a year of photography in my back garden and beyond.

For helping me put across my passion for gardening on the screen, I have been lucky enough to work with Tim Shepherd and Paul Hutchings, my regular cameramen, who can give even the dullest job a starry sheen, and a cheerful band of sound recordists and occasional cameramen, who have all said 'ooh' and 'ah' in all the right places.

On the production side, Dick Colthurst, Claire Markwell, Mark Flowers, Belinda Cherrington, Rachel Malin and Toby Musgrave have all come to know me and gardening better. I hope the experience has left them as happy as it has left me. As for my producer Kath Moore, she has been one of the most rewarding task masters I have ever met. Conscientiousness and good fun do not always go together. On this occasion they most certainly did.

And finally, to all the locals in my neck of the woods who allowed me to use their gardens in the programmes and within these pages, a big thank you. They gave us hospitality, encouragement and, just occasionally, strange looks. I hope that now it all becomes clear.

The photographer would like to thank Helen Yemm for her assistance with this project and the following owners and designers for kindly giving permission for their gardens to be photographed:

Abbey Dore Court, Herefordshire (Charis Ward) p 130; Abbey Road, Hampshire (Fred and June Dod) pps 46 and 110; American Impressionists Garden, Giverny, France (designer: Mark Brown) p 58; Barleywood, Hampshire (Alan Titchmarsh) pps 61, 80, 89, 92, 99 (*1*), 105, 124, 138, 156, 177, 198 and 238; Beth Chatto Gardens, Essex (Beth Chatto) pps 36, 77 and 96; Church Lane, London (Paul Kelly) pps 100 and 128; Earl's Court Road, London (Camilla Shivarg) p 101 (*bottom*); Eastgrove Cottage, Worcestershire (Malcolm and Carol Skinner) pps 11 and 237; East Ruston Old Vicarage, Norfolk (Alan Gray and Graham Robeson) p 225; Glen Chantry, Essex (Sue and Wol Staines) pps 17 (*all*), 63, 94, 101 (*top*), 108, 133 and 134; Great Dixter, East Sussex (Christopher Lloyd) pps 107 (*all*) and 192; Hatfield House, Hertfordshire (Lady Salisbury) p 10; Hollington Herbs, Berkshire (Judith and Simon Hopkinson) pps 187 and 257; *Home Front* garden, Hackney (designer: Diarmuid Gavin) p 13; Ketley's, East Sussex (Helen Yemm) pps 28 and 123; Lady Farm, Somerset (Judy Pearce) p 99 (*3*); Landor Road, Warwickshire (Maurice and Wilmur Green) pps 35, 88 and 125; Merton Hall Road, London (Gay Gray) p 251; Peachings, Hampshire (Gill Siddell) pps 19, 71, 127, 164 and 173; Perch Hill, East Sussex (Sarah Raven) p 54; Roger's Rough, Kent (Richard Bird) p 99 (*2*); Rose Cottage, East Sussex (Fergus Garrett) p 114; Squires Hill Lane, Hampshire (Sarah and Andrew Coyle) p 103; Spencer Road, London (Anthony Goff) pps 86–87, 193, 197 and 241; Sticky Wicket, Dorset (Pam Lewis) p 255; St John's Road, Staffordshire (Maureen and Sid Allen) pps 29, 98 and 229; Tower Street, Hampshire (Jesse Delaney) pps 2, 27, 67 and 85; Upper Mill Cottage, Kent (David and Mavis Seeney) pps 77 (*top*) 116 and 223; Waterperry Gardens, Oxfordshire p 97; Wellhouse Road, Hampshire (Verity and Andrew Bronwitt) p 168.

This book is published to accompany the television series entitled *How to be a Gardener*, first broadcast in 2002. The series was produced by BBC Bristol.
Executive producer: Dick Colthurst
Producer: Kath Moore

Published by BBC Worldwide Ltd,
Woodlands, 80 Wood Lane, London W12 0TT

First published 2002
Reprinted 2002 (nine times)
Reprinted 2003, twice
Text copyright © Alan Titchmarsh 2002
The moral right of the author has been asserted

Photographs copyright © Jonathan Buckley 2002

Except the following photographs from: **BBC WORLDWIDE/SUSAN BELL**: p 135 (*bottom*). **HOLT STUDIOS**: photos by Nigel Cattlin pps 34 (*left*), 143 (*12a*), 213 (*2 and 4*), 214 (*5, 8 and 9*), 216 (*10 and 11*), 219 (*3, 4 and 5*) and 231 (*1, 4 and 8*); Alan and Linda Detrick p 245; Phil McLean p 214 (*7*); Rosemary Mayer p 143 (*12b*); Primrose Peacock p 143 (*11b*). **MATTHEW MORGAN**: pps 141 (*2a, 3a, 3b, 4a and 4b*), 142 (*5a and 5b*), 145 (*2a and 2b*), 146 (*5a and 5b*), 149 (*4a and 4b*), 219 (*2*), 231 (*5*) and 244. **TOBY MUSGRAVE**: p 45. **OXFORD SCIENTIFIC FILMS**: photos by Niall Benvie p 39; H.L.Fox p 231 (*2*); Mark Hamblin p 228; Geoff Kidd p 216 (*12*); Satoshi Kuribayashi p 231 (*7*); Colin Milkins p 214 (*6*); Robin Redfern p 221; James H.Robinson p 231 (*2*). **PHOTOS HORTICULTURAL**: p 24 (top row: *left* and *centre*; middle row: *left*, *centre left*, *centre right* and *right*; bottom row: *left*).

BBC Worldwide would like to thank the above for providing photographs and for permission to reproduce copyright material. While every effort has been made to trace and acknowledge all copyright holders, we would like to apologise should there have been any errors or omissions.

ISBN 0 563 53740 X

Commissioning Editor: Nicky Copeland
Project Editors: Charlotte Lochhead and Khadija Manjlai
Copy Editor: Lin Hawthorne
Art Director and Designer: Isobel Gillan
Artists: Sandra Pond and Will Giles

Typeset in Sabon and Akzidenz
Printed and bound in France by Imprimerie Pollina s.a-L 91128
Colour separations by Kestrel Digital Colour, Chelmsford